He
Changed
My
Life

He
Changed
My
Life

Edited and Arranged by L. Brent Goates

Bookcraft
Salt Lake City, Utah

Library of Congress Catalog Card Number: 88-70652

ISBN 0-88494-657-6

First Printing, 1988

Printed in the United States of America

Contents

Preface   ix

Introduction   1

1. I Know He Was a Prophet of God   7
   Ezra Taft Benson

2. On Following Counsel   11
   Thomas S. Monson

3. Lost in the Service of Others   15
   Glen L. Rudd

4. He Was Most Like the Prophet Joseph   23
   Marion G. Romney

5. God Spoke to Harold Every Day   26
   Oscar W. McConkie, Jr.

6. He Spoke to Me Spirit to Spirit   32
   Gene R. Cook

7. The Blessing That Preserved the Next Prophet   38
   Mark E. Petersen

8. First Impressions   40
   Boyd K. Packer

9. His Influence Stretches Across My Life   42
   Hugh W. Pinnock

10. Favorite Thoughts and Quotations of
    President Harold B. Lee   46
    Franklin D. Richards

11. He Touched Every Fiber of My Being   51
    J. Thomas Fyans

12. My Greatest Compliment   54
    Vaughn J. Featherstone

13. Counsel on Giving Counsel   59
    John H. Groberg

14. Fulfillment of Prophecy   62
    Devere Harris

15. Use Medicine and Priesthood Blessings   64
    Victor L. Brown

16. My Last Visit with President Harold B. Lee   66
    Keith W. Wilcox

17. Our Miracle Girl   75
    Francis M. Gibbons

18. My Personal Appreciation of Harold B. Lee   78
    James B. Allen

19. A Courageous Prophet with a Tender Heart   83
    Wendell J. Ashton

20. He Seemed Eager to Serve Us   90
    Wallace G. Bennett

21. Blessings from Obeying the Counsel of Prophets   94
    Rodney H. Brady

22. He Taught the Unbounded Power of the Priesthood 102
    M. Elmer Christensen

23. A Healing Handshake   108
    R. Viola Davidson

24. We Were Better Because He Made Us Feel Special 110
    John K. Edmunds

25. Ruth, Come Walk with Me   118
    Ruth Hardy Funk

26. I Remember Best His Humble,
    Unpretentious Friendliness   127
    L. Ray Gardiner

27. Memories of a Student in Oxford, Idaho   131
    Joseph Clifford Gibby

28. He Has Kept a Light Burning in My Life   135
    Diana Bird Holt

29. I Have Tried to Be Like Him   140
    C. Dennis Smith

30. Testimony—In the Heart or in the Head?   145
    Elliott D. Landau

31. "He Looked and Acted Like God"   148
    Robert J. Martin

32. He Made a Difference in My Study of
    the Scriptures   151
    Steven R. Pogue

33. The Most Inspiring, Uplifting Experience
    of My Life   155
    Gerald B. Quinn

34. He Wrote His Record upon My Heart and Life   159
    Glenna L. Reese

35. He Became a Prophet When Ordained an Apostle   162
    Paul E. Reimann

36. My Mentor and Dear Friend   164
    John M. Russon

37. An Unforgettable Lesson on Delegation   168
    John Schreiner

38. Changing Teaching in the Church and in My Life   171
    Rex A. Skidmore

39. He Answered All My Questions   175
    Richard B. Sonne

40. Blessings from Traveling with a Prophet   178
    Asael T. Sorensen

41. He Awakened in Me a Desire to Gain a Testimony   182
    Betty B. Stohl

42. Memories of My Dearest Friend   185
    Walter Stover

43. My Most Influential Teacher   189
    J. Clifford Wallace

44. Early Signs of His Greatness   192
    Harriet E. Jensen Woolsey

45. Unifying the Joseph Smith Family   196
    Buddy Youngreen

46. He Taught Us the Vision of Eternal Families   205
    Elaine A. Cannon

47. Remembering a Brother   213
    George W. Cornell

48. He Treated Me as the Savior Would Have   218
    Leo D. Jensen

49. Choice Memories of a Prophet   221
    Paul H. Dunn

50. A Call Never to Be Forgotten   231
    James E. Faust

51. Two Remarkable Healings   233
    Theodore M. Burton

52. The Blessings of Being Tutored by a Friend   237
    Neal A. Maxwell

Index   241

Preface

On 6 October 1972, the day President Harold B. Lee was sustained as the President of The Church of Jesus Christ of Latter-day Saints, he offered in his acceptance sermon his own humble formula for assessing his accomplishments: "The only true record that will ever be made of my service in my new calling will be the record that I may have written in the hearts and lives of those with whom I have served and labored, within and without the Church" (in Conference Report, Oct. 1972, p. 19).

The biography of his life and labors, *Harold B. Lee, Prophet and Seer* (Bookcraft, 1985), was approached in an autobiographical manner, using the writings of President Lee from his diaries, correspondence, family records, and life sketches. It was, as much as was possible, an intentional attempt to allow Harold B. Lee to describe his own life and labors.

The author recognizes that this approach is one-sided. Except for the sheer volume of pages required, one would hope that a much more balanced work could have been offered in the biography. At the time of that publication, we promised the counterbalancing material to come forward in a later book. This volume is the fulfillment of that pledge and offers the opposite approach, relating the experiences of those with whom President Lee labored, speaking of how they viewed his life and service. Many key episodes only briefly described in the biography now come into full flower through eyewitness accounts.

There is an obvious difference in the two approaches. If one of our authors were to describe an interview with President Lee, it just might be the most inspirational and memorable experience of a lifetime; yet the same event would occupy but a few terse lines in the diary of President Lee. Thus it is our intention in this book to present the enlarged, personalized versions as seen by a small sampling of individuals blessed by his ministry, some of which are also related in the biography.

For these reasons this book could well be perceived as an extension of the original biography of President Lee. The two books combined will best provide a complete and balanced record of his illustrious service to the Church and its member-ship.

In this book, fifty-two witnesses step forward and give their own accounts of how their lives were changed and uplifted by this man of God. Their testimonies fit under Harold B. Lee's for-mula for assessing the value of his labors: the "record that I have written in the hearts and lives of those with whom I have served." This document abundantly declares the majesty of his accomplishments as measured by the exacting test of his own design.

Yet the present book possesses its own unique and practical identity. Not only do these precious stories come as inclusions to the true record of President Lee's life, but each story is of valuable, practical worth to the reader. To facilitate making application in one's daily life of the wisdom and truth in these many stories, an index has been included, referencing the morals to the stories and filing them under easy to identify common subjects. It is hoped that in this way the stories will live beyond an entertaining and enjoyable moment of reading to perpetuate the miracles from his leadership and power and bring about further opportunities whereby new generations can attest that *He Changed My Life*.

Introduction

If we work upon marble,
it will perish;
if we work upon brass,
time will efface it;
if we rear temples,
they will crumble into dust;
but if we work
upon immortal souls,
if we imbue them
with principles,
with the fear of God
and love of fellowman,
we engrave on these tablets
something which brightens
all eternity.

—Daniel Webster

L. Brent Goates

A Measure of
True Greatness

When the fading embers of mortality are finally snuffed out, those remaining sit and ponder the meaning of the deceased one's life. The speaker at the funeral service attempts to evaluate the significance of the life of the one being honored. Did he lead a successful life? The answer depends upon how one defines success in mortality. Could he properly be called great in the eulogy? It is difficult to evaluate greatness, yet we all seem to know when it touches our lives. In William Shakespeare's *Julius Caesar*, Antony made an evaluation of Brutus immediately after his death, and paid him this tribute:

This was the noblest Roman of them all. . . .
His life was gentle [noble], and the elements
So mixed in him, that Nature might stand up
And say to all the world, "This was a man."
(Act 5, scene 5, lines 68, 73–75)

Library shelves are filled with volumes dealing with the subject of greatness. Philosophers, historians, essayists, and poets

have exhausted themselves and their readers in analyzing it.
Who rightly should the world venerate as its ageless heroes?
What is it that lifted them above the masses to a place in immor-
tality?

In the early 1920s, Les Goates, then a young sports editor
and columnist for the *Deseret News*, wrote a tribute to Babe Ruth.
While placing him on the pedestal of greatness, Les Goates also
surveyed world history for others of enduring power:

> A garrulous old gentleman named *Socrates* remade the
> mental process of the world by his incessant questioning. *Gali-
> leo* got an idea the earth was running around the sun, and not
> the sun around the earth, and revamped the study of the
> heavens. *Napoleon* believed in the red star of destiny which he
> saw shining for him at night, and he completely changed the
> method of warfare and for his brief but brilliant hour dominated
> the earth.
>
> And so it has been ever and always in the history of man.
> Great personalities spring up from obscure places, flash their
> genius upon the stage which we call the world, and drive,
> inspire and dominate—then fade away. But always they leave
> their imprint upon a remade world.
>
> An *Edison* arises to dominate with dynamos. A *Ford*
> launches a new industrial era. A *Pasteur* blesses humanity with
> a new method of fighting disease. A *Bach* changes the course of
> music. They live their lives, pass on, and others take their
> places, while a world of endless generations, blessed by their
> deeds and fascinated by their courage, seeks a key to the riddle
> of their amazing personalities. But there is no answer, for the
> world's great, each in his chosen way, has been a law unto him-
> self, refusing always to conform and daring always to sail out
> on uncharted seas.
>
> There is but one *Shakespeare*, one *Lincoln*, one *Mark Twain*.
> There are no seconds. Grand opera will never know another
> *Caruso*, and the prize ring will never know another *Dempsey*.
> And baseball also has its lone figure, sitting upon the Olympian
> or, shall we say, myopian heights of hero worship. One man
> sits alone there, and the baseball world will never know his
> likes again, *George Herman Ruth*, the inspiration of the boyhood
> of young America.
>
> For thirty years the mighty Babe dominated the thought of
> baseball's millions. The boy athlete, taken out of an industrial
> school for orphans, became an international figure. His star cir-

cumnavigated the globe so that many in foreign lands knew of him more than they knew of the leaders of his country. All this time he vied with the *Edisons,* the *Fords,* the *Roosevelts,* the *Vanderbilts,* and the *Pershings* for front-page position in the newspapers of the land. The people wanted to know about him, his daring, ruthless, rushing powerhouse tactics, so as to catch the thrill of his personality.

The Church also has seen greatness of such enduring quality in the works of Elder James E. Talmage. At the funeral services for Dr. Talmage, Elder Melvin J. Ballard, of the Council of the Twelve Apostles, said: "In this ministry he produced many volumes that shall be read until the end of time, because that which he has written is so clear and so impressive that it shall ever be among the cherished treasures of those who love the works of God. Yet these contributions he gave freely to the Church, without any earthly reward." (*The Parables of James E. Talmage,* comp. Albert L. Zobell, Jr. [Salt Lake City: Deseret Book Co., 1973], p. 71.)

J. N. Larned concluded that these three ingredients must be present in the truly great person:

1. Great endowments, so much beyond the gifts of faculty or power to common men that they surprise our wonder and admiration, whatever their nature may be.

2. Great opportunity for the adequate exercise and demonstration of such endowments, without which they remain undeveloped, as well as unknown.

3. Great motives and purposes in the use of whatever the great endowments may be, so that they be not wasted on worthless employments, or defiled by an evil use. (*A Study of Greatness in Man* [New York: Houghton Mifflin Co., 1911], pp. 31–32.)

The third element places morality as a requisite for one who could truly be called great. Thus to Larned, an early twentieth-century educator and author, Napoleon was a prodigy without greatness, Cromwell was imperfect in greatness, Washington was impressive in greatness, and Lincoln was simplest in greatness.

Leadership that borders on greatness, then, may be as much a matter of what that person *is* as what he *does*. Of course, the characteristics of successful leadership are legion, but surely this list would include: the skill to demonstrate a vision so that others, too, can see it and share in its objective; example; confidence; commitment to the goal; persuasion; charismatic qualities that develop discipleship; courage to initiate against opposition; caring for others; determination; and perseverance to never give up.

All of these qualities would no doubt be possessed by one who became a great leader. "But where, then," asks Larned (page 28), "shall we look for the final mark and measure of a really great superiority in one man over the mass of his fellow men?"

The model, great leader, whose life could really be called successful, is one who makes a difference in the lives of others. It must be said of him that this world was made better by his passing through it to lead and give love, and to be loved by his peers.

One method of assessment might be to analyze the consequences had this one life not been lived. The classic film *It's a Wonderful Life,* starring Jimmy Stewart, illustrates this method by allowing Stewart's character a look at his world as it would have been had he not married, had children, and influenced friends and family members—as if he had never been born. The result was a powerful insight into the worth of an individual's life and offers a creative means for evaluating a person's contribution to his world.

We all take inspiration from the performance of great and accomplished men. Even more to be admired, and worthy of greatness, however, is a woman praised in a fast and testimony meeting. A sister described the Beehive teacher she had when she was young. Not only did this teacher, the late LaPreal Swallow, teach powerful gospel lessons, but she offered a personal service to each member of her class. She offered to teach anyone interested to play the organ. This student accepted the offer, and her life and value in Church service has been resplendent because a teacher wanted to give all she could instead of merely teaching lessons in the classroom.

When we give something to someone else, even in the smallest degree, we are serving in a Christlike way. Through such service we contribute new understandings and provide opportunities for growth and lasting improvement and enrichment in the lives of others.

President Spencer W. Kimball, in his impressive article "Jesus: The Perfect Leader" (*Ensign*, Aug. 1979, pp. 5–7), told how the Master involved his disciples to give them development, and how he loved people enough to make demands of them that were real but reasonable. Yet the Savior made his assignments with sensitivity. Of greatest import, however, was this vital ingredient:

> The Savior's leadership was selfless. He put himself and his own needs second and ministered to others beyond the call of duty, tirelessly, lovingly, effectively. So many of the problems in the world today spring from selfishness and self-centeredness in which too many make harsh demands of life and others in order to meet their demands. This is a direct reversal of the principles and practices pursued so perfectly by that perfect example of leadership, Jesus of Nazareth. (*Ensign*, August 1979, p. 6.)

The epitome of leadership and service in mortality is to bring about change that perfects and uplifts others. If we would dedicate our lives to such Christlike service, our leadership and example can make a difference in the lives of our fellowmen.

King Benjamin's farewell address had such a profound effect upon his subjects that they became spiritually begotten: "And now, because of the covenant which ye have made ye shall be called the children of Christ, his sons, and his daughters; for behold, this day he hath spiritually begotten you; for ye say that your hearts are changed through faith on his name; therefore, ye are born of him and have become his sons and his daughters" (Mosiah 5:7).

There can be no more important work on earth than to bring about such a magnificent change as conversion, which leads to eternal life for all peoples. This is the ultimate change, being uplifted in a way that finally unites us with our Savior and our Heavenly Father in the celestial kingdom of God.

In the following pages the greatness of President Harold B. Lee, in using his talents and choices of time and energies to lead souls in their upward strivings, is attested to by fifty-two stories that represent hundreds of similar experiences. It is my hope that President Lee's example will provide us with the vision and inspiration to so serve one another that we might fulfill the greatest aspect of true leadership and magnify our opportunities of mortal existence. We must join in such a righteous quest under the slogan, "I want to live and serve in such a way that I can make a difference in the lives of my friends and family."

Such service is the highest and noblest of earthly pursuits, and he who does it well deserves to be called great.

1

Ezra Taft Benson
President of the Church

I Know He Was a Prophet of God

President Harold B. Lee was a rare spiritual giant, raised up for a time that demanded stalwart leadership and courage. He was called of God to his high and holy calling as prophet, seer, and revelator and without doubt was "ordained to that very purpose in the Grand Council of heaven before this world was" (Joseph Smith, *Teachings of the Prophet Joseph Smith*, sel. Joseph Fielding Smith [Salt Lake City: Deseret Book Co., 1938], p. 365).

I knew Harold B. Lee from our boyhood years. We were high school classmates together at the old Oneida Stake Academy. It was then I first came to love and respect him. In his youth I could sense his strength of character, his courage, and his sense of purpose. Even as a young man he was serious minded; there was no foolishness in him.

Growing up on a small farm near Clifton, Idaho, where struggle and sacrifice were a part of everyday life, President Lee developed a philosophy of hard work and self-reliance. He came to know, as the scriptures teach, that men should earn their bread by the sweat of their own brow, not by the sweat of their neighbor's brow.

When the Great Depression came to this nation in the early 1930s, Harold B. Lee was serving as a young stake president. While others looked to the government for relief, he developed work projects for the unemployed members, which provided them with the necessities of life. Self-reliance, hard work, and priesthood cooperation were the bases for that successful rehabilitative effort. Later, when called as the first managing director of the Church welfare program, the same philosophy became the cornerstone for this dynamic Church program.

I suppose the proudest moment of my association with Harold B. Lee came when my former boyhood friend was named as the newest member of the Council of the Twelve. I was seated in the audience and was so pleased I could not hold back the tears. Following that session of conference, I worked my way to him, and we threw our arms around each other. We both had tears of joy in our eyes. I told him how proud I was of him. Since that day, I have admired his courage on matters of principle, his deportment as a priesthood officer, and his always-timely counsel to his brethren and Church members. His spiritual demeanor before his associates was constant evidence to all of us of his closeness to the Lord.

We who knew him best saw him struggle with mighty problems that weighed heavily on him. We saw on many occasions how he would supplicate the Lord in earnestness for answers. He once said, "I have learned by my own experiences that the heavier the responsibilities, the greater is my dependence on the Lord." Answers came, and those of us who were participants in some of those struggles are witnesses, to use President Lee's own words, "that aided by God's holy power, doubts can be resolved into certainties, burdens can be lightened, and a literal rebirth can be realized as the nearness to [our] Lord and master becomes more certain."

He gave the Church constant testimony and reminder that our only safety would be in following those whom God has appointed to preside in his Church. "Follow the Brethren, listen to the Brethren," was his admonishment.

But of all the impressive admonitions he gave to the Church, none impressed me more than his declaration to fathers, "The greatest of the Lord's work you brethren will ever do as fathers will be within the walls of your own home" (in Conference Report, Apr. 1973, p. 130).

I have shared that statement frequently—and the philosophy it represents—with members of my own family. Would that all parents in Zion might follow this counsel.

Beneficently, our wise Father in Heaven endowed Harold B. Lee with many gifts of the Spirit suited to strengthening the faith of others and building the kingdom. Reposed in his character were all those attributes mentioned by the Lord as qualifications for the ministry: "faith, virtue, knowledge, temperance, patience, brotherly kindness, godliness, charity, humility, diligence" (D&C 4:6). Because these virtues abounded in him, he was not "unfruitful in the knowledge of the Lord" (D&C 107:31).

If ever a man deserved a biography of his life, because that life was worthy of emulation, it is Harold B. Lee. There is not one word of exaggeration in his biography on film, *The Long Odyssey.* I am grateful it has been done, and I hope that every member of the Church will see it.

With all my heart I loved him as a brother. I knew the spiritual qualities of Harold B. Lee, one of the great prophets of the Church. I have told my brethren that he is one of the greatest souls I have ever known, and I have known many whom I consider to be great men. Harold B. Lee was a prophet of God. I never doubted it. I am sure of it.

It was one of the greatest disappointments of my life when I learned of his serious illness and of his passing. I had assumed that Harold B. Lee, a young man, would probably be the last President of the Church that I would serve under—and I know that Spencer W. Kimball felt the same way.

I loved Harold B. Lee as I have loved few men in this world. I have been on the old farm in Clifton, Idaho. I later became a county agent and knew his family. I know his children. I know his wife. I know his background. He was a prophet of God. I know this as well as I know that I live. May God bless the memory of Harold B. Lee and his posterity and loved ones. I am grateful beyond measure for my association and friendship with this noble servant of our Heavenly Father. I bear witness that he was a prophet of God.

2

Thomas S. Monson
Second Counselor in the First Presidency

On Following Counsel

Toward the end of World War II, I enlisted in the United States Naval Reserve. My training took place at the Naval Training Center in San Diego, California, where I later became attached to that facility permanently. As the months went by, I worked diligently to achieve the seaman 1st class rating, followed by the petty officer classification—yeoman 3d class. I had excellent opportunities at the Naval Training Center serving as the personal secretary and administrative aide to the classification officer, Lt. Commander Joseph M. Santos.

One thing I did learn in the navy was that the commissioned officers represented a privileged class, followed by the petty officers, with those below the rank of petty officer being grouped together with fewer privileges. Upon my discharge from the navy, I reenrolled at the University of Utah and later entered the United States Naval Reserve unit at Fort Douglas, Utah, so that I might qualify to receive a commission in the United States Naval Reserve. I felt this was added insurance so that if there should be another conflict I would at least have the opportunity to be a commissioned officer.

I labored to qualify in every respect for consideration as a commissioned officer. Upon graduating from the University of Utah, I submitted a list of my credits, a personal reference from my employment supervisor from several summers earlier at the United States Naval Supply Depot in Clearfield, Utah, and any other personal reference I could obtain in order to make my application as impressive as possible. My first application brought forth a request for additional information. This I obtained and then awaited the outcome.

In the meantime, Frances and I were living at 608 South Second West and were members of the 6th–7th Ward of the Temple View Stake. In March of 1950, there arrived in the mail from Washington, D.C., my commission as an ensign in the United States Naval Reserve. It was a beautiful certificate with the script lettering of my name and then those words—"a commissioned officer." At last my ambition had been achieved. Contained in the cover letter was a statement to the effect that I had thirty days to accept the commission. I smiled at this sentence realizing how strenuously I had labored to qualify.

Within days, Bishop John R. Burt came to our home and extended to me a call to serve as second counselor in the bishopric of the 6th–7th Ward. He mentioned that our bishopric meeting would convene each Monday night at 7:00 P.M. Immediately I recognized that this was the exact time that my Naval Reserve drill meeting was held each Monday evening, but determined to say nothing.

After praying and worrying about the conflict between my reserve obligations and my new position as a member of the bishopric, I determined to visit with my former stake president and revered Church leader, Elder Harold B. Lee. As I sat in Brother Lee's office, I explained to him that I was a member of the Naval Reserve and held the rating of yeoman 3d class, that I had just received a commission in the Naval Reserve as an ensign, and that at the same time a call had come to me to be a member of the bishopric. He, of course, knew of the latter call inasmuch as he had set me apart to that position.

I explained to Brother Lee that war clouds were on the hori-
zon in the Far East and that if our headquarters unit of the
Naval Reserve were to be activated I, no doubt, would be called
to active duty. Elder Lee pondered for some few minutes and
then leaned toward me and said, "Brother Monson, place that
commission in an envelope and mail it back to Washington,
D.C., with a letter indicating that you are not in a position to
accept it. Then, write a letter to the commanding officer of the
12th Naval District in San Francisco, to which your reserve unit
is attached, and indicate that you would like to be discharged
from the reserve."

I responded, "Elder Lee, you don't understand. There will
be no problem at Washington, D.C., in withdrawing the commission that has been extended to me, but I have no reason to
think that the 12th Naval District will in any way honor my
request for discharge from the reserve."

Elder Lee countered, "Brother Monson, have more faith.
The military is not for you."

I returned to my office and the activities of that day feeling
that Brother Lee surely did not understand the complexities
involved in my situation. However, I so respected his judgment
that I complied with his counsel. With tears in my eyes, I posted
to Washington, D.C., the beautiful commission and letter indicating that I could not accept the commission of an ensign in the
United States Naval Reserve. I then sent a letter to the commander of the 12th Naval District, requesting discharge from
my reserve unit.

Within a few weeks, my discharge through San Francisco
arrived in the mail. My discharge was among the last processed
before the Korean War broke out in all its fury, and my Naval
Reserve unit at Fort Douglas was activated and sent to the Far
East.

Within seven weeks of my call as second counselor in the
bishopric, our bishop was called to the stake presidency, and I
was called to serve as the bishop of the ward. Again I went in to
see Elder Lee and told him the outcome of the counsel he had
provided. Brother Lee smiled and said, "There is safety, Tom, in
following the servants of the Lord. Had you not followed the

counsel I provided, difficult as it may have appeared to you at the time, you would not have been called by the Lord to be the bishop of your ward.''

I have often contemplated what the course of my life might have been had I not received and followed the advice of Elder Harold B. Lee.

3

Glen L. Rudd
Member of the First Quorum of the Seventy

Lost in the
Service of Others

In 1941 Elder Harold B. Lee was called, sustained, and ordained an Apostle and a member of the Council of the Twelve Apostles. He had served for five years as a stake president, the youngest in the Church at age thirty-one, when called, and for five years as the first managing director of the Church welfare program. That five years of service was spent mostly in traveling throughout the stakes, introducing and teaching the concepts of the welfare program. As a member of the Welfare Department staff, I was privileged to meet with him often and to travel with him many times on these teaching assignments.

For over thirty-two years he traveled to and fro over the earth as an Apostle of the Lord Jesus Christ, always alive and awake, but always totally lost in the service of others.

Our son Glen Lee was named after President Lee. Lee graduated from high school in June of 1961. About that time, he began to suffer from numbness and cold in his hands and feet, and he began to stumble and fall down. We took him to our friend Dr. Rees Anderson for medical attention. However, after two weeks his condition worsened. I was in New York and flew home to find him unable to walk and in a dangerous situation.

Again we took him to Dr. Anderson, who engaged a consultant, Dr. Madison Thomas, a neurologist. He immediately admitted Lee to the hospital. We were told that he was suffering from an unusual disease known as Guillain-Barré syndrome, which is similar to polio except that it attacks the nervous system rather than the muscles. Dr. Anderson told me on this Friday afternoon that all of the nerves and muscles of Lee's body were beginning to fail and that he would need to be hospitalized so that if his breathing became a problem he could be placed in an iron lung. He told me that he had known of only two cases before ours, and both of them had been fatal. He then said bluntly, "Except for a miracle, your boy probably will not make it." Lee was then eighteen years of age and was planning to go on a mission in about six months.

I left the doctor's office and went straight to the Church Administration Building to consult with Elder Harold B. Lee, who had been our family friend and associate for many years. I told Brother Lee the desperate circumstances, and he asked if we had administered to Lee. I told him we had done so. Then Brother Lee said, "He will be all right, at least until Sunday. I don't want to go to the hospital right now to bless him, but if you will come to my house Sunday morning, the two of us can go then to the hospital to administer to him."

He didn't tell me what he was going to do, but I knew Brother Lee well enough to know that he wanted to fast and pray and prepare himself to give Lee a special blessing. Brother Lee told me two or three times that he knew my two boys, Lee and Matt, as well as he did any boys in the entire Church. He felt as close to them as if they were his own grandsons.

When I left his office, I felt better but, of course, was still shaken by the seriousness of our son's condition. I went back to the hospital to join Lee and his mother, who sat at his bedside constantly at that stage. There was a large iron lung sitting in the hall outside of his room on the seventh floor of the hospital, just waiting for emergency action. Lee was unable to talk at this point, except in whispers, and he was unable to move any of his limbs or his head. He just lay there and tried desperately to communicate with us. This was a tremendous crisis in our family. Lee was our eldest son. At a time of his life when he should be experiencing marvelous social and spiritual highlights, he was stricken with this dreaded, potentially fatal disease.

The next morning was Saturday, and I left his hospital room and went down to the lobby. There I met by accident President Henry D. Moyle, who at that time was a counselor in the First Presidency of the Church. We visited briefly and then Brother Moyle asked, "Why are you here?"

I said evasively, "Just visiting someone who is sick."

He pressed, "Who? One of your family?"

I then admitted that it was my son Lee. For some reason I had been reluctant to talk about our problem. But he made me tell him what the situation was, and he grabbed me by the arm in his characteristic aggressive manner, saying, "Let's go up immediately and give that boy a blessing!"

As we entered the room, he went over to Lee and looked him straight in the eye saying, "Lee, I have just talked with your mission president!"

Then I watched tearfully as our fine son tried to ask a simple question, "Who?"

I could barely hear him ask this word and told President Moyle that Lee wanted to know the name of his mission president.

President Moyle told him that his mission president was in New Zealand. President Moyle then told Lee that he had come to call him on a mission and to set him apart as a missionary to serve in the New Zealand Mission, the same mission in which I had served. President Moyle then turned to me and said, "Come, let's give him a blessing."

I anointed Lee, and President Moyle sealed the anointing and set him apart as a missionary to serve in the New Zealand Mission, promising him good health and a full and complete recovery from his illness.

At this time Lee was unable to move any part of his body except his eyelids, and the only way he could communicate that he was hearing us was by moving his eyes. We were told by the hospital attendants that everything had ceased to function except the vital organs of his body, and they anticipated that those organs would quit also at any time. Despite this extremity, Lee managed to get through that Saturday.

Early on Sunday morning I called for Brother Lee, and we went to the hospital. There he gave Lee a marvelous blessing and promised him a complete recovery and the restoration of his health. From that moment on, conditions began to markedly improve. Within a day or two, there was no longer any need for the iron lung to be kept a few feet from his bed. Lee responded slowly, but affirmatively, and within a matter of a few weeks we were able to take him home.

After one short relapse, Lee was making reasonably good progress. By the end of the summer, he was able to partially use his hands and arms, though still flat on his back and unable to otherwise move. His progress was excellent, except that he had lost the ability to do many of the movements he had learned as a child. He had to learn all over again how to crawl, how to walk, how to button his clothing, tie his shoes, and other simple functions of daily care. Though he learned quickly and well, it was a difficult, tough time as we tried to help him become more self-sufficient.

My other son, Matthew, and I would carry him into the living room and put him on his hands and knees to give him a chance to try to move from that position. Sometimes he would be frozen there for twenty minutes, and we would finally have to turn him over bodily because he couldn't move his muscles enough to fall onto his back or onto his side. By his nineteenth birthday in October, we were able to get him out of bed and into a wheelchair for visits in the living room. Soon after that, he was on crutches; and by the time the snow was leaving in February, he was able to walk quite well, even though he didn't have good control over his balance.

He would lie in bed for hours lifting dumbbell weights to build up the muscles in his arms. He tried to walk as much as he possibly could to rebuild his leg muscles. Brushing the last remaining snow aside, we arranged for him to bounce a basketball in our backyard. He insisted on doing this by the hour, and after two weeks, he was able to throw the ball up toward the hoop and gradually regained his strength and body coordination.

Now it appeared to everyone, including the physicians, that Lee was going to have a complete recovery from his illness, as had been promised by his priesthood blessings. At this stage he began to ask questions about going on his mission, since he was now four months beyond the time he had planned to leave for the mission field. By spring of the year, he was pressing continuously to go. I talked with Brother Lee about it, and we stalled as long as we could, but finally Brother Lee agreed with us and the doctors that he could plan to leave for his mission in the summer of 1962.

Lee departed for New Zealand in June of that year. He completed a splendid mission and returned home well in 1964, marking the fulfillment of a remarkable prophecy through priesthood blessings. Even today his doctors have only the one explanation—a mighty medical miracle from God.

Brother Lee was a great man! I know that, and I suppose most everyone else does. Yet, I suspect that few persons realize what a tremendous individual he really was.

Elder Lee was a man who had little time to sightsee or relax when he traveled. His work was never-ending: always he was teaching, explaining, counseling, blessing, and encouraging the Saints. Year after year he moved from city to city, state to state, country to country, and continent to continent, always the slave of a schedule of appointments and demands, rarely having time to do anything that would be pleasurable to him. He was almost always filling the plans made by circumstances or by others. It mattered little how he felt or whether he was well enough to do the job. The job had to be done, and he had to do it.

He was a strong, vigorous man, but like the Apostle Paul, he had his "thorn in the flesh." Headaches, fatigue, and more than his share of minor and major irritations and sicknesses constantly plagued him. He was one of those unusual men who achieved much and remained firm in spite of, or perhaps because of, his acquaintance with adversity, sorrow, difficulty, and disappointment.

The Saints and his brethren, however, were always blessed, encouraged, and lifted up, generally unaware of the problems that he endured. When his biography was published, many of his closest companions in the Council of the Twelve were surprised to learn of his chronic ailments. He was never one to complain or to seek sympathy. He went about his daily tasks in an uncomplaining, quiet manner.

Typical of this attitude was the circumstance of his visit to us when I was presiding over the Florida Mission in 1967. A serious health problem had been bothering him. Because of overwork, he spent three days in the hospital in Salt Lake City. After receiving a blood transfusion, he left the hospital so that he might come and fulfill his responsibilities and the schedule set up for him. But as he was preparing to leave, another personal heartache occurred. Another friend, relative, and loved one passed away. But he had the schedule to keep, and he flew across the country to begin his tour in the Florida Mission. For eight days he was again "lost in our problems." There were buildings to dedicate; five in all. There were decisions to make on Church expansion and growth and on buildings yet to be built. There were 221 missionaries to interview and to encourage. There were blessings to be given to the sick wherever he went, as well as other types of blessings. There were special interviews with members of the Church. Every day required traveling either by car or airplane. He was up early and went to bed late. Every moment involved another question and another problem to solve, and always he had the inexorable schedule to keep.

In all of this, hardly a personal moment was provided for himself. Yet, he was always concerned for the comfort and happiness of Sister Joan Lee, his wife, and her sister, Edna Cazier, who came as a guest companion. He was always most concerned also with the safety and comfort of Sister Rudd, and me, as the mission president. Meanwhile, he was ever willing to carry on and finish the work.

After eight rugged and intensive days, three or four long air rides, and over 2,300 miles traversed in a car, his visit to the Florida Mission was completed. This would have been a wonderful opportunity for him to rest and relax under the warm Florida sun, but no, he had another plane waiting for him to take him to New York for meetings beginning almost immediately, which would lead to the division of the New Jersey Stake.

Once more, he was consumed in the care and service of others. After many interviews and hours of strenuous work, which he invested only after receiving a priesthood blessing himself, he completed the division and reorganization of the New Jersey Stake. He was so exhausted physically and mentally, however, that he knew he could not keep his business appointments in New York City and flew back home to Salt Lake City. His safe arrival was made possible only by a miraculous blessing by the laying on of hands on his head inflight, by personages unseen and unknown. President Lee described this miracle in a general conference sermon on 8 April 1973.

Under emergency conditions, he immediately was admitted to the hospital, where studies demonstrated stomach surgery was imperative. Physicians ruled out his participation in the April 1967 general conference. Following the conference, he was operated on and over half of his stomach was removed.

Brother Lee recovered. He renewed his vigorous, unyielding schedule for many years. The Lord had a great work for him to accomplish and he did it. Yes, Brother Lee continued to be "lost in the service of others" throughout the balance of his life. Always was he alert and awake to the tasks at hand and those ahead.

A great, spiritual giant was Brother Lee. In his warm heart there was room for all the troubles and problems that came his way. Always there was room for patience, understanding, and kindness. There continued to flow from him wisdom, advice, counsel, encouragement, and admonition, which the Saints of the Church and the General Authorities so very much needed.

President Lee was born to become a servant of his fellowmen. He did not fail his destiny. All of us whom he served owe his memory our love and gratitude. He could have stayed home from his visit to our Florida Mission when he knew he wasn't well, but he came to us and, again, magnified his calling and blessed us mightily. As a result, increased devotion and dedicated service was multiplied among the thousands of persons he served.

Brother Lee was no doubt one of the great men of this dispensation, and I have missed him as much as or more than any other man since he passed away. Many times in my assignments since his death, I have felt very close to him.

As I become older, I think about the great men that I have known very well, and I am quite pleased to recognize that it has been my good fortune to be reasonably close to many great and fine men. At times I discussed this subject with President Marion G. Romney, and I know how he felt about it for many years. It was always a thrill to me to have him tell me about the great men of the Church, and then he would tell me about each President, but when he came to his friend, Harold, he always said, "But, Harold was a seer."

President J. Reuben Clark, Jr., who was the teacher of President Lee, was another great man of this century. President Clark had a tremendous influence on the life of President Lee, possibly greater than any other person.

I know what I have said of President Lee is true, for I remember hundreds of personal moments with him. He was my stake president while I was an Aaronic Priesthood boy and a young elder. We were friends for over forty years. He was a great friend to me and treated me like his own son. His greatness has been unmatched in my experience.

4

Marion G. Romney
President of the Quorum of the Twelve

He Was Most Like
the Prophet Joseph

Harold B. Lee was no ordinary man. His influence in Church councils was effective from the beginning. It continued to increase until the day of his passing. All the programs of the Church operative during the nearly thirty-three years he served as one of the General Authorities bear the mark of his prophetic genius.

He loved the youth with a divine compassion. He sorrowed over the rebellious and unrepentant and rejoiced over the returning prodigal.

He was one of the most powerful men in modern Israel. The source of his strength was in his knowledge that he himself lived in the shadow of the Almighty. To him, his Heavenly Father was a senior partner, daily giving him guidance. Few indeed had had

The first three paragraphs were taken from a letter to the author, 15 April 1980. The text that follows comes from an interview with the author, 7 March 1980.

contacts with heaven as direct and regular as did he. He knew that the gospel of Jesus Christ is eternal truth.

Harold B. Lee was a unique man. I was well acquainted with him, and I have been acquainted with many great men during my last forty years with the General Authorities. Very few men enjoyed a friendship like we had with President Clark and Harold. We were as close as men could be.

I have never had a closer relationship with any man than I did with Harold. It goes back to our earliest married years when he invited me to his house, and I invited him to our house where I had made some of the furniture in my home.

In one aspect of his life and his character he was different from any other man that I've ever been with. I felt with him like I'd imagine the Prophet Joseph Smith was, with respect to the inspiration that came to him. Joseph Smith spoke by the power of the Spirit out of a personal knowledge and association with the Father and the Son. Brother Lee, in my judgment, was more like the Prophet Joseph Smith in this respect than was any other man I've ever associated with. He seemed to get the inspiration of the Lord spontaneously.

He didn't approach his decisions and counsel like a lawyer and argue or reason things out. President J. Reuben Clark, Jr., was painstakingly slow in making a decision. He would study it out and, using his great mind, would come to his conclusion. In contrast, Harold just seemed to me to speak directly from inspiration and could jump, as it were, from peak to peak as he went along in his teachings and his interpretations of the gospel and in his answering of questions.

I remember reading once that the Prophet Joseph Smith wrote that he with Oliver Cowdery and W. W. Phelps were laboring one afternoon (1 October 1835 in Kirtland, Ohio) on the Egyptian alphabet, and "during the research, the principles of astronomy as understood by Father Abraham and the ancients unfolded to our understanding" (*History of the Church* 2:286). And that's the way Brother Lee used to get inspiration, as I associated with him and heard him time and time again. He just spoke as the inspiration of the Lord enlightened his mind, without the reasoning and arguments that so many of us go through as we labor. I have always felt that no man I've ever met in my life was as near the Prophet Joseph Smith in that respect as Brother Lee. He obtained his knowledge immediately from God by revelation. He was a seer.

I miss him. It seems to me to be impossible that Harold is gone. I'm surely looking forward to the time when I will see Brother Lee again and associate with him. It will be a happy reunion, I'm sure. I'll be glad to join him and go on with our intimate association.

5

Oscar W. McConkie, Jr.
Former Regional Representative

God Spoke to Harold
Every Day

I was a missionary in New England. President S. Dilworth Young was the mission president.

I was assigned the area of Amherst, Massachusetts. We were staying with the Reverend Kenneth Beckwith, a prominent Congregational Church minister. His wife, Betty, was a frequent speaker in local church services.

Betty agreed to read the Book of Mormon. She told me with wonder about her experience in reading the account in the book of 3 Nephi of our Lord's coming to the inhabitants of this continent.

She said she had always been interested in the scriptures. When but a young girl she would read the New Testament in bed by use of a flashlight. When her parents would check to see if she were asleep, she would put the Bible and the flashlight under the covers and feign sleep. She would then continue her reading. She loved the New Testament.

Her favorite part of the New Testament was the seventeenth chapter of John. Christ's intercessory prayer touched her to the depth of her heart. She felt she should not even read this chapter unless she was in a particularly sanctimonious mood.

But, said she, "I was more moved and more motivated in reading the eleventh chapter of Third Nephi than I have ever been in my life, even than when reading the seventeenth chapter of John."

It was a wonderful religious experience.

Shortly after the time when Betty Beckwith experienced reading the Book of Mormon, I got word that Elder Harold B. Lee of the Council of the Twelve was coming to tour the New England Mission. He would be in Springfield, Massachusetts, to speak to the Saints there.

I asked Betty if she would drive my companion and me to Springfield to attend the meeting at which Elder Lee was scheduled to speak. "You know many of the prominent Protestant ministers," I reasoned; "this is your opportunity to meet a living member of the Twelve Apostles."

She drove us from Amherst to Springfield and attended the meeting with us.

Elder Lee commenced his sermon, not unlike the introduction of many of the Saints, "Would each of you in the congregation please pray for what you want me to speak about?"

I looked at Betty. Her head was bowed in prayer.

Elder Lee spoke. It was a talk on baptism. The Spirit of the Lord was there. It was a spiritual experience.

After the services, I introduced Betty to Elder Lee.

"You spoke on just what I was praying you would speak on," she said.

"I know somewhat of your prayers," replied Elder Lee. He then spoke directly to her. As he spoke, it was apparent that he knew more about Betty and Ken Beckwith than I did; and I had stayed at their house at intermittent times during the preceding months. It was more than insight. It was more than warm human sensitivity. He was speaking to her soul.

As we drove back to Amherst, Betty burst out with, "That man knew things he just shouldn't have known!"

President Lee was a talker, quite unlike my brother Bruce, then a member of the First Council of Seventy. I loved to be in his presence and listen to him recount his experiences. He shared himself.

For a few years I was secretary of Elbert Farms, a Church farming enterprise. The Brethren wanted one of their lawyers to serve as secretary to set the agenda, keep the minutes, and be aware of legal matters as they might arise. President Lee was the presiding officer conducting the board of directors' meetings. We met quarterly.

It didn't take me long to discover that President Lee came fifteen minutes early to his meetings. So I came twenty minutes early. I liked to be with him because he talked.

He usually was full of spiritual experiences that had recently occurred. Some of them were startling. Some seemed very tame to me.

President Lee would say, "I had one of my great experiences this morning." He would then tell me what happened. Some sounded like the New Testament accounts. About others, I was led to say to myself, "That's not nearly as significant or unusual as other stories he's told me. Why does he think that is so great?" It finally dawned on me that here was a servant of the Lord. He had just had a personal experience with one member of the Godhead, the Holy Ghost. Of course, at that time, he thought that particular experience was one of his great ones!

This particular account happened years and years before all of this. President Lee was then the president of a stake. He told it to me when he was a young member of the Quorum of the Twelve.

I had just returned home from my first mission. My older brother Bruce phoned me and asked if I would accompany him to a stake conference he was assigned to attend in Idaho. I had been gone for two years, and this would be an opportunity to renew our love and friendship.

Parenthetically, I might add that, as a typical young returned missionary, I did think it quite appropriate that a General Authority should invite me to a conference with him. It wasn't until the trip home that I discovered that Bruce was checking me out and had counsel for me.

After Bruce asked me, he got a call from Elder Lee, "Would you drive me to my northern Utah conference and pick me up after? It's right on your way." Of course Bruce was happy to do so. He told Elder Lee that he had asked me but would postpone that. Elder Lee would not hear of it, "Bring Oscar along."

Bruce phoned me. One of the members of the Twelve was coming. I was to sit in the back seat and behave; speak only when spoken to.

It didn't work out that way. Elder Lee insisted that I sit in the front seat with them. And, like I said, he talked. I asked questions.

Poor Bruce! How he must have felt to hear his younger brother say, "Elder Lee, you're twenty years younger than the next senior Apostle to you. It seems apparent that you one day may be the President of the Church. My question is, has the Lord ever told you that you were going to be President of the Church?"

Elder Lee said, "I'll tell you a story.

"When I was a stake president, I called on a woman in the stake who had a devil in her. As I came into her house, the devil said through her mouth, 'I know you, you're the President of the Church.' I said, 'No, I'm the president of the stake.' But the devil said again, 'You're the President of the Church.' "

Elder Lee then told us of casting out the devil.

He did not answer my question. But, in Elder Lee's open, sharing nature, he shared an experience in which a devil seemed to know. The devils also knew and trembled before the Savior, who while in his mortal ministry, came to the country of the Gadarenes, where two evil spirits hailed him as Jesus, the Son of God, and asked why he had come to torment them before their time. (See Mark 5:1–2 and Luke 8:26–39.)

Earlier, I had been in the U.S. Navy. I was eighteen years old, and it was the first time I had been away from home. During my senior year at East High School in Salt Lake City, I signed up for an officer's training program. Having passed the physical and mental examinations, I reported for duty a week after graduation.

My unit was stationed at the University of New Mexico in Albuquerque. My father saw me off at the train station. He nearly missed the train departure because he was buying me a going-away present, a wristwatch. He breathlessly gave me my present and final instructions on keeping the commandments, "Remember who you are. I love you."

I knew my father loved me more than anyone else in the world did. However, there were great anxieties in my breast. The McConkie household had been a sheltered home. How prepared was I for the real world? particularly the navy world?

In point of fact, this was of such concern to me that I had gone to Father a few days before and asked for his blessing. As the train pulled out of the station, I pondered that blessing. I had had a lot of fears. Father had taken me and Mother into the bedroom. Mother sat on the end of the bed, with a yellow legal pad. She wrote as Father spoke the words of his blessing, "Oscar, my son, unto you it is given to bear my name . . ." Then came the peace of comfort, advice, and encouragement.

Navy life was harsher than the football locker rooms of high school athletics—the most jarring experience I'd had to that point in my life. Some of my new associates had come from other high schools around the country. Others had been selected from the fleet. These were the "old salts." The old salts told of experiences beyond my ability to conjure up. It was indeed a worldly world.

Father typed up my blessing and sent it to me. It served as refuge against the world. Still, my father sensed that I needed more. He wrote me long, concerned, instructive letters each week.

Father was called to preside over the California Mission in 1949. He and Mother and my younger brother moved to Los Angeles. My older brothers, Bruce, Brit, and James, were also in the armed services. My only sister's husband, Bill Pope, was in the army. We were flying missions from bases in England, fighting in the Battle of Bastone, and in the war in the Pacific Ocean.

The letters came to all of us each week. The letters served as a balance. War and wickedness there was; but, there was also God and his workings with men.

I'm pondering now the effect on me of one of those letters. Here is the essence of that letter:

Elder Harold B. Lee, of the Council of the Twelve Apostles, was assigned to tour the California Mission. The mission president made the arrangements to make the best use of an Apostle's time and get the most benefit from the visit of such a dignitary.

Father wanted as many of his missionaries as possible to have the opportunity to meet and shake the hand of a living Apostle of our Lord. After the scheduled Church service, he would have the missionaries in the area line up to meet Elder Lee.

Father had one missionary who had deported himself in such a way that he knew he should release him from missionary service and send him home. But, Dad's king-sized personality would not permit it. He was going to save each of those missionaries given to his charge, screaming and hollering if necessary. There was nothing he couldn't handle, and he was not going to send any missionary home.

Elder Lee spoke to the missionaries in the zone where the errant missionary was laboring. No hint was made of his misdeeds.

The missionaries in the zone lined up after the meeting to greet and shake Elder Lee's hand. A few words were spoken between Elder Lee and each missionary. Father and Elder Lee started to get into the mission car to leave the area.

Elder Lee stopped. He looked at Father and said, "Oscar, why haven't you sent that elder home?"

Father knew that the heavens had whispered to the apostolic servant. As Father told us of the mission tour of Elder Harold B. Lee, he wrote to his sons, "God spoke to Harold every day."

We knew God was in his heaven, and notwithstanding our present circumstances, all would be right with the world.

6

Gene R. Cook
Member of the First Quorum of the Seventy

He Spoke to Me
Spirit to Spirit

When President David O. McKay died, on 18 January 1970, the President of the Council of the Twelve, President Joseph Fielding Smith, was called to be the new prophet of the Lord. Elder Harold B. Lee was the next senior Apostle to President Smith and was called a few days later to serve with President Smith as the First Counselor in the new First Presidency. Elder Lee told us of an experience that happened to him during these two days, when the reorganization of the First Presidency was being considered.

One of the Church brethren approached Elder Lee and asked "Is it correct what I have heard that they're going to make Joseph Fielding Smith the President of the Church?"

That wasn't a very good question to ask of Elder Lee at that time. Elder Lee answered politely and confirmed that he thought that would be the case.

This message is taken in part from a talk given at a Church Employees Devotional entitled "We Thank Thee O God for a Prophet," November 20, 1981; used by permission.

But the man persisted and said, "How can that be? I can't believe that. How can we sustain Joseph Fielding Smith? He's ninety-three years old. Why, he's so old I'm not sure he is really quite with it." The man continued developing this point—how could a man of that age, his body weak and worn down, still direct this Church?

President Lee listened for a while, but his sharp mind was spinning. He responded, "My good brother, do you know what it takes to be a prophet of the Lord?"

The man said, "Well, I guess I really don't know exactly."

"Well," said Elder Lee, "what do you think it would take?"

The fellow then said, "Well, I suppose he'd have to know all about genealogy, the missionary program of the Church, and all the missionaries and what they're doing and how to supervise them. He would need to know about the Primary and the Relief Society and the building and construction programs." He named quite a few other major functions of the Church.

When he finished Elder Lee said, "That's all wrong." He could sometimes say that quite pointedly. The man was taken back a bit. Then Elder Lee answered his question by stating, "Shall I tell you what it takes to be a prophet? There's only one capacity; just one. And that is to be able to hear the voice of the Lord. That's all. He's got all the rest of us to do the work. He just has to do one function. Do you suppose that this great living Apostle, who has been sustained a prophet for six decades, longer than any other man on earth, might be able to do that?"

The brother was feeling a little low by then, but Elder Lee continued, "Do you suppose that Joseph Fielding Smith, who was a home teaching companion of President Wilford Woodruff, might know something about that?"

By this time the man, in some humility, was on the retreat.

President Lee retold this story at times to teach a great lesson. We have since had another great prophet who became bent with age, but President Spencer W. Kimball still continued many long years effectively giving the Church the "voice of the Lord" as only he could do.

Brother Lee had so many tremendous characteristics that I have tried diligently to emulate. He was a mighty prophet, a gifted teacher of righteousness. He was most quotable. What he said impressed because it came from the Lord. He would make statements like this: "You cannot lift another soul until you are standing on higher ground than he is. You must be sure, if you would rescue the man, that you yourself are setting the example of what you would have him be. You cannot light a fire in another soul unless it is burning in your own soul." (Conference Report, Apr. 1973, p. 178.)

Of course that places the burden on each of us to be worthy. I used to love his great statement that he quoted so often to the Brethren and others in the Church that were faithful Latter-day Saints already; he would say, "You will know you're beginning to be converted when your heart begins to tell you things your mind does not know."

Two other experiences taught me memorable lessons from President Lee. I was blessed to be the executive secretary for a period of time to the First Council of Seventy when as a council we were in the process of trying to recommend how the First Quorum of Seventy would be called and how that prophecy would come into place. Men had worked on that project for 150 years. The Brethren were struggling to get revelation on how to do it and when and in what way it should be done. In those days they called some leaders as mission representatives of the Council of the Twelve, twenty-nine of them, to begin working in that direction. I was called to be one of those, and I was worried and concerned because I was then a very young man. I guess I felt much like Enoch did when he was called, that maybe they called the wrong person.

President Lee, in his perceptiveness, taught this concept always, and did so to me personally, saying "As a mission representative don't ever go alone to a stake conference." And, of course, immediately some would think, "You mean I'm going to have a companion go with me—another General Authority?" Of course he didn't mean that. He would say, "No, don't ever go alone. If you have the Lord with you, you need not worry. You'll find many times, Brother Cook, when you go to stake conferences week after week after week, you'll get off the airplane, you'll be in the stake president's car, and within five minutes you'll know, generally speaking, the stature of the stake and where they are spiritually, because this is the man who leads the stake. In some instances they'll be in such good condition, that if it wouldn't disappoint the Saints, you could get back on the plane and go home and not even give your talks or lessons because they are under way, headed in the right direction. It wouldn't make too much difference one way or another.

"In other cases, you'll know within a few minutes that the Lord has sent you there for some specific purposes and all you've got to do is find out what they are and teach that stake president so he'll teach his stake members."

President Lee was constantly stressing revelation. He wanted us to move ahead on our feelings by what we sensed inside, with the assurance that the Lord would not deceive, if we had such faith.

I have never forgotten a general priesthood meeting that was held the night following the solemn assembly when President Lee was sustained as the prophet, seer, and revelator and President of the Church. Many others, like me, will still remember his sermon on Saturday night, 7 October 1972. It was a marvelous priesthood meeting, a truly unique experience.

In that particular priesthood meeting, President Lee taught most effectively and with penetrating power, that

> There is another danger that confronts us. There seem to be those among us who are as wolves among the flock, trying to lead some who are weak and unwary among Church members, according to reports that have reached us, who are taking the law into their own hands by refusing to pay their income tax because they have some political disagreement with constituted authorities . . .
>
> "Let no man break the laws of the land . . . until he reigns whose right it is to reign, and subdues all enemies under his feet." (D&C 58:20–22.)
>
> I want to warn this great body of priesthood against that great sin of Sodom and Gomorrah, which has been labeled as a sin second only in seriousness to the sin of murder. I speak of the sin of adultery . . . and besides this, the equally grievous sin of homosexuality, which seems to be gaining momentum with social acceptance in the Babylon of the world, of which Church members must not be part.
>
> While we are in the world, we must not be of the world. (Conference Report, Oct. 1972, p. 127.)

He spoke that night of many such specific issues of our day, stating the doctrine so clearly that nobody could misunderstand. It was a powerful priesthood meeting. I was overpowered as I sat in the audience listening to that sermon by the Spirit. I had a tremendous surge of feelings, and I witness that I had heard the prophet of the Lord speaking.

I pondered those feelings and the message that night as I went home. The next morning, as I went to the Sunday Tabernacle Choir broadcast, I parked my car and walked over to the underground tunnel leading to the Tabernacle. I wasn't paying too much attention to what was going on because I was really thinking about what had been said the night before. I had my head down watching the ground and just about bumped into President Harold B. Lee on the walkway. He was walking alone, which was very uncommon, on his way over to the Tabernacle. He warmly said, "Come and join me and let's walk over together."

As we started walking together, I tried to express to him some of the feelings I had experienced the night before, but I had a hard time saying it. I was rather emotional about it and couldn't quite get the words out. Finally President Lee stopped me and said, "Gene, you don't need to say anymore. I know what you're trying to say, and I understand." Then he said, "May I share something with you?"

Of course I was eager to hear more, and what he told me illustrates the spiritual caliber of that great prophet. He gave me this background: "There were a lot of statements made last night that perhaps in policy or clear teachings have not been stated before, and I worked over them to be certain that it was correct and right and that the First Presidency was in full agreement with them. I wasn't really worried about that, Elder Cook. You know that. I wasn't worried much about that, other than it be right in concept.

"What I was worried about was that I wanted every last priesthood holder to *feel* in his heart the great witness and outpouring of the Spirit. That's all I wanted, and it didn't matter too much what was being taught, just as long as they felt with great power the Spirit of the Lord.

"Remember, Gene, that it's more important what you feel than what you know."

We walked on, arrived at the Tabernacle, and I sat down in the audience. We had a half hour or so before the general session started, and I felt I ought to write all that down because I was really impressed by what President Lee had told me. I wrote it all. It took about thirty minutes to do it. When I finished, the thought came to me, "What are all these six pages?" He couldn't have said all that. He was only with me three or four minutes."

Then I learned another great lesson. It was indeed all from President Lee. He didn't say the words, but he spoke to me in those few minutes in the Spirit in such a way that it was as if he had spiritually played an orchestra in perfect harmony inside of me and played a hundred notes while maybe saying only four. That's speaking by the Spirit. I learned some marvelous truths that day about how he did it to me and maybe how I can do it to other people, to play that harmony inside of them by the Spirit, moving them to repent, to bring their lives nearer perfection.

I am constantly thankful to President Lee for teaching me spiritual communication, and I am still striving to be like him.

7

Mark E. Petersen
Member of the Quorum of the Twelve

The Blessing That Preserved the Next Prophet

It was at general conference time, April 1972, when President Spencer W. Kimball was so critically ill and was trying to determine whether to have the open-heart surgery that physicians were advising. He could not make up his mind about submitting to surgery because, as I remember it, the doctors had told him there would only be a 50 percent chance of recovery.

He had come to President Lee to ask whether he should be operated on. President Lee then invited him and Camilla and all of the members of the Twelve and the First Presidency to come to the council room on the fifth floor of the temple. There we would pray about it and give Brother Kimball a blessing in the hope that this blessing would answer the question.

We knelt in prayer in the council room. Then Brother Kimball took the chair in the middle of the room where it was placed. We gathered around him, and President Lee gave him a blessing.

President Kimball was so weak that it was difficult for him even to walk. His face was gray. He was tremendously worried and almost thought that his career had about come to an end, so he was very much filled with anticipation as he sat down on the chair and the Brethren laid their hands upon his head.

President Lee, inspired as he was, gave President Kimball a marvelous blessing and advised him to have the operation on his heart. In the blessing, President Lee prayed for the doctors that they would have unusual skill and inspiration. Then he blessed President Kimball with recovery and promised him that he would be made well again and be able to carry on a great mission, that the Lord still had a great work for him to perform, and that the Lord would make him well and fully fit him to accomplish this great purpose.

Everyone was in tears by the time the blessing was over. The Spirit was there, and we felt that the Lord had spoken through President Lee.

The subsequent events, of course, absolutely fulfilled the promise that President Lee made to President Kimball. We are all familiar with the remarkable ministry President Kimball performed after this surgery as the prophet and President of the Church.

I think this was the most spiritual occasion of my life in connection with President Lee.

8

Boyd K. Packer
Member of the Quorum of the Twelve

First
Impressions

Shortly after we were married, I was called as an assistant stake clerk in the North Box Elder Stake. The stake presidency consisted of John P. Lillywhite, president; with Verl Willey, first counselor; and Eberhard Zundal, second counselor.

One of our visitors to quarterly conferences, as they were held in those days, was Elder Harold B. Lee. Two general sessions of conference were held, one in the morning and one in the afternoon. Between these sessions, we were invited to go with the stake presidency and stake clerk to the home of Eberhard and Laura Zundal for a luncheon. Donna and I, who lived just a few blocks from President Zundal, hurried home to see to our little children. Her mother was tending them for us.

We arrived at the Zundal's just a few minutes after the others had arrived. Brother Lee had left the house to come out to the car to get something from his briefcase. As we drove up, he stood on the sidewalk and waited for us.

As we met on the sidewalk, he pointed to the house and said, "Those are great men in there. Never lose an opportunity to learn at the feet of such men as these."

I was greatly impressed at his statement and became a little choked up. I told him how grateful I was for the opportunity to learn at the feet of such men as President Lillywhite, President Willey, and President Zundal. He then looked at me, as Brother Lee could look at people, and said, "God bless you, my boy. One day you will carry great responsibility."

This was a powerful statement coming from a member of the Quorum of Twelve Apostles, and it greatly influenced my life.

In countless subsequent meetings over the years and in time associating with him in the ranks of the General Authorities, his influence on my life has been profound. He was always teaching. If one had the sensitivity to listen, his lessons were always substantive, never trivial, always helpful.

9

Hugh W. Pinnock
Member of the First Quorum of the Seventy

His Influence
Stretches Across
My Life

I t has been interesting to me to observe the deep respect that so many of our brethren have had for Elder Harold B. Lee during his ministry. I remember the reverence with which he was held by my mission president, A. Lewis Elggren, in the Western States Mission. Incidentally, I take pride in the fact that I served in the same mission where Elder Lee had served.

One of President Lee's favorite stories of his mission happened when he was preaching on the corner of 16th and Larimer Street. He reported that a football team came past in a bus where he was conducting a street meeting and slowed down in order to give fifteen cheers for Jesus.

While serving in Denver, Colorado, I was editor of *Westate News*, our mission newspaper. I had allowed to be published a scripture that was misquoted humorously. Elder Lee read that article and immediately phoned President Elggren in Denver, telling him that this statement was not appropriate in a mission newspaper or anywhere else. I learned a lesson about sacred subjects that I have not forgotten during the thirty-two years that have transpired since that time. That same experience is helping me today in my responsibilities with Church magazines.

When I was dating my future wife, Anne Hawkins, our conversations would often focus upon men that I admired. Like hundreds of young college students, I had made President Lee my hero, and I would rejoice in telling Anne about his ability to regulate and build up the Church, just as I tell our children today about this wonderful leader.

My experience with this great man became more personal and intimate in 1968. At the October general conference of that year, James E. Faust and I were called as Regional Representatives of the Twelve and as members of the Priesthood Leadership Committee. Elder Thomas S. Monson, youngest member of the Quorum of the Twelve in seniority and age, was our chairman. We began then a five-year period of service in which our paths crossed frequently with President Lee.

Wendell J. Ashton, advertising executive, and Neal A. Maxwell, vice-president of the University of Utah, were the senior members of that committee. Elder Maxwell and Elder Faust had the basic responsibility of training Regional Representatives. Wendell Ashton and I had the task of developing training materials for stake presidents and bishops.

In seeking a means to properly train bishops, we learned that Elder Lee had provided his son-in-law, L. Brent Goates, then serving as a bishop, with a comprehensive outline of the duties of that office. We borrowed this material because of its brilliance, simplicity, and scope. It defined the responsibilities of a bishop by drawing five circles of his stewardship. This became the heart of the *Bishop's Training Course and Self-Help Guide*, which was disseminated throughout the Church. Much of this material is still used to great advantage.

At this time, President Lee was serving as Acting President of the Twelve and had many responsibilities relating to the First Presidency due to his seniority and because of the ill health of

President David O. McKay. With this influence, he placed special importance on the *Bishop's Training Course* and on teacher development.

One day Elder Lee called me into his office and asked how we were progressing on the *Bishop's Training Course*. I told him that we were moving the project along but that we were concerned about home teaching and activating the "inactive." Elder Lee replied, "Brother Pinnock, would you define for me the 'inactives' of the Church?"

I said, "Well, they are those who do not attend their Church meetings on Sunday, they don't hold callings in their wards, and they are not helping with such responsibilities as home teaching."

He answered, "Brother Pinnock, you have described me exactly."

In his sage and characteristic manner, he had taught me another powerful lesson. Since that time I have been most careful in discussing those persons who are not as involved in the Church as they should be. I felt embarrassed, but I had been taught effectively.

Once I shared a stake conference assignment to Tacoma, Washington, with Elder Marion G. Romney. I asked him, as we traveled together, about effective leaders he had known. Elder Romney answered, "The finest leader I have ever known is Harold B. Lee. He is a seer."

After the *Bishop's Training Course* was completed and we had worked on several other projects, I was called with my family to serve as a mission president in Pennsylvania. At the general conference of April 1973, while crossing the underground parking area, President Lee called me over, saying, "Hugh," the first time I can ever remember his using my first name, "do you have any idea why we have called you on a mission?"

Feeling that he had a reason that would help me understand more thoroughly my calling, I said, "No, sir, and I would appreciate your telling me why."

He answered, "We want to keep you out of trouble." Then he laughed for what seemed to be several minutes. It was exceedingly rare to see him enjoy himself and to respond in that manner.

He later gave me his sincere thinking in a firm, tender, and caring manner. He reminded me that much of our service in the Church and many of our callings might be for reasons other than those for which we had thought or hoped.

Indicative of his masterful teaching was his marvelous way of communicating when we were heading in the wrong direction or not measuring up to his expectations.

One afternoon, the leadership committee had presented four or five ideas, all of which he rejected. He sent us on our way, reminding us that he would not have to tell us no if we had been better prepared and more in tune with our responsibilities. That was difficult for all of us on the committee to accept, but thereafter we were always better prepared because of that experience. His standards of excellence became our standards, and that is effective leadership and teaching.

President Lee's amazing memory for details not only kept us alert but always communicated the fact that he was vitally interested in those projects that he had assigned to the leadership committee.

We always knew exactly where he stood. On one occasion, a Regional Representative of the Twelve had taken upon himself more responsibility than he had been implicitly or explicitly given. President Lee made certain that this individual was contacted immediately; he didn't even wait for an hour to pass. The individual was instructed to behave more appropriately or he would not have the privilege of serving longer as a Regional Representative. Operating in that environment helped all of us to be better servants. He motivated all people who knew him to lift their performance and to be at their best at all times.

As I look back now over these and many more experiences like them, stretching back to my earliest days in the mission field, I can see how my life has been dramatically changed through my association with President Harold B. Lee. How I cherish the molding influence of this mighty man of God!

10

Franklin D. Richards
Member of the First Quorum of the Seventy

Favorite Thoughts
and Quotations of
President Harold B. Lee

The young man who came to our door to sell us a set of books on Bible study was so gracious, so persuasive, that we bought them in spite of the fact that it was a strain on our budget. This was our first contact with Harold B. Lee.

Little did we know that in years to come he would become a very dear friend and would have a tremendous influence in our lives.

We spent fifteen years in Washington, D.C. When we came back to Utah, we had a great desire to learn how to more effectively teach the gospel. We felt the best way to do this was to become stake missionaries. Harold B. Lee set Sister Richards and me apart as stake missionaries. This was the beginning of the most wonderful years of our lives.

In the next few years, we had many occasions to associate with Elder Lee and his sweet wife, Fern. We grew to love and admire them both and learned to appreciate his great spiritual power, his deep sense of caring for others, and his unselfish devotion to the work of the Lord.

In 1960 I was called to preside over the Northwestern States Mission. A wonderful opportunity was given to us in May of 1960 when Elder Lee and his wife were assigned to tour our mission. We had just completed developing the six missionary discussions, and Elder Lee reviewed them for doctrinal correctness and gave us some very constructive suggestions. He subsequently recommended their use to several mission presidents. The mission tour required two weeks, and we had the closest association with these two great people. We held meetings in all of the districts and held conferences with all of the missionaries.

How motivated and inspired the missionaries were as he taught them the gospel and instructed them in the way they must live to fulfill their obligations to their Heavenly Father and be worthy of his blessings.

How precious to us were the hours we spent traveling together. In this close intimacy, we felt his love for us personally and his desire to help us. In every way he was truly a man of God with all of the great qualities necessary to make him a true prophet. What a rare and wonderful privilege this association was for us.

When I was called to be a General Authority, Elder Lee took time to advise and counsel me. His example, as well as his counsel, had a tremendous influence in my life, and I will ever be grateful for our friendship and association.

In 1979 I was asked to give a ten-minute spiritual thought at a meeting of the First Quorum of the Seventy, and I chose to share these thoughts with the Brethren on that occasion so that they might know the great influence President Harold B. Lee had been in our lives.

That I might not lose the gems of thought and counsel President Lee had given to us, and to keep them in ready access for reference in years to come, I have recorded them. Hardly a week goes by still that I do not quote some of these statements publicly, inasmuch as they are certainly as appropriate today as they were at the time President Lee first pronounced them. Following are a few of the most precious of his teachings that have been an inspiration to me over the years and to many others to whom I have related them. I have placed them under various topics.

Doctrine and inspirational thoughts:
- Every dispensation is introduced by a powerful revelation of the Godhead.
- You cannot kindle a fire in anyone's heart until it is burning in your heart.
- How do we sanctify ourselves? By keeping the law.
- All blessings come COD. When you keep the law, the Lord is bound.
- "What does the Church think?" means "What does the President of the Church think?"
- If we were facing death, what unfinished business do we have? If today we died, is there something we should have done? *Today* is the only day for sure.
- An executive is one who knows how to train an organization to carry on when he is away. It embraces the ability to delegate, communicate, and check up.
- You may be the only standard work of the Church that many may see.
- We are illiterate so far as the standard works of the Church are concerned.
- The all-important thing is not whether the Lord is on your side but whether you are on the Lord's side.
- Reoccurrence to fundamentals is essential to perpetuity.

On missionary work:
- Church activity is the soul of spirituality. Adult Aaronics are really prospective elders. "Use me or lose me" is the motto of inactives. To work with "inactives," we must identify, involve, and instruct. Teach the difference between a job and a calling in the Church. Make a man feel he is needed, and he will respond. (Regional Representatives' seminar, 30 Sept. 1971.)
- A sincere and true testimony is the most powerful proselyting tool we have.
- "Let your light so shine that men may be led to glorify your Father in Heaven" means "Let your light so shine that men shall be led to join the Church or the kingdom of God."

- Don't prepare a lesson, but prepare yourself to give it. The discussions are instruments in the hands of the Holy Ghost to teach the people.
- Have your contacts ask God if Joseph Smith is a prophet of God, not if the gospel is true.
- The greatest miracle is seeing the lives of people change after they accept the gospel.
- The Holy Ghost lives and is operating to bring souls into the Church. Cultivate an ear to hear the Lord's promptings.

On counsel:
- Don't get so tied up in details that you can't get the message of the Spirit.
- Now you have the whip hand, but don't you ever use it.
- Give what you have to give; it may be better than you think.
- Confine your testimonies to the words of the Lord and not to the works of the devil.

On faith:
- "I said to a man who stood at the Gate of the Year: 'Give me a light that I may tread safely into the unknown,' and he replied—'Go out into the darkness and put your hand into the hand of God. That shall be to you better than a light and safer than the known way'." (Quoted by King George VI, during a radio broadcast to the British Empire.)

On the United States of America (from an address at Ricks College, 27 Oct. 1973):
- The United States is a great nation. It is a nation that was founded upon an inspired declaration we call the Constitution of the United States, and the Lord said it was written by men whom he raised up for that very purpose.
- This [the United States] is the cradle of humanity where life on this earth began in the Garden of Eden. This is the place where the New Jerusalem is. This is the place where the Savior will come to his temple."

- Men may fail in this country. Earthquakes may come; seas may heave themselves beyond their bounds; there may be great drought and disaster and hardship. But this nation, based as it was on a foundation of principle laid down by men whom God raised up, will never fail.
- While it is true there are dangers and difficulties that lie ahead of us, we must not assume that we are going to lie down and watch the country go to ruin.
- This country is torn with scandal, criticism, faultfinding, and condemnation, and it is an easy thing for many Americans to "clamor onto the bandwagon."
- We should not be heard to predict ills and calamities for the nation. On the contrary, we should be providing optimistic support to the nation. We must be careful that we do not say or do anything that will further weaken this country. I ask the Latter-day Saints not to find fault, downgrade, or speak pessimistically about the country.
- This Church is one of the most powerful agencies for progress in the world, and we must all sound with one voice. We must tell the world how we feel about this land and this nation.
- There's not an agency that has as powerful a voice as the Church and kingdom of God and the holy priesthood that speaks to the world.
- It is the negative, pessimistic comments about the nation that do as much harm as anything. We should not be so concerned about finding out what's wrong with America, but we should be finding out what's right about America.
- I have faith in America! You and I must have faith in America if we understand the teachings of the gospel of Jesus Christ.

11

J. Thomas Fyans
Member of the First Quorum of the Seventy

He Touched
Every Fiber
of My Being

My first encounter with Elder Harold B. Lee occurred in San Antonio, Texas, in the early 1940s. He had come there to dedicate a chapel. I was a full-time missionary, serving as the district president in the Spanish-American Mission. Elder Antone R. Ivins of the First Council of the Seventy was touring the mission. He arrived in San Antonio at the same time as Elder Harold B. Lee of the Quorum of the Twelve Apostles. A missionary meeting and Spanish-speaking member meeting were planned. I was asked by President Haymore, my mission president, to conduct these meetings.

There are two aspects about that occasion that I will not forget. One was the overwhelming responsibility and privilege of conducting meetings with the mission president and two General Authorities present. The other unforgettable aspect was the deep impression I received from the Spirit upon hearing the remarks of Elder Lee. So much was I affected that, at the close of my mission and upon my return home, my sweetheart, Helen

Cook, and I sought the privilege of his performing that very sacred ordinance of sealing us together as companions for the eternities in the house of the Lord. (This was at a time when the General Authorities were more involved in the performing of sealings in the temple.) His counsel at this very special time has influenced me and my family to this very day.

Three years later, I had been called to be a bishop of the Butler Ward in the East Jordan Stake, just south of Salt Lake City. My ordination to the office of bishop was to occur in conjunction with a quarterly stake conference. How thrilled I was to learn that Elder Harold B. Lee would be the conference visitor and would officiate in my ordination.

In the Saturday evening leadership meeting, Elder Lee made an inspiring presentation on the five areas of responsibility of a bishop. He drew five circles and illustrated in a very effective manner the span of responsibility of a bishop. I still have my notes taken over forty years ago in that instructive and uplifting meeting while sitting at the feet of a special witness of the Lord.

Many years later, the content of Elder Lee's presentation was taken to the whole world in stake conferences. I had the privilege of making these presentations, and an awareness of his influence accompanied me wherever I went.

As a young bishop, I was blessed to be in his office and personally instructed by him. I still remember the scriptures he quoted to me, including Doctrine and Covenants 78:14, where we are taught that "the Church may stand independent above all other creatures beneath the celestial world." This instruction from Elder Lee has stayed with me for over four decades and has influenced me dramatically in my perspective, both personally and in my Church responsibilities.

In 1961, mission presidents from all over the world attended a special seminar. Elder Lee was to present ideas on leadership training in the mission field. As one of the mission presidents, I returned from South America to attend. Circumstances brought us together. Elder Lee invited me to share his time on Sunday morning and express some ideas we were using in the Uruguayan Mission. When he introduced me as "one of his boys," I was awestruck and warmed to the very depth of my soul. My father had passed away when I was a young man, and here was someone I deeply admired accepting me in this very special relationship.

He was instrumental in the calling of brethren to be Regional Representatives. For some reason beyond my comprehension, I was included in the original group. It was very special to be lifted heavenward year after year in the seminars in which Regional Representatives were instructed by this spiritual giant of the kingdom.

His inestimable contribution in the great task of correlation was observed by me, because I was invited to be present in his office in the northeast corner of the second floor of the Church Administration Building. Such Brethren as Elder Spencer W. Kimball, representing missionary work, and Elder Marion G. Romney, charged with home teaching, were present in these meetings. Who can place a value on this privilege?

It was President Harold B. Lee who called our home on a Saturday before Christmas 1971 and invited me to come downtown where I was to be called as the first executive director of the Internal Communications Department. A few days later, when the four directors of Internal Communications were to be called, we were summoned to the First Presidency meeting room on the north side of the main floor of the Church Administration Building. This is a beautiful room where the leaders of the world are greeted by the First Presidency. As we entered the room, the two counselors in the First Presidency, President Tanner and President Lee, were in their places. President Joseph Fielding Smith was ill and did not attend the meeting. President Lee stood and walked across the room. Taking me by the arm, he placed me in the seat between the two counselors, which is normally occupied by the President of the Church. How could any act be more uplifting, challenging, and humbling? He was a master teacher in work, action, and thoughtfulness. His influence has touched every fiber of my being.

12

Vaughn J. Featherstone
Member of the First Quorum of the Seventy

My Greatest Compliment

During the late fifties and early sixties, I served as stake superintendent of the Young Men's Mutual Improvement Association in the Salt Lake Hillside Stake. Elder Lee, an Apostle, visited the stake with Elder Marion G. Romney, his associate in the Quorum of the Twelve. The stake conference was a profoundly spiritual one with these two mighty Apostles in attendance. At the conclusion of the Sunday morning session, I lined up along with hundreds of others just to shake hands with Elder Harold B. Lee. I had heard him speak before. I had read many of his talks. I wanted to do everything he suggested we do. I have often thought that he must have been my line leader in the spirit world. I loved, admired, respected, and adored him, though he didn't know me.

As I walked through the long line, I noticed that no one was talking while waiting. Most people had tear-filled eyes as did I. When I got to Elder Lee, I had so many things I wanted to say to him, and I wanted to tell him how he had impressed me. But no words came. I stood in front of this great soul with tears flowing freely, shook his hand, and moved quietly by. Everyone else did the same. No one could speak. I felt a love radiate from him, and I knew he loved every one of us.

It was no wonder, with the love and admiration I felt for him that my call to the Presiding Bishopric was so special. One day in 1972, while I was serving as a stake president in Boise, Idaho, my wife answered the phone, and the person on the other end said, "President Harold B. Lee and President Nathan Eldon Tanner would like to speak to your husband."

Merlene sent one of the boys down to the school to get me. My daughter and I were riding a small Honda 70. When I answered the phone, President Lee introduced himself and said that President Tanner was also on the line. I greeted them and asked, "What can I do for you brethren?"

President Lee said, "Elder Featherstone, we are asking you to make one of the most momentous decisions of your life."

I caught my breath and responded, "What is it, brethren?"

President Lee said, "On April 6 at general conference, the Lord is making a change in the Presiding Bishopric. Victor L. Brown has been called to be the Presiding Bishop, and the Lord has called you to be his counselor."

I think it was at least sixty seconds before my emotions would let me speak. (The Brethren must have letters to sign while we recover.) Finally I said, "I will do anything the Lord calls me to do."

President Lee then said, "President Featherstone, you may tell your wife, but not another soul."

I took my wife into the living room, and we had about as sweet and tender, spiritual and emotional, few minutes as we have ever had. She asked if we could tell our two sons who were on missions, and I told her President Lee's counsel was to not tell a soul. She said, "Can we hint?" And I said, "No." April the sixth was only one week away.

On Wednesday I went to Salt Lake City. Thursday morning I was sustained as second counselor to Bishop Victor L. Brown. My wife had stayed in Boise and kept the children out of school. She said, "Your father may be called upon to give a prayer or something at conference; and if he is you will want to hear him."

After the announcement of my call, she went directly to the phone to call our two missionary sons. Ron had been in the mission field over a year and was the mission secretary. He answered the phone like this, "Hello, Elder Featherstone, secretary of the Gulf States Mission speaking. Is this my mother calling?"

And she said, "Yes, Ron, but how did you know?"

He said that someone in the mission had just called and told him that his dad had been called as a General Authority. They had a great talk and some very tender thoughts were exchanged.

Later she called Dave, who was in the Virginia Roanoke Mission. She didn't get hold of him until about 2:30 in the afternoon. After she greeted him, she said, "Dave, have you heard the news?"

He said, "I haven't heard any news, but I know my dad was called to be a General Authority."

She said, "Dave, how did you know that?"

He said, "My Heavenly Father told me about three days ago."

Sunday, after the afternoon session of conference, the new Presiding Bishopric and the new Assistants to the Twelve were invited to the upper room of the Salt Lake Temple to be ordained and set apart. Our wives were invited to attend this special, sacred occasion. As each member of the Presiding Bishopric was ordained, I listened carefully. Just before my turn came, I offered a special prayer in my heart, "Heavenly Father, if it doesn't make a great deal of difference to thee, I would be truly grateful if President Harold B. Lee could ordain me and set me apart." When it was my turn, President Lee said, "I will ordain President Featherstone." My heart leaped within my bosom—to have this man of God that I admired and respected so much lay his hands on my head and ordain me to this high calling.

After the meeting was over, my wife and I were walking out, and President Lee was nearby. Merlene told him of the experience our missionary son had of knowing three days ahead that his father had been called as a General Authority. President Lee stopped us in the hall of the temple and asked my wife to repeat the story to those who were nearby.

While I was serving as stake president, there was a chapel in each of the three Boise stakes that was ready for dedication about the same time. I contacted the other stake presidents and, with their approval, wrote a letter to President Lee to see if he could dedicate these three buildings in the three separate stakes. We were delighted beyond measure when he accepted and confirmed the dates. We were scheduled in early June, and our correspondence took place in February and early March. It was that April when I was called into the Presiding Bishopric. Immediately assignments came to me to be the visiting General Authority at stake conferences. The week of the three dedications I was assigned to a stake conference in Logan. I called L. Aldin Porter, then a Regional Representative and now a General Authority, and asked him to host President Lee and to stay right with him for the two days. Aldin Porter is such a great soul that I wanted President Lee to become better acquainted with him, and I thought Brother Porter should handle it and have that great privilege.

Monday, after stake conference, I received a telephone call from Bishop Brown. He said, "President Lee wants to see you in his office. He said that he expected you to be in Boise and to host him. You invited him."

I said, "Bishop Brown, I had a conference assignment." And he responded that he was aware of that.

I made an appointment to see President Lee, and when he invited me into his office, he said, "I expected you to be in Boise and to accompany me everywhere I went." I explained about my stake conference assignment, and he said, "You could have had that changed. I expected you to be there."

Every way I could, I tried to get off the hot seat. For about twenty minutes he lectured me. Then he said, "It would have been a good opportunity for me to get to know you." As I left, I felt rebuked, but loved. I apologized several times, humbly. As I left his office, in spite of the slight rebuke, I loved him even the more because somehow I knew that he had a sincere love for and interest in me.

Because of President Lee, I have always worn a white shirt, tie, and suit when possible in giving blessings. He taught in a magnificent way the need to purge the Church and handle the transgressor and yet to do it in absolute and total charity. His wisdom was brilliant, his understanding of doctrine immense, and his commitment absolute. Everything he said to do I wanted to do with all my heart and soul. I would have marched through hell for this great hero in my life.

I have a portrait of President Lee on my office wall that I prize with all my heart. He signed it, "Bishop Vaughn J. Feather-stone, esteemed brother, colleague, faithful servant of the Lord. With confidence and esteem, Harold B. Lee." I know of no greater compliment than to be esteemed by President Harold B. Lee.

13

John H. Groberg
Member of the First Quorum of the Seventy

Counsel on
Giving Counsel

Shortly after returning from my mission to Tonga, my sweet-heart and I were married, and I continued my educational pursuits. I graduated from Brigham Young University and then attended Indiana University, where I obtained an MBA degree in 1960. I then returned to Idaho Falls, my hometown, and began working in business in that city.

We were most fortunate to serve in a rapidly growing ward made up mostly of young families. Like the other young couples in the ward, we had two children at the time, one three years old and one who was a year old. There were, however, people of all ages and economic patterns represented in our ward membership. The ward grew rapidly from about five hundred members to nearly twelve hundred members in a period of eighteen months, at which time it was divided.

In December 1961, I had been sustained as the bishop of the Idaho Falls 26th Ward. In March of 1962, after I had served as bishop for about three months, it was time for our stake quarterly conference. In those days bishops were set apart only by General Authorities, and rather than send all the bishops to Salt Lake City to Church headquarters, they waited for the General Authorities to come to the next quarterly stake conference to handle the ordinance work. Accordingly, I had served about three months without being set apart. Our conference visitor was Elder Harold B. Lee of the Quorum of the Twelve, who made arrangements in advance to ordain me a bishop and set me apart.

At the conclusion of the stake conference, the setting apart meeting was held. It was a most inspirational meeting, and stronger spiritual feelings I had seldom felt. Elder Lee was so kind and so wise and also so very prophetic in the statements he made and the spiritual insights he received. I remember him saying how he had never felt better about a group of bishops. (There were three or four of us being set apart at that time.)

When he had concluded giving us some instructions, he asked, "Now, do any of you have any questions?" Since I had been serving for several months, I did have a few questions— one in particular. But, for whatever reason, I just didn't feel it appropriate for me to take Elder Lee's time with my question. After the meeting had been dismissed, Brother Lee, while shaking hands with various ones, saw me and came over to me and said, "Young man, you have a question; I can tell. What is it?"

His bold action surprised me, but I did have something on my mind. There was a young wife in our ward whose husband had been accused of a serious crime. In fact, he had been sentenced and sent to the state penitentiary, and she had come to me wanting to know about obtaining a divorce. She wanted to leave the area because of the embarrassment she would experience if she remained in the neighborhood.

I had not given this woman an answer, saying instead, "Stake conference is coming up. I'll see you after conference." But in my mind I was thinking that if anyone was ever justified in obtaining a divorce, it would be this sister. I expressed those thoughts to Elder Lee when he gave me that opportunity.

He looked at me very kindly, but very firmly, and almost putting his finger on my nose, he said, "Young man, let me tell you something, and don't you ever forget it. Never, under any circumstances, advise anyone to get divorced. Do you understand that?"

"Yes," I said.

He then added emphatically, "And, by the same token, don't ever, under any circumstance, advise anyone to marry a particular person, or at a particular time. Do you understand that?"

"Yes," I said.

Then he went on to explain more fully, "It may seem strange not to do the obvious. It may seem to you that this girl is justified, and she may be; but don't you tell her to become divorced. Those are personal decisions that must be made by the individual, for it will be that individual who will carry the consequences of the action taken. You can point out to them the alternatives—here's what will likely happen if you get divorced, and here's what will happen likely if you don't. But the decision must be theirs to make.

"As soon as you, or any bishop or ecclesiastical leader makes a decision like that for someone, then we have released him or her from responsibility. And as sure as anything, somewhere down the line, events won't go quite right and then that person will be able to say, 'If it hadn't been for Bishop So-and-so, or Brother So-and-so, maybe things would have been different.'

"Now, do you have that principle in mind? Never, under any circumstances, advise anyone to obtain a divorce, or not to get divorced, or to get married or not to get married. Point out the differences, but make certain that person makes the final decision."

Needless to say, I have remembered that sage advice over the years. I love President Lee. My very first association with him was to have his hands placed on my head, ordain me a bishop, and give me a beautiful blessing, and then to have him seek me out by inspiration to answer a question which he knew by the Holy Spirit that I needed to have answered to fulfill my calling. This experience has always been a great blessing in my life.

14

Devere Harris
Member of the First Quorum of the Seventy

Fulfillment
of Prophecy

On 15 June 1969, Father's Day, I was installed as president of the Idaho Malad Stake by Harold B. Lee, President of the Council of the Twelve, and Neal A. Maxwell, Regional Representative of the Twelve. When I was asked to take this assignment, I was amazed but not totally surprised.

Two weeks before this date, I awoke out of a deep sleep at 3:00 A.M. with a strange feeling, so I awakened my wife and told her that I was going to be called as the president of the Malad Stake. She responded, "I don't think you have anything to worry about. We live eighteen miles from Malad, and they will call someone closer."

I prayed continuously throughout the remainder of the night and into the next day that I would not be called to be president of the stake, because of my feeling of inadequacy. However, the very next night, at the same time, 3:00 A.M., I awoke out of a deep sleep, and again I awoke my wife and told her that I had the same spirit once more and that we might just as well accept the fact that we would be called.

Stake conference weekend arrived, and in a meeting on the Saturday night of conference, the stake clerk came and placed his hand on my shoulder and said, "President Harold B. Lee would like to see you and your wife in the stake president's office."

As we entered the room, President Lee took my wife by her hands and asked her if she were willing to sacrifice for the Church. She said that up to that time she had never had to do that but felt sure that she would if asked. Then he said, "The Lord wants your husband to be president of the Malad Idaho Stake."

We were then trained by President Lee in many great and important leadership principles. We recognized his great ability to be so directed by the Lord that he could fulfill the prophecy that had already come to us and teach and train us by the same Spirit.

Because of a challenge President Lee gave me that day, my life was changed. Due to his inspired direction, much of my life since then has been directed toward temple activities, later leading to my becoming president of the Idaho Falls Temple and ultimately being assigned as a General Authority to serve as a managing director in the Temple Department of the Church.

15

Victor L. Brown
Member of the First Quorum of the Seventy

Use Medicine and Priesthood Blessings

I have a strong overall impression from serving seventeen months as the Presiding Bishop of the Church under the leadership of President Harold B. Lee.

Our Presiding Bishopric could not have had a more supportive and inspiring leader. The manner in which President Lee faced up to difficult problems and the wisdom and skill with which he handled controversial matters were an inspiration to us. He had a very unusual power of recall. It seemed that no question could be raised but that he could recall many scriptures that would answer the question. His memory seemed unfailing.

One of the great opportunities of my life has been to receive training from President Lee, as well as from other Presidents of the Church under whom I have served.

In 1970 my physician informed me that I had contracted cancer and that it would be necessary for me to go to a Midwest university hospital for special surgery and treatment. I asked

President Lee if I might have a priesthood blessing before going. The First Presidency and the Quorum of the Twelve laid their hands on my head in the Salt Lake Temple and gave me the requested blessing.

Afterward, I turned to President Lee and suggested that to me it seemed there was no longer a need for me to have the operation. I felt that a blessing under the hands of the First Presidency of the Church and the Council of the Twelve was sufficient to heal me.

President Lee's response was to me one of the great spiritual teachings of my life. He indicated that it was my responsibility to obtain first whatever medical attention was necessary, after which the Lord would bless me. He said there was no question but that I should do whatever my physician recommended.

Sometime after the surgery and treatment, when it appeared that the problem had been completely corrected, my doctor informed me that the mortality rate for the type of cancer I had was extremely high, particularly for those at my relatively young age at the time. Now, approximately seventeen years later, there has been no recurrence. The counsel President Lee gave me has been vindicated, and the answer to the blessing given to me by the Brethren is evident.

President Lee's reply of seventeen years ago taught me a profound lesson about the relationship of receiving priesthood blessings after doing everything possible that we could do to help ourselves. I have always been extremely grateful for this counsel, which I have used myself and passed on to many persons whom I have counseled.

16

Keith W. Wilcox
Member of the First Quorum of the Seventy

My Last Visit with President Harold B. Lee

My first personal experience with President Harold B. Lee occurred in February of 1960. I had been called on 30 November 1958 to be president of the Weber Heights Stake in Ogden, Utah. Elders Marion G. Romney and William J. Critchlow, Jr., had come to the South Ogden Stake conference to divide the stake, to create a new stake, and to call new stake presidencies. Elder Critchlow, president of the South Ogden Stake, had been called as an Assistant to the Twelve earlier that year. What happened was a never-to-be-forgotten experience.

The South Ogden Stake was at that time a stake of almost 9,000 members. The newly created Weber Heights Stake, the 272nd stake in the Church, began with 4,339 members. It was composed of the South Weber, Uintah, Ogden 34th, 37th, 50th, and 55th wards. I was then serving as bishop of the Ogden 50th Ward. It was quite overwhelming to be called as the first president of the Weber Heights Stake. But it was a wonderful opportunity to work with my counselors in calling new leaders and in attending to our many new responsibilities.

Our meetings were held in the 34th and 37th ward chapel, but three wards were meeting in this building. It was considered to be our stake center, although it had been designed as a two-ward building. Two classrooms were put to use, one as a high council room and one as a stake office. It soon became apparent that more adequate facilities were needed. The stake was growing rapidly.

We studied properties within the stake very carefully and found a beautiful location for a new stake center on Country Hills Drive, east of Harrison Boulevard. It was a large, open field of farmland. The balance of this area was later purchased by Weber State College for the location of the Dee Events Center. But we were able to obtain sufficient acreage for a stake center, and I yielded to the promptings of those around me to design this stake center, doing it with minimum fee, loving the work, and creating a building that satisfied the suggestions of the newly organized Church Building Department, under the direction of Brother Wendell Mendenhall.

Brother Mendenhall and his assistants, John H. Vandenberg and Howard Barker, were studying different ways of building ward and stake centers. A fixed pattern had not been established. One they wanted very much to try was a stake center with the gymnasium and cultural activity area being detached somewhat from the regular mass of the building. In my design, these functions would be housed in a separate building. Other forms being studied placed the gymnasium building, or cultural hall, integrally with the chapel.

It was a time of experimentation. Those in the Building Department were very happy when I presented my suggested solution for the Weber Heights Stake Center. It was different. It functioned well. In addition to space for two wards, stake offices, and a small cultural hall, there was a detached gymnasium, which also served as a space for stake events. A kitchen was included in the building. The baptismal font was also located in this building. We knew this stake center would be of tremendous help to our wards, our stake, and possibly to other stakes.

We had taken the general proposal for this new stake center out to the wards for consideration. We invited our bishops to our office and individually reviewed the design and cost with each bishop in great detail. There was harmony, I thought, among all of our bishops, high councilors, and other stake and ward leaders concerning the great advantage of building a new stake center.

The time came when the bishops were to present to the priesthood bearers of each ward the proposal to build this stake center and the approximate amounts each ward would be asked to raise to contribute to the building cost. We estimated the total cost to be $600,000. The total design had thirty thousand square feet of space. We were very excited about proceeding. It would be a great blessing to the wards and to the members of the stake.

The next Sunday when the proposition was presented in each ward, I was shocked to learn that in two of our six wards there had been strong objection to the proposal. In fact, in one of the wards, the bishop had actually encouraged the members to vote against it, and they had done so. Another ward had about a fifty-fifty vote, with the bishop expressing strong reservations. There also had been a few negative votes in some of the other wards. Obviously, we had not obtained sufficient approval or acceptance to proceed.

The reception to this proposition left me quite dumbfounded. I felt betrayed. These same ward leaders had, in our private meetings, given full support. Yet in proposing it, they had not shown that kind of enthusiasm at all. Lack of support had resulted in this divided opinion. I didn't know what to do. My wise counselors urged that we not move too quickly, that we study the matter further. Fortunately, Elder Harold B. Lee was to be the visiting authority in our stake conference on 5 and 6 March 1960. This was about two weeks after the voting had taken place.

As our conference began, I really was at a very low point. After all of the marvelous organization success and the experience of launching a new stake, we had run into what seemed to be an impossible situation. Luckily, or as the Lord had impressed us, we did not do anything until President Lee came to our conference.

I was greatly affected by being with President Lee. He was so down-to-earth, so kind, and so insightful. We held our presidency meeting and our priesthood meeting in a delightful way. I rejoiced at being in the presence of this great spiritual leader, whom I had admired so much over a long period of time. I felt a great lift in his presence.

When there was time to chat privately with Elder Lee, I opened up the subject of what had happened in the voting on our proposed stake center. I described this in detail, fully expecting President Lee to give me guidance on how I could readjust the wards to be sure of leadership that would support the proposition. I spent some time in going through the detail of what had happened. President Lee, I'm sure, could tell that I was very upset and needed guidance.

I was caught off guard when President Lee laughed after I finished my discussion. He chuckled, with a smile on his face, and then he said to me, "President, this is not so different. The same thing happened not long ago in a stake in Idaho. This can happen. Don't feel badly."

Then President Lee said, "Let me give you some counsel on how to handle this." He then told me that, in effect, I had taken a stone or boulder from the bottom of the canyon and rolled it and pushed it until I had moved it to the top of the hill. At the last moment, the stone had gotten away from me. Instead of rolling over the hill, as intended, it had rolled backward and there it was, back in the bottom of the canyon. This was my situation that day.

President Lee then counseled me on what to do. I was not (and he emphasized *not* twice) to release any of my bishops. He said they were good men. They simply needed to be better educated and understand more fully the need I had explained. They possibly were concerned that as time went on this building would not be their permanent stake center. Now, he admonished, I should go down to the bottom of the canyon again and get that stone. I was to take enough time, all that was necessary, to move it to the top of the hill. It would possibly take several months, but when I had the stone to the top, I was to be sure this time that I didn't lose control. I was to be sure that it was pushed over the brow and that it rolled down the other side. I was not to allow it to get away from me again as it reached the top.

Well, I thanked Elder Lee profoundly. The image he had created in my mind was powerful. He had given me very exact and unforgettable directions on what to do. I was lifted tremendously by the conference. We had achieved an attendance figure that was much higher than any other stake conference we had held, this being the fifth quarterly conference since our organization, each being attended by a General Authority.

We did as Elder Lee advised and, at the appropriate times, met again with ward and stake leaders, satisfied their feelings, and listened to their counsel. We could feel their support growing. They knew and agreed that we really needed a new stake center. In a few months it all came to a head again, and this time we had 100 percent approval in proceeding with the project. The construction proceeded exceptionally well, and this stake center became the building that the Weber Heights Stake uses to this day. It was later dedicated by President David O. McKay, at the request of Elder William Critchlow, Jr., and fulfilled our needs completely. It has also served multistake activities quite often.

I shall always be grateful for the wisdom I received from this great man at that time. I could have made some very serious mistakes as a very new and inexperienced stake president, but his great wisdom and counsel made the difference. How I appreciated the inspired guidance of this great Apostle of the Lord.

One of the most memorable, spiritual experiences of my life happened on Friday, 21 December 1973. I had business in Salt Lake City that day with the building board of the state of Utah, concerning a special education building I was designing for Utah State University in Logan, Utah. I also had been selected as the architect for a large addition to the Olympus High School in Holladay, Utah, and had visited there later that morning. On the way back to my home in Ogden, I stopped at the Church Administration Building. My wife, Viva May, had given me three loaves of homemade bread, wrapped as Christmas gifts, to give to Presidents Lee, Tanner, and Romney. Each of these brethren had been in our home and had been very complimentary about my wife's cooking, especially enjoying her home-made bread. I knew these gifts would be welcomed.

I first went to President Tanner's office. He was in a meeting, and I left his loaf of bread with his secretary. I walked across the hall and found the same situation existed with President Romney. I then walked into the First Presidency's general office, gave the loaf of bread to one of the secretaries, and asked if she would give it to President Lee. She suggested I give it to Brother Arthur Haycock, President Lee's executive secretary. I was very surprised when Brother Haycock said, "Why don't you give it to him yourself?" With that, he phoned President Lee and, after explaining my gift, said, "Go right in." That was something I hadn't expected.

I took the loaf of bread, opened the door, and President Lee was there sitting behind his desk. He looked up and smiled at me. As I walked into the room, he rose from his chair. He walked around his desk, took my hand, gave me a warm embrace, and said, "I greet you as my friend, even as Christ greeted his disciples as his friends."

I cannot remember having experienced a greater thrill—to have the prophet of the Lord greet me in such a way. I will never forget that marvelous moment, having the prophet look me in the eye and being considered his friend.

President Lee then quoted from the Doctrine and Covenants. He was a master of the scriptures, and he quoted section 84, verse 77, "And again I say unto you, my friends, for from henceforth I shall call you friends, it is expedient that I give unto you this commandment, that ye become even as my friends in days when I was with them, traveling to preach the gospel in my power."

President Lee went on to thank me for the work I was accomplishing for the Church and the responsibilities I was carrying. He mentioned a new project, which I had been asked to design, the Language Training Mission (LTM) at Brigham Young University, which later became known as the Missionary Training Center.

I told President Lee that I had enjoyed a great spiritual experience in the design of the LTM and explained to him what a remarkably short time it had taken to design the buildings, due to the inspiration that had come to me from the Lord during the design period.

President Lee responded by telling me that he, also, had received some spiritual experiences recently. He said, "I'd like to share one with you." He pointed to a plaque he had received from Ricks College on which had been inscribed some words of prophecy that he had given there. He indicated that he had received by revelation at that time some insights pertaining to this country that had been a very choice experience. He explained what it was. The United States would not fail. America had a great destiny. He discussed several events that had happened, which had led him to the inspired conclusions he announced in his Ricks College sermon. I was electrified in hearing such marvelous statements from our prophet.

Then he shared with me another remarkable experience that had very recently occurred. He said that President Tanner had come to him and indicated that he had experienced a dream the night before in which he was given to know that he should suggest that President Lee write a letter to President Richard M. Nixon concerning the stress he was under at the time, from what later became known as the Watergate scandal. President Lee said he accepted that counsel and was quite amazed when, a little later, his other counselor, President Romney, came in to see him and told him that he was impressed to suggest that the First Presidency write a letter to President Nixon. Then, President Lee said to me that he also had received the same impression and was preparing to write such a letter when his two counselors brought the same idea before him.

President Lee found, after his first attempt, that this was not an easy letter to write under the circumstances that existed. He decided to reflect further on the task while he went for a few days of rest at the Church's Laguna Beach home on Emerald Bay in California.

Five days later, President Lee was finally able to dictate a suitable letter to President Nixon. This difficult to compose communication was read and approved by the First Presidency and then mailed, via a protected route, to be placed in a daily file for "the president's eyes, only."

The text of the letter reminded President Nixon of his visit to Salt Lake City in July 1970, and what President Lee had told him then, when he was conducting at the request of President Joseph Fielding Smith. In the letter President Lee said:

> The bitter hostility you have faced the last few months has reminded us of the conversation we had in July 1970, when you visited in Salt Lake City. At that time we mentioned the story related by President Lincoln, who, in defending General Ulysses S. Grant, said, "If we were watching a man on a tight-rope crossing Niagara Falls carrying all that we hold dear, we would not shout at him or criticize him, but would pray for him with all our might." We then told you that we would pray for you as we always pray for the president of our country, since the president holds in his hands much of what we regard as dear and precious.

President Lee then told me that he had felt impressed in his letter to convey a message to President Nixon, that he, as president of the United States, had no need to fear, as long as his decisions had been based on religious principles. I have pondered that many times since first hearing it from President Lee during our visit that day. As our conversation came to an end, President Lee told me he had received a very appreciative letter back from President Nixon.

As noted in my journal, in which I wrote about this experience in great detail, I had been with the President about twenty-five minutes. I remember as I left his office that Brother Haycock looked a bit agitated. There had been many intervening telephone calls, which I had noticed as the lights fluttered on the telephone on President Lee's desk. There were people waiting for him. I hadn't intended to be in his office for this length of time, and I'm certain Brother Haycock had not expected that to happen. Yet, it became for me a very choice memory and one that I shall always cherish.

It was only five days later, on December 26, that the terrible news hit the Church concerning the passing of President Harold B. Lee. It was almost unbelievable. I couldn't have been more shocked. I was too stunned to even contemplate the significance of such a loss to the Church and the world. I felt so badly about the news that it was very difficult to sleep.

I look back and remember the great opportunity I had just a few days before his death of being in President Lee's presence. I marvel at the wonderful experience of being personally taught by him and visiting alone with him. He was truly a great man, a great spiritual giant of our day. I had been tremendously impressed with the spirituality I felt that day in the presence of a prophet of God. It was an experience that will live in my mind for the remainder of my life and one for which I am extremely grateful.

I remember talking to President Tanner a few days after President Lee's funeral. I mentioned that I just hoped I could live a worthy enough life that the time would come when I could again visit with this great man. President Tanner simply responded by saying, "Stay on the course you are on, and that will happen."

17

Francis M. Gibbons
Member of the First Quorum of the Seventy

Our Miracle Girl

My wife, Helen, and I first met President Harold B. Lee in Palo Alto, California, in 1948 while I was attending Stanford University. We belonged to a study group that included President Lee's daughter, Maurine, and her husband, Ernie Wilkins, who also was a Stanford student. Usually, when President Lee had a conference assignment in that area, the Wilkinses would arrange a meeting of the study group in their home, where we were privileged to receive counsel and instruction from the prophet in an intimate, relaxed setting.

At the time, we were childless, although we had been married for several years. In early 1950, during one of Elder Lee's visits to Palo Alto, Helen felt inspired to seek a blessing from him. In it he blessed her that the vital functions of her body would be quickened by the Holy Spirit to begin the processes that would result in motherhood and specifically blessed her, "even as Hannah of old," and counseled her to covenant with the Lord in her secret prayers as Hannah had done. He also blessed her with peace of mind and faith and that if there should be a space of time before she conceived that we should spend that time in service to the Church, to open our hearts to other children and to prove ourselves worthy of parenthood. He also conferred a special blessing on the doctors who would serve her, that they would be specially inspired in exercising their medical skills in her behalf.

We endeavored, as best we could, to comply with all the conditions Elder Lee had mentioned. We were very active in the ward, filling assignments in Relief Society and Sunday School. We did baby-sitting for our friends, took Helen's young brother into our home, and even applied to adopt a baby through the California placement service. As far as we can determine, Helen conceived about the time of our visit to the California State agency in San Francisco.

Everything went well with the pregnancy until about three weeks before the expected delivery, when Helen developed a severe pain in her side. The doctor thought her complaints were merely the reaction of a woman pregnant for the first time who did not realize what to expect in carrying a child. Nevertheless, after the complaints continued, he hospitalized Helen to conduct tests, which revealed nothing.

The evening before the baby's birth, the doctor visited Helen in the hospital again and, finding no clues to the root of her trouble, went home. He later told us that he became uneasy as he thought about Helen and that he felt compelled to return to the hospital. When he arrived and examined her again, he discovered that the baby was in distress, which caused him to decide immediately on a Caesarean section. The doctor contacted me at home to obtain my consent. I barely had time to arrange for a neighbor, Mac VanValkenburg, to accompany me to the hospital where we administered to Helen.

After the doctor had taken the baby, he discovered the root of Helen's pain. Somehow, circulation had been cut off to one ovary, resulting in a strangulated ovary. By that time, the lack of circulation had caused the ovary and all the surrounding tissue to become gangrenous, requiring its removal. Had he induced labor as he had thought to do earlier in the evening, or had there been a delay of as much as a half hour in taking the baby, it is almost certain that Suzi would have been born dead or with serious brain damage because of the lack of oxygen, and Helen would have lost her life.

After the delivery, a nurse told Helen that someone should go to church the next day, Sunday, and thank God that she and the baby were alive and well, which I did, as it was fast Sunday.

A few months after the birth, I wrote President Lee a letter, detailing the circumstances of Suzi's miraculous birth and of the unusual way in which his blessing to Helen had been fulfilled.

Many years later, and shortly after I began my service with the First Presidency, President Lee said that one morning before a First Presidency meeting he had been looking through his "miracle" file and had found the letter I had written to him almost twenty years before, telling about Helen's blessing and Suzi's birth. He asked about Suzi then, as he often did thereafter; and when she was sealed to Timothy A. Burton in February 1972 in the Salt Lake Temple, President Lee graciously performed the sealing.

The day before President Lee's death, he called me at home to wish me and the family a merry Christmas. Almost the last words I ever heard him speak in mortality were to ask, "How is our miracle girl?"

I understand that experiences of this kind were repeated time and again during President Lee's ministry. He was and is a true prophet of God, richly endowed with spiritual perceptions and sensitivities possessed by few of God's servants.

18

James B. Allen
Chairman, History Department,
Brigham Young University

My Personal Appreciation of Harold B. Lee

In beginning the welfare program, President Harold B. Lee relied upon the organization of the priesthood, and it was the need to use the priesthood to its fullest capacity that made him so interested in correlation. In welfare work he demonstrated a penchant for organization and administration. In the late 1940s, as a member of the Council of the Twelve, he presented to the First Presidency a special committee report on the organization of the Church. The First Presidency had asked for the study in order to find ways to simplify the programs of the Church and at the same time improve effectiveness of their work. In 1960 the First Presidency made a similar request to the General Priesthood Committee, of which Elder Lee was chairman. In addition, the committee was asked to work out a correlated system of

Originally printed in *Dialogue: A Journal of Mormon Thought*, Autumn–Winter issue, 1974. Used by permission.

gospel study for the entire priesthood and auxiliary program of the Church. From then until his death, President Lee was best known among the general membership of the Church for his leadership in helping to develop the correlation program.

When the Church Correlation Committee was organized in 1961, Elder Lee was appointed chairman, and he held that responsibility until January 1972. In this capacity he employed all of his talents and knowledge to help refine Church administration so that a systematic program for teaching the gospel to children, youth, and adults could be implemented. In addition, he led out in inaugurating and perfecting a system for better communications between Church leaders at all levels of administration. At the heart of his philosophy was the idea that all programs of the Church should be placed more fully under the direction of the priesthood, and this objective found place in many of his sermons, particularly in his later years.

Grand as his contributions to the organization and administration of the Church may have been, however, they were no more important than the personal impact he had upon the lives of individual members. My own experience is only one example. I am sure he influenced different members in different ways, but for me three memories have special significance. In each case I was part of a group, and Elder Lee had no idea that I was there, or even who I was. Maybe it was because I was looking for something special at the time—but whatever it was, his ideas found place in my heart and became highly personal and spiritual to me.

The first came in the summer of 1954, when I was a young seminary teacher attending the Brigham Young University summer session for all teachers in the Church school system. This was a special summer, because for five weeks Elder Harold B. Lee was our instructor. I don't know how his instruction affected others, or what they remember from it, but as a young teacher I was particularly concerned with the fact that there were so many differing points of view within the Church on so many issues. The differences as such did not bother me, for I had already been reconciled to the fact that the Lord did not expect complete uniformity among his Saints on everything. But I badly wanted to hear a Church leader say that not everything written in so-called Church books had to be accepted as scripture.

Maybe that was why I was impressed with what happened on June 22, the day our instructor talked about the creation of the earth. My notes from that day are filled with statements such as these: "God has not revealed *how* the world was created. All the ideas we have presented are *theories* and must be accepted as such." The idea that the first chapter of Genesis is the story of the spiritual creation and the next is physical "is *theory*—some learned men in the Church are not in accord." The idea that a day in the story of creation "is a thousand years, etc., is a theory." Then, and most important because this was really his message to the teachers that day, "Don't present theories as though they were facts. We criticize scientists who teach theories as facts. It is just as dangerous for religion teachers to do so."

"But what," someone asked, "about all the books that are written on various subjects, often by prominent men in the Church—what if we disagree?"

His answer? "Where an idea is in complete accord with scripture, then accept it—but if not, then write the name of the author in the margin; it is his theory."

To most of us today such things may seem commonplace, but as a guide for helping students realize that all the answers to all the problems are not in, and that even the most learned men in the Church may still disagree, it was soul satisfying indeed.

A similar, though more deeply spiritual, experience came in 1967, when B. West Belnap, former dean of the College of Religious Instruction, passed away. Elder Harold B. Lee was the major speaker at the funeral. I remember that he had caught, and tried to portray, one of the deepest concerns of Brother Belnap; and the way he portrayed it was of special importance to me, a teacher of both history and religion at BYU. Elder Lee described one of his last visits with Brother Belnap in the hospital—when Brother Belnap knew he probably would not live. I can't remember the exact words, but the idea went something like this as he reported Brother Belnap's final message: "I have been thinking as I lay here about all the people I know, and about all the disagreements they often have over points of doctrine, and this and that. But as I contemplate my fate, I realize now more than ever that these things, in the long run, really make no difference. What matters is that we love one another. All other things are transient and passing, for it is only really getting to know and love each other for the good that is within us all that will matter in our eternal relationships.'' Again, what a powerful message to those of us who were often caught up in the endless, often meaningless, debates over this and that fine point of doctrine.

But there were some things that President Lee knew beyond a doubt, and the experience that affected me most, and has been the most long lasting, came on an occasion when he was fervently declaring such knowledge.

It was in the spring of 1961. I remember it well because that year I was teaching an Institute of Religion class in the New Testament to a group of southern California college students. Somehow, we found ourselves discussing for two days the question of the role of the Apostle in the early Church and were asking just what an Apostle's responsibility really was. I had pointed out that after the fall of Judas, the New Testament Apostles had chosen another, Matthias, to be a witness with them of the resurrection of Christ (see Acts 1:22–26). I had taught my class that one of the basic responsibilities of modern Apostles was also to bear witness of the living Christ. But I had not heard such a testimony from a living Apostle for quite some time—at least not that I remembered.

So it was that I attended a quarterly conference in the Los Angeles Stake, and Harold B. Lee was the conference visitor. On that particular morning, I was in anything but the ideal mood to receive inspiration. My wife and I were late arriving at the meeting and had to sit in the cultural hall, where it was noisy. And our three children, ages six, five, and four, were anything but soothing in their behavior as they squirmed, wiggled, whispered, crawled, and climbed over us. By the time Elder Lee got up to speak, my wife and I were both tired, and we were discussing which of us would attend conference that afternoon while the other took care of the children in the city park. As I remember it, I won. I would get to take care of the children.

Then Elder Lee began to speak, and at his first statement, my mental reservations about the inspiration of the conference went even deeper. He announced that all the Primary presidents in the stake were to contact all the Primary teachers, who were to call all the parents in the stake between conference meetings (and the stake covered almost half of Los Angeles), and have them bring their Primary children to conference that afternoon, for he wanted the children to sing two certain songs.

"Elder Lee," I remember thinking, "what are you trying to do? Not only is this an impossible task for the Primary ladies, who have to feed their own families and get back in less than two hours, but I don't think that many people who aren't here now will even want to come." I was sure (well, at least fearful) that his plan would fail. As my wife and I looked at each other with some dismay at the thought of another session of squirming, crawling children, I was in a frame of mind in which inspiration is not usually said to come. But we did return that afternoon, and the Primary children did sing, and the whole experience was beautiful. I wouldn't have missed it for the world.

Then, after making this request, Harold B. Lee, in his role as an Apostle of the Lord, began one of the most memorable sermons I have ever heard. As he recounted a recent trip to the Holy Land, he told of his deep and spiritual feelings as he walked where Jesus walked, and renewed again his own communion with the Master. It almost seemed as if the message were just for me, partly because of what I was doing in the institutes, for seldom before or since have the chills gone up and down my spine or has the Spirit touched my soul, as on that day. Elder Lee knew and because Elder Lee knew, I knew, and because I knew, hopefully other people, too, would know.

Welfare? Yes. Correlation? Yes. Administrative skill? Yes. *But the most valuable contribution of any man is in the uplifting influence he has on the lives of others.* If my experience was any example, the influence of Harold B. Lee will be lasting and profound.

19

Wendell J. Ashton
Former Regional Representative

A Courageous
Prophet with a
Tender Heart

President Harold B. Lee was a friend of mine for approximately forty years before his death in the closing days of 1973. Few men have influenced my life as he did. He was truly a mighty prophet of the Lord at a period of time when The Church of Jesus Christ of Latter-day Saints showed momentous growth and development.

I first knew him through my father, Marvin Owen Ashton, who through his service as a member of the Presiding Bishopric labored with Elder Lee in the beginning days of the Church welfare program during the 1930s. One of the early direct influences of Harold B. Lee on the course of my life came in 1958, when as a member of the Council of the Twelve, he reorganized the presidency of the East Millcreek Stake in Salt Lake Valley. At that time he called O. Layton Alldredge as president of the stake and then reached out for me when I was serving distantly as a member of the general board of the Sunday School, to be the first counselor to President Alldredge. I felt it was through Elder Lee's influence that this calling was made since I had little acquaintance with President Alldredge and had lived in the stake only about one year.

I was a seventy when I was called to the stake presidency, and Elder Lee ordained me a high priest and set me apart as a counselor in the stake presidency. I shall never forget the wonderful blessing he gave me at that time. Among the promises made was that if I remained faithful in the Church, my basket would always be full so far as my personal finances were concerned. That particular blessing has certainly been true since that time. The Lord has blessed me and my family abundantly in material ways.

While President Lee did not say so openly, he hinted that another, higher calling in the stake would come later. Two years afterward, President Alldredge was called to preside over the South African Mission, and Elder Delbert L. Stapley of the Council of the Twelve installed me as the president of the East Millcreek Stake. I later had an even closer relationship with President Lee when I served on the adult committee of the Church Correlation Council under his direction.

The next time he had a profound influence on my life was a summer day in 1972, just a few days before the death of President Joseph Fielding Smith. At the time, President Lee was First Counselor to President Smith, and President N. Eldon Tanner was the Second Counselor in the First Presidency. President Lee invited me to meet with them in his office on a Sunday morning. President Smith was very infirm at the time and did not attend.

President Lee was the spokesman for the First Presidency and told me that the Brethren desired me to organize and direct the Public Communications Department of the Church, just then being formulated. I remember asking President Lee if this were a Church calling or a business proposition. I shall never forget his response, "If anyone has been called by the Lord, you have, Wendell."

With that statement, I immediately concluded my affairs with my advertising agency, in which I had the highest income in the firm and likely among the highest in the advertising profession in Utah. When I began my duties as managing director of the Public Communications Department of the Church, President Lee had just become the President of the Church.

He told me at that time, in my new role, that I was to be the spokesman for the Church with the news media of the world. He directed representatives of the news media to me and insisted that I speak for the Church with network television representatives, major newspapers, and wire services.

The question of blacks not holding the priesthood was a key issue with the news media at that time, and there were frequent inquiries regarding the subject and the position of the Church. I recall President Lee's statement at that time, and I quoted it often to the media. He said that blacks had not yet received the priesthood because the Lord had not directed that they should receive it. He said that he felt that the time would come when they would receive the priesthood, but that time would come only as the Lord directed.

President Lee told me that his office would always be open to me, and I need not go through channels to reach him directly in his position as President of the Church. He discussed with me some of his innermost thoughts and invited my opinions on different issues.

Among his many qualities of leadership, President Harold B. Lee was a master at handling situations well in difficult meetings and interviews with the news media. He would courageously, but graciously, stand his ground when the Church was challenged.

I recall his response to an NBC television network newsman when President Lee first became President of the Church. The newsman asked him how he received revelation as the prophet, seer, and revelator of the Church. President Lee responded that revelation came in a number of ways. Referring to the scriptures, as he most always did, he noted that revelation could come as an inner feeling, through a message from the Lord, through a heavenly message in the middle of the night, or through other ways. He stressed that only the President of the Church receives revelation for the entire Church, but each Church leader is entitled to inspiration or revelation in his own stewardship. He explained that this applied to a stake president, a bishop, a Relief Society president, or a father in his home.

He encouraged fathers to give special blessings to their children. One of his favorite stories, and a favorite of mine that I liked to tell, was an encounter his daughter Helen had while she was bottling apricots late at night and had sent her boys to bathe while she worked with the ripening fruit. They came ready for prayers but the mother was still tied to her fruit and suggested that they say, for this night, their own prayers. Her four-year-old asked, "Which is more important, Mommie, prayers or apricots?"

Another memorable experience that I observed with President Harold B. Lee was while he was President of the Church. A group of about eight leaders of the Pentecostal Church, which was holding a world conference in Salt Lake City, called at the Church headquarters. They met with President Lee and me in the First Presidency's room of the Church Administration Building. I recall that pleasantries were exchanged. Then one of the younger members of the Pentecostal delegation asked President Lee if the Book of Mormon was mentioned in the Bible. He attempted to embarrass President Lee through his questioning —obviously aimed at winning favor with his senior associates in the Pentacostal hierarchy. President Lee stood his ground by explaining the Book of Mormon and our scriptures generally. He held the upper hand but was gracious in putting the young Pentecostal leader in his place.

In the summer of 1973, I accompanied President Harold B. Lee and his wife, Joan, to the Hill Cumorah Pageant. While there, he conducted a special meeting of members of the Church who gathered in the Sacred Grove. I recall President Lee explaining to the congregation there in that sylvan setting that Joseph Smith could not behold the Father and the Son with his natural eyes. He explained that the boy, Joseph, was transformed in that First Vision in a way that he could, indeed, behold the manifestation.

In April 1973 we scheduled a press conference in New York City where President Lee was to announce the construction of a new thirty-six-story building in the Lincoln Center area of Manhattan, which would house a new stake center for the New York Stake. On the morning of 12 April, Brother D. Arthur Haycock drove us to the home of President Lee on Penrose Drive in the Federal Heights area of Salt Lake City so that we could take Elder and Sister Lee with us to the airport.

This was my second visit to his home. The living room of the Lee home, where we gathered, was pin neat. The beige carpet, a large beige couch, and off-white walls were highlights of the decor. On one wall of the living room was a huge color portrait of President Lee by Los Angeles photographer Merritt Smith. President Lee explained that Sister Lee had placed the portrait there. It was a striking pose, with the President standing beside a large globe of the world.

As we entered the living room, we were advised that the airline had called and reported that our plane for New York had been delayed; therefore, we had some time on our hands. President Lee showed us a small replica of Michelangelo's *Moses* on his piano. It had a small plaque explaining that the replica had been presented to President Lee in February 1973 by the Olympus Stake M-Men and Gleaners. There was a beautiful inscription on the plaque, indicating that the Church youth looked to President Lee's leadership in this day even as the children of Israel had looked to Moses for his leadership centuries ago.

With no demands on his time, President Lee sat at the large, grand piano that he had given his wife as a wedding present and began to play. We gathered around him, and he showed us the music that he had started to play. It was titled "The Link Divine," and he held the music with his left hand and played with his right hand. The words to the song were written by Alfred H. Hyatt, with music composed by Piccolomini. President Lee began to choke up as he played, and he explained to us that this song had been sung at the funeral of his first wife, Fern, and also at the funeral of his daughter Maurine. Brother Haycock explained also that the Tabernacle Choir had sung this selection as the final musical presentation in the closing session of the last April general conference. The song had followed a most touching concluding talk by President Lee, in which he strongly bore his personal testimony of the divinity of the restored gospel.

President Lee was a young seventy-four years of age, and his voice was rich as he talked in the privacy of his home that morning. His hair was graying; his height was about five foot eight inches; his weight about 150 pounds. That was a choice, intimate glimpse of the prophet in his prime.

When we arrived in New York City, President Lee invited F. Charles Graves, who was in charge of the New York City office of the External Communications Department of the Church, to join us in family prayers in the President's suite in the towers of the Waldorf Astoria Hotel. We noted that the hotel management had sent to their suite two big bowls of huge, fresh strawberries, along with a bottle of President Lee's favorite cranberry juice, cradled in ice, as a welcoming gesture.

What a spiritual experience it was to hear the prophet of the Church express gratitude to our Heavenly Father and ask for his blessings on our activities of the next day.

I always admired President Lee for both his wisdom and his courage and also for his unfailing care for people. He truly was creative in his thinking and was a powerhouse in organizing the Church at headquarters for greater efficiency and worldwide administration.

He always felt at ease conversing with people of the highest levels in government and business, and yet he was so tender and considerate of the lowly. He had grown up among the poor living alongside the Jordan River in the western part of Salt Lake City, and he became the champion for the common man in the Church.

President Lee could be very tough, if the situation called for it. Some people felt that he expressed too much sharpness at times. However, I loved and admired him for his fortitude and unflinching commitment to building the kingdom of God on earth. He could be a lion in seeing a job through its many obstacles.

I especially admired President Lee for his thoughtfulness and his deep concern and kindness to President Spencer W.

Kimball when President Kimball was having his struggles with his heart and cancer problems. Harold B. Lee truly was a courageous, well-organized administrator, but also a man with a tender heart.

I shall never forget the evening of 26 December 1973. I was at home in my study at about 9:00 P.M. I received a phone call from President Marion G. Romney, who was at the LDS Hospital. He told me that President Lee had just passed away. Not knowing that President Lee was even ill, I was shocked, yet it was my responsibility to notify the news media. I worried that the report of President Lee's passing was not really true, but I did notify the media, and the word went out across the world.

I lost that night a warm and highly esteemed friend. The Church and the world had lost a mighty leader.

20

Wallace G. Bennett
Former Mission President

He Seemed Eager
to Serve Us

I cannot express how much President Harold B. Lee meant to our family. We imposed on him, I am certain, but he was so willing and seemed even anxious at times to be of service.

In March 1956, I was involved in a freak accident in which our eldest son, then three and one-half years old, jumped on me while we were romping on the floor. He landed on my spleen and ruptured it. A few days later my doctors decided that I should have surgery, and the spleen was removed.

During the night after the surgery, I bled internally and had almost hemorrhaged to death by morning when the surgeon came to see me on his rounds. I was rushed to surgery again, and after the bleeding artery was closed off, I received several pints of blood.

Before I went to surgery the second time, the physician told my wife, Theda, that my condition was critical. He advised her to call my parents, Senator and Mrs. Wallace F. Bennett, who were then living in Washington, D.C., and to tell them that I might not have long to live. She did so.

Theda also phoned the Church Administration Building and asked for one of the Brethren whom she knew well. It was a Saturday morning, though, and the one she asked for was not in his office. The switchboard operator, however, kindly put her in contact with Elder Harold B. Lee, whom she had not met. Theda told Brother Lee who she was, described my condition, and asked if there was any chance he could come to the hospital sometime during the day to give me a priesthood blessing. He came to the hospital almost immediately, accompanied by one of the secretaries to the Council of the Twelve.

In the blessing he gave me, Brother Lee promised that I would regain my health, recover from the operation, and complete my mission on the earth. My wife, Theda, asked him why there had been such a long pause early in the blessing when he was getting started. He said he was waiting for the inspiration of the Spirit, and that he could feel the presence in the room of my grandfather, President Heber J. Grant, and others.

On the following Thursday, he came to the hospital to visit with me. He was somewhat surprised to find me sitting up in a chair eating my lunch. He remarked that my recovery to that point had been rather miraculous.

Sometime later, we met on the sidewalk one day. He asked me how I was and if I had suffered any ill effects from that episode. I assured him that I was in good health and that there had been no lingering consequences. He then told me that the Lord had healed me and that I should remember that experience throughout my life as an evidence of the Lord's power and his love for me.

We had other experiences with President Lee, too. He administered to Theda several times. He came to her bedside at our home when she suffered from meningitis. He blessed her and told her that the Lord had already been mindful of her or she would have died. He blessed her also when she underwent a spinal fusion. He advised her to return home to Salt Lake City for surgery when we were in England on our mission and promised us that she would be well again. He blessed her mother; he blessed our son.

We went to him once when I had a medical problem that was potentially quite serious. He asked us to come to his office on the day after Christmas, and he gave me a priesthood blessing. We then went to the medical specialist in Los Angeles, to whom we had been referred. A complete examination and biopsy there revealed no problem. Elder Lee referred to this experience when he spoke at our missionary farewell and described it in these words:

> They were faced with one of the most difficult decisions, I suppose, that a man and a woman can be faced with on this earth—the possible loss of divine powers caused by a serious and critical operation. The doctor, before he could perform the operation said, "You must bring your wife. I must talk with her, and she must understand the nature of this operation because it affects her life as well as yours."

President Lee then related our experience with the blessing he gave us and how I had been healed by the power of the priesthood. He concluded:

> Time passed. They came back from this experience with a radiance and the knowledge that beyond the powers of doctors and the skill of physicians there is a power that overrules. Today they bear testimony with a strength and fortitude and a determination that indicates the kind of faith and blood from which they've come.
>
> So, I come tonight with a little more than just a relationship of a General Authority to one being called into the mission field. I come with a feeling almost akin to blood relationship, because I've seen them walk through the fire. I've seen them go like Nephi of old, when he was given the tremendous responsibility and he said, "I, Nephi, crept into the city and went forth. . . . And I was led by the Spirit, not knowing beforehand the things which I should do." (1 Nephi 4:5–6.) They will now have to do that many times again.

We loved being with President Lee briefly in England, in September 1972, when Lord Thomson of Fleet, a wealthy and influential British newspaper owner, entertained him at a luncheon. This was followed that night with a missionary meeting attended by over four hundred missionaries. His example was always a great learning opportunity for us, and on this occasion we especially observed how solicitous he was of his wife.

We will always be grateful for his interest and concern for us, his willingness to give blessings, and for the way he built our faith. He always made us feel that he was pleased to be of service, instead of our occasional requests being an imposition or an intrusion. We treasure our memory of our association with President Harold B. Lee.

21

Rodney H. Brady
Former Government Official

Blessings from Obeying the Counsel of Prophets

In early June of 1970, I was approached by the newly appointed secretary of the U.S. Department of Health, Education, and Welfare, Elliot L. Richardson, to determine my interest in joining his top staff in Washington, D.C., possibly as assistant secretary for administration and management. That appointment, being of subcabinet rank, would require that I become the chief administrative and management officer of a department of the federal government with approximately 115,000 employees and annual expenditures approaching $100 billion, accounting for approximately one-third of all federal expenditures.

At the time I received this inquiry from Secretary Richardson, I was serving as vice-president for administration and as a member of the executive committee of the aircraft division of the Hughes Tool Company, a large Los Angeles headquartered company engaged in research, development, and production of aircraft and support equipment. My wife, Mitzi, and I, along with our two sons, Howard, age three, and Ryan, age one, were happily and comfortably settled in a newly purchased home in the Westwood area of Los Angeles. At the time, I was serving also as bishop of the Westwood Ward of the Church.

During the days following this initial inquiry from Washington, I spent many soul-searching hours evaluating the pros and cons concerning my interest in this appointment. I sought the advice of Elder Thomas S. Monson of the Council of the Twelve, and coupling his counsel with my own careful deliberations, my wife and I decided to pursue the opportunity to join the administration in Washington. Thus, during the months that followed, I made numerous trips from Los Angeles to Washington to discuss with Secretary Richardson, HEW officials, and presidential aides at the White House the details of this appointment, which, after thoughtful prayer, I decided to accept.

Though the public announcement of my appointment was not to be made until December, rumors and speculation regarding my pending appointment started to circulate in late October and early November. In mid-November I received a message from the office of President Harold B. Lee, First Counselor in the First Presidency of the Church, indicating that he and several other General Authorities would like me to stop by Church headquarters for a visit the next time I was in Salt Lake City. The message indicated that the Brethren would like to visit with me about my appointment in Washington. Therefore, in connection with one of my subsequent flights between Los Angeles and Washington, D.C., I stopped over in Salt Lake City, spending part of the day of 23 December 1970 visiting with several of the Church leaders, including President Lee.

Though I had met President Lee on several prior occasions, my principal contact with him in the past had been through his second wife, Sister Freda Joan Jensen Lee, who had been a close friend of my parents and who had taught me in a Mt. Jordan Stake teacher training course during my youth. Thus, as I entered President Lee's office in the southeast corner of the main floor of the Church Administration Building, he greeted me with some familiarity, shook my hand warmly, and then asked that I sit down with him in the conversation area of his nicely appointed office.

During our twenty-minute visit, President Lee guided the conversation to a variety of subjects, including differences between the Church welfare program and the government's welfare program. As I stood up and was about to leave, President Lee said to me, "Bishop Brady, as you are about to undertake a very special assignment in the government, would you like to have me give you a special blessing?"

I was overwhelmed at the thought of receiving a special blessing at the hand of an ordained Apostle of the Lord, who was also a member of the First Presidency of the Church. Thus I responded, "Yes, President Lee, I would very much like you to give me a special blessing."

President Lee then placed a small chair in the center of his office, in front of his desk, and asked that I be seated. He then placed his hands upon my head, paused for a moment, and pronounced a blessing upon me.

The blessing that President Lee voiced that day I recorded from memory approximately one hour after it was given as I sat at a table on the mezzanine floor of the Hotel Utah, next door to the Church Administration Building. Included in that blessing were these most pertinent words:

> I feel inspired to counsel you, Brother Brady, that while you are in Washington you should concentrate all of your energies toward accomplishing that assignment which you have been called to fulfill. Beware of those who will tempt you to become involved in other endeavors prior to your completing this assignment. Beware of those who will encourage you to depart from those principles of honesty, virtue, and character that you know to be right. Beware of those who will tempt you with pride and vain ambition, for they can destroy you.
>
> I encourage you to stay close to your family and stay close to the Church, for the Lord has great and important assignments in his kingdom for you if you will live worthy of these callings. If you live worthily, Brother Brady, I can see the Brethren in the highest councils of the Church relying upon you often to assist them in building and administering the kingdom.

Of course I was on a "spiritual high" as I left President Lee's office that day. As I reduced to writing my best recollections of the words President Lee pronounced during that blessing, I was especially struck by the unity of advice contained in President Lee's blessing with that which I had received from Elder Monson six months earlier.

My family and I moved to Washington in late December of 1970, and during the next year, I, with the superb support, leadership, and assistance of Secretary Elliot L. Richardson, was able to accomplish in just one year far more than I had hoped to be able to accomplish in four or five years. Not only did I receive broad recognition for my administrative and management accomplishments within the Department of Health, Education, and Welfare, but my subcabinet colleagues throughout the executive branch honored me by supporting my election to the position of chairman of the subcabinet executive officers group. The White House staff, and even President Richard Nixon himself, made note of our administrative and management accomplishments at HEW. In fact, on 2 December 1971, I received a personal letter from the president, commending me for the high quality job I was doing as the chief administrative officer at HEW.

A few days after receiving the letter from President Nixon, I received a telephone call at my office at HEW from the office of Attorney General John Mitchell. Attorney General Mitchell had been appointed chairman of the committee to reelect the president for the election of November 1972. My name had been suggested as one of those who should be considered to play a major role in managing that election campaign. Since my response to this inquiry was somewhat guarded, I was asked to "think it over" and to "consider the possible assignment that might come your way if the president is reelected."

As I sat in my large executive chair in my impressive Washington office "thinking it over" that day, I started to dream of the grand and powerful future that might be ahead for me if I answered this inquiry in the affirmative. Secretary Richardson dropped by my office that afternoon on another matter of business, so I discussed the inquiry with him. His response was somewhat cool and not encouraging, which I interpreted as disappointment that I might be leaving the Department of HEW before our management improvement job was fully complete.

As I arrived home that evening, I immediately went to my well-organized personal files and pulled out two documents that my memory suggested might have some bearing on this decision, one being my notes on my visit with Elder Monson eighteen months before and the other being my written record of the blessing I had received at the hand of President Lee twelve months before. As I reread these documents, I was awestruck by the specific way in which the advice of these two inspired Apostles addressed this particular decision.

First, Elder Monson's advice was to "avoid contracting 'Potomac Fever'" and second, President Lee in his prayer stated, "While you are in Washington you should concentrate all of your energies toward accomplishing that assignment which you have been called to fulfill. Beware of those who will tempt you to become involved in other endeavors prior to your completing this assignment. . . . Beware of those who will tempt you with pride and vain ambition, for they can destroy you."

In accordance with this inspired advice, which was sufficiently direct to cause me to make the decision at that moment, I dropped to my knees in the privacy of my study that evening and poured out my soul to the Lord, thanking him for confirming to me through his Holy Spirit that the words of his servants were appropriate to this decision.

Upon arriving at my office the next day, my first action was to place a call to the office of the attorney general, where I left a message indicating my desire that my name be withdrawn from any further consideration to serve with the committee to reelect the president.

The rest is well-known history. In July of 1971 the Democratic National Headquarters at the Watergate was broken into, and the men involved were apprehended. President Nixon was reelected by a landslide victory in November 1972, and in 1973 the infamous events called "Watergate" were slowly uncovered, leading to the congressional hearings in early 1974 that culminated with the resignation of the president of the United States in August 1974. Several of my subcabinet level colleagues and White House staff aides who had joined the committee to reelect the president, along with the attorney general and the president, himself, were implicated in the affair.

As for myself, I continued to serve in the position of assistant secretary for administration and management at HEW until I had guided through to their implementation the improvements I had gone to Washington, D.C., to accomplish. In the summer of 1972, I notified both Secretary Richardson and the president that I would be returning to private business in California immediately after the November 1972 elections, which I did. Soon after our return to Los Angeles, I was called as a counselor in the presidency of the Los Angeles Stake and subsequently as the president of that stake.

As the events of Watergate unfolded in the two years following my departure from Washington, I often asked myself the question, "Had I become involved with the committee to reelect the president early in 1972, would I have had the insight, the moral courage, or the power to have had an influence upon the decisions and events that ultimately transpired?" My own personal conclusion regarding what was best for me, my family, the Church, and the country concerning whether I should have involved myself in these events is absolutely clear. The counsel of the two inspired Apostles had indeed blessed and protected me and my family from great temptation and great danger.

How thankful I am for my testimony that we have today upon the earth servants of the Lord who have been called by him to serve and counsel us. How thankful I am for a knowledge of the scriptures that make it clear to us that "he that receive [my servants] receiveth me, and he that receiveth me receiveth him that sent me" (Matthew 10:40); and "whether by mine own voice or by the voice of my servants, it is the same" (D&C 1:38).

While serving as assistant secretary of the U.S. Department of Health, Education, and Welfare and as a member of the president's subcabinet in Washington, D.C., from 1970 to 1972, I would receive a letter about a month before each general conference of the Church from President Harold B. Lee, inviting me to be a special guest of his at the conference. Happily, I was able to accept President Lee's invitation for the October conference of 1971. On this particular occasion, President Lee invited me to stop by his office at the Church Administration Building for a visit one hour before the morning session of conference, which I arranged to do.

As I entered his first-floor office, I could not help but recall the spiritual blessing I had received from him the previous December in the same office when I was about to undertake my assignment in Washington, D.C.

During my October 1971 conference visit with President Lee, we discussed at length some of the same topics that we had covered in our earlier visit; that is, the expansion of the Church and the federal welfare programs. I was able to update President Lee on my experience with the federal and state welfare programs, federal domestic policies, and impressions regarding President Richard Nixon, Secretary Elliot Richardson, and other key government leaders.

After our thirty-minute visit, there came a gentle knock on the office door. President Lee asked that I see who was at the door. To my surprise, I discovered our visitor was President Lee's wife, Sister Freda Joan Jensen Lee, my close friend.

After we embraced warmly, Sister Lee reminded President Lee that it was time that they should make their way to the Tabernacle for conference. Generously, President Lee asked that I accompany them to the Tabernacle through their "special way," which I soon discovered was by way of a tunnel from the underground parking plaza of the Church Administration Building, under Hotel Utah, under Main Street, and under much of Temple Square, surfacing beneath the choir seats of the Tabernacle.

When we reached a point about midway through the tunnel, President Lee asked that we excuse him for a few minutes. As Sister Lee and I waited for his return, I could not help but inquire as to where President Lee had gone. Sister Lee responded, "Before the beginning of conference, Harold likes to spend a few minutes visiting with the Lord in the temple."

As President Lee reappeared a few minutes later, his face shown with a special radiance, and his countenance seemed especially serene. He then took Sister Lee by the hand and quietly escorted her to the end of the tunnel, then to the General Authorities' lounge behind the rostrum of the Tabernacle. After introducing me to many of the other General Authorities, President Lee asked that I sit near the pulpit, next to Sister Lee, in a special area reserved for conference guests.

Though the opportunity to view a session of the general conference of the Church from the stand of the Tabernacle, and to feel of the spirit of the Brethren from so close at hand was awe inspiring, the experience of the day that had the greatest effect upon me was President Lee's emergence from the temple bearing the special countenance of a prophet who had just visited with the Lord.

22

M. Elmer Christensen
Former Regional Representative

He Taught the Unbounded Power of the Priesthood

I have had the privilege of meeting with President Harold B. Lee many times in my life. I visited the Pioneer Stake when I was a member of the YMMIA General Board while he was still serving there as the stake president. When he was managing director of the Church Welfare Committee, I met with him many times in connection with food processing problems in the welfare program. At that time I was serving as Utah State chemist.

When the Church first started to process canned foods, such as corn, tomatoes, peas, and beans, the Church distributed the foods in bare cans without labels. I met with President Lee to advise and assist in the development of a labeling system that would be attractive, informative, and legally acceptable. He later sought my assistance in a program of routine examinations and testing of welfare products for purity and quality. I was able to incorporate such a testing program into the regular state food inspection work. For several years I was able to be of such assistance to him and the Church Welfare Committee. This brought us into rather intimate and frequent contact. It was always a pleasant experience to associate and work with President Lee.

I did not realize how much Elder Lee really appreciated that service until I accompanied him to a stake conference in the Sharon Stake in 1965. I was then serving as a member of the General Home Teaching Committee. He spent some time in his remarks during the conference referring to my service to him and the committee when the welfare program was just being launched. I thought he was far too complimentary of me, but that was his routine manner of relating to valued friends.

When I was called to serve as president of the Cottonwood Stake, the visiting General Authorities were Elders Lee and Stephen L Richards. Elder Richards did most of the interrogation during the interview, but Elder Lee asked me two perceptive questions that impressed me so much that I have always remembered them. The first question was, "Who do you feel should be called to be the new president of this stake?" I suggested Brother Marius O. Evans, who was then serving as the first counselor.

His next question was, "In view of your past experience in Scouting and your enthusiasm for it, what emphasis would you place upon the Aaronic Priesthood program, in relationship to the Scouting program, if you were called to be the stake president?" I knew that Elder Lee was aware of my work in Scouting for almost thirty years. I immediately recognized his concern for the Aaronic Priesthood program at that time when the two programs were almost competitive in some areas of the Church. I replied that I would endeavor to interpret the attitude of the General Authorities and give each program the emphasis they felt they should have. He seemed to be satisfied with my answer.

In 1957 I was serving as a member of the Granite District Board of Education. We had a written board regulation that prohibited students or employees of the district from smoking cigarettes on school property. That policy was one of long-standing in the district.

During that year the Building Maintenance Department employed a recent immigrant from Hungary to work on the building painting crew. He was found smoking cigarettes one day and was warned to desist by his foreman. Later, he was found smoking again while painting one of the buildings and was warned by the district supervisor, Leland Davey. He was advised that his services would be terminated if he did not comply with the regulation. He was caught smoking a third time and was dismissed from employment.

The next morning the action received prominent attention in the local newspaper. Subsequently, a delegation of citizens from the district met with the Board, protesting the action. The meeting became very noisy, insulting, and tense. Four of the five board members were Church leaders, two of them being stake presidents. I was determined to adhere to the regulation and uphold the action of the district supervisor, but one of the board members made a motion that the board rescind the regulation forbidding smoking on the job and reinstate the painter. The vote was four to one in favor of the motion. I later agreed to make it unanimous.

I felt terrible, and realizing that the majority of the citizens of the district were members of the Church, I felt that we had "let them down." The next morning I called Elder Lee's office and asked for an appointment with him. I felt he deserved an explanation of our action, and I wanted his opinion as to what we should do in the future.

I spent a considerable amount of time with him and rehearsed all of the details of the previous evening's experience. He listened patiently, without comment, until I was finished. I expected him to defend our traditional no-smoking regulation, but he said nothing about it. Instead, he recalled several experiences he had had in dealing with the public while he was serving in the Salt Lake City Commission, explaining the citizen complaints he had to deal with and the differences of opinion on moral issues between him and those with whom he worked. It was a rich educational experience for me.

He did not make any specific suggestion for future action but did say that in dealing with the public on civic matters, the attitudes and opinions of all segments of the city, or area, had to be carefully weighed and considered, and decisions should be

made on the basis of fairness and justice. I felt greatly relieved
and appreciated his calmness and patience and the wisdom of
his counsel.

On 27 February 1965 I accompanied Elder Lee to the Sharon
Stake conference in Utah County. He introduced me to the
Stake priesthood leaders as the "dean of stake presidents" in
the Church. At that time I was still serving as president of the
Winder Stake, even though I had been a member of the Church
Home Teaching Committee for eighteen months. We were
scheduled to hold a Saturday evening session of the conference,
but Brigham Young University was playing an important basketball game that night in Provo. Elder Lee had just the right solution to the conflict. He suggested that the evening session be
held early for a limited number of presiding leaders, after which
we could all go to the game together. This we gratefully did.
Elder Lee had an extra ticket that he gave to me, and I sat next to
him during the game. I have never enjoyed a game as much as
that one, although I can't tell you now who won. It was the company and the circumstances that made it so special. Elder Lee
was acknowledged over the public address microphone, and
individually by many friends that night, and was a hero for
making everyone happy by reducing the pressures between duty
and pleasure.

I was also privileged to accompany Elder Lee to two stake
conferences while I served as a member of the Church Home
Teaching Committee. One conference was held in November
1964 in the Utah (Provo) Stake. In that meeting with the stake
presidency, Elder Lee invited me to discuss with them the supervision of the home teaching program in their stake. I emphasized the need to urge families to become more involved in
home-centered activities. The president responded that there
was practically no time for families to do very much at home,
because they were involved in ward and stake activities every
night of the week.

Elder Lee then volunteered a revolutionary, courageous
observation. He said that the Church would, apparently, have to
formally set aside one night of the week as a "home night" and
not permit anything to interfere with it. He said, "We will just

turn out the lights in every meetinghouse in the Church on that night.''

That was the first time that I had heard any General Authority make that suggestion as specific and as positive as Elder Lee did. Within a short time after this experience, the General Authorities made it a general Church policy that Monday nights would be family home evening, with no outside interferences allowed. I have since felt that Elder Lee was inspired to make that observation in Utah Stake and that he was responsible for its adoption as a Churchwide policy.

The most outstanding impression that President Lee has left with me was his tremendous respect for, and confidence in, the power and role of the priesthood in caring for the personal and general needs of the Church. The decisions he made as a leader and the expressions of his beliefs provided irrefutable evidence of his conviction of the divine nature of the priesthood.

As a youth I had been an active participant in the auxiliary programs of the Church, and I developed a strong appreciation for them. As a leader in the YMMIA, I learned of a prediction that President Joseph F. Smith made in his opening address at the 1906 April general conference when he said:

> We expect to see the day, if we live long enough (and if some of us do not live long enough to see it, there are others who will), when every council of the Priesthood in the Church of Jesus Christ of Latter-day Saints will understand its duty, will assume its own responsibility, will magnify its calling, and fill its place in the Church, to the uttermost, according to the intelligence and ability possessed by it. When that day shall come, there will not be so much necessity for work that is now being done by the auxiliary organizations, because it will be done by the regular quorums of the Priesthood. The Lord designed and comprehended it from the beginning, and He has made provision in the Church whereby every need may be met and satisfied through the regular organizations of the Priesthood. It has truly been said that the Church is perfectly organized. The only trouble is that these organizations are not fully alive to the obligations that rest upon them. When they become thoroughly awakened to the requirements made of them, they will fulfill their duties more faithfully, and the work of the Lord will be all the stronger and more powerful and influential in the world. (Conference Report, Apr. 1906, p. 3.)

This statement surprised me. I was willing to accept it as a prophecy but felt that its fulfillment lay far into the distant future. It also was difficult for me to understand how the priesthood could accomplish the task, in view of their many other responsibilities.

I lived to see the day when the Lord would raise up a prophet and leader who had the vision and the courage to make that prediction come true. In my opinion, that man was President Harold B. Lee. The smooth and efficient manner in which the transition was made demonstrated his outstanding ability as a capable organizational leader.

President Lee was a man of many virtues. He loved and understood people. He was a ready friend to all he met. He patiently listened to those who sought his advice and always had practical, helpful counsel to impart to those in need. When our first child and daughter, LeRae, was married in 1952, we asked Elder Lee to perform the sealing ceremony. They remember in great detail, to this day, the practical and helpful counsel he gave to them at that special time.

I know all of these statements are true because I was a frequent recipient of his wisdom and kindly spirit.

23

R. Viola Davidson
Wife of a Serviceman Convert

A Healing
Handshake

My husband, Floyd Thomas Davidson, was a U.S. Navy career serviceman, very handsome and blessed with natural leadership abilities. He was not a member of the Church when we were married, but the year 1954 brought a wonderful change to our lives.

Floyd was aboard the *USS Hornet* on a round-the-world tour of duty. On board that ship an outstanding Latter-day Saint servicemen's group was organized. He mingled with these men and wanted to be like them. Soon his conversion neared, and he planned to be baptized when they arrived in Japan.

The group was excited to learn that Elder Harold B. Lee, of the Council of the Twelve, was touring the Orient and was to preside at a servicemen's conference in Tokyo. Floyd, too, wanted desperately to attend this conference, but he had developed a most painful, swollen, infected arm. The ship's physician also was a member of the Latter-day Saint group and gave him permission to go ashore for the conference since he would be there to attend him if necessary.

Floyd was uncomfortable throughout the meeting, but after the conference he lined up to meet and shake hands with Elder Lee. He told him that his aircraft carrier would be in Manila at the time Elder Lee would be visiting the Philippines and that he hoped he would see him then and be able to tell him that he had been baptized a member of the Church. While on the train en route back to the ship in Yokosuka, he suddenly realized that the severe pain was gone and his arm was healed. It had been almost unbearable all during the meeting.

A few days later, I received a telegram from Yokosuka, dated 27 August 1954, that said, "Baptized this morning, Now your Latter-day Saint husband. Love, Floyd."

He was privileged to see and visit with Elder and Sister Lee in Manila. Elder Lee told a general conference audience in the Salt Lake Tabernacle on 3 October 1954 that Floyd came to them with his arm completely healed and reported his baptism, saying:

> Something happened to me after I left that conference in Tokyo. My arm was swollen and was painful all through the meeting, but after I had shaken hands with you, I got on the train going back to the boat. Suddenly the pain ceased, my arm was healed, and now I am going back to that lovely wife who has been praying that I would straighten my life. I smoked, and I drank, and I did a lot of things to cause her sorrow, and I am going back to that sweetheart of mine, and I am going to spend the rest of my life trying to prove myself worthy of her love. (Conference Report, Oct. 1954, pp. 128–29.)

For thirty years my husband was a living testimonial of how Elder Lee changed his life. Floyd became a wonderful husband and father and an outstanding member of the Church, serving in many positions, including that of bishop and high councilor.

His health began to fail during 1979–80, and he passed away on 3 November 1984. I am so grateful for his true and lasting conversion and his worthiness that led to our marriage for "time and all eternity."

24

John K. Edmunds
Former Temple President

We Were Better Because He Made Us Feel Special

Following my appointment as President of the Chicago Stake on 12 May 1945, it was my special privilege and blessing to have President Harold B. Lee, then a young Apostle, as one of our early stake conference visitors. Elder Lee and my wife's brother, Marion G. Romney, were very close friends. As a result of this friendship, I had become acquainted with Brother Lee in the midthirties, about the time he was called by President Heber J. Grant to implement a Church welfare program.

President Lee had served as a stake president, and I was most anxious to receive his counsel and advice at the beginning of my term as stake president. He came prepared for service and performed a great and significant work in our stake. He stayed at our home. The discussion of the affairs of the Chicago Stake began almost as soon as I met him at the train on the Saturday of conference. I unloaded my problems and projects upon him, and we discussed them at great length during the afternoon. After he had met with me personally, my counselors, Dr. Ariel L. Williams and Henry A. Matis, joined us. President Lee counseled us at length with respect to our duties and opportunities. Then there followed meetings with the stake presidency, high council, and the priesthood leadership of the stake. At the conclusion of this long day's work, President Lee retired late. However, he was up again early Sunday morning holding more meetings, which continued through the day and included two general sessions of conference and meetings with the seventies and stake missionaries. Then there were interviews with various priesthood officers and prospective officers. The final meeting of the day was an evening meeting, a special fireside with our military servicemen from the Great Lakes Naval Training Center and from other military centers in northern Illinois.

No time was wasted during those two days; no time given to sight-seeing or entertainment. I was greatly impressed by the time and energy President Lee gave to the conference business. Offering me much by way of encouragement, President Lee departed Monday for New York.

In those days the railroad was the accepted means of transportation for conference visitors from Salt Lake City. There were then four stakes east of the Rocky Mountains: Denver, Chicago, New York, and Washington. The conference schedules were so planned that the latter three stakes held conferences on successive weekends, it being a waste of time for the General Authority to return to Salt Lake between these conferences. President Lee left Chicago to attend the conferences in New York and Washington. He informed me about his itinerary and arranged for me to meet him in Chicago as he returned to Salt Lake City.

I met President Lee at the railway station two weeks later by appointment, and we had dinner together at a restaurant in my office building at One La Salle Street. I reported to him on the progress that had been made in implementing the recommendations he had made two weeks earlier, and he seemed greatly interested and pleased. As I sat across the dining table from him, I became seriously concerned over the marks of strain and fatigue I observed in his face. The tired eyes and the obvious drain on his energy caused me to say, "You look very tired, Brother Lee. This must have been a hard assignment for you."

He said it was. Then without divulging any confidences, he related some of the problems that had confronted him during the days in New York and Washington. When he finished, my concern had reached such a point that I, perhaps inappropriately, offered the suggestion that he ease up a little in his stake conference work. "Otherwise," I said, "your health might break under the strain."

He looked at me a minute, as if considering what I had said. I could almost see him formulating his memorable answer, "I have thought about this, John. I am faced with three alternatives. First, I could eliminate some of the extra meetings, interviews, and other work at the stake conferences and conserve my energy. The work calls for meetings with the stake presidency, the high council, the Saturday night priesthood meeting, and two general sessions on Sunday. The other meetings could be eliminated.

"Second, I could hold all the meetings but put more of the work load upon the stake president and others during the conference.

"Or, third, I could go on holding all the meetings that I deem advisable. I could hold all the conferences with stake leaders and officers, conduct interviews, ordain and set apart stake officers, try to solve the personal problems I find in the stake, and do all I could to be helpful.

"I think of Albert E. Bowen and the other Apostles and think of the long service they have given. Many of them are now old and do not have the strength they once had. I am one of the youngest of the Twelve and feel that it is my hour in life to give everything I have to the Lord's work.

"So, John, I have decided to hold all the meetings I consider advisable, as I did at your stake conference, doing whatever I can to be helpful and giving my full strength and energy to my calling."

There was nothing more to be said. I think I shall never forget that beautiful experience at the dinner table and the impression this great and devoted Apostle made upon my life.

During the years that followed, my association with President Lee became ever closer and more intimate. There were other stake conference visits; there were unscheduled visits at my office between trains as he went east or west through Chicago.

Eighteen years later, upon my release as stake president in 1963, I feared our close association might come to an end. Fortunately, however, I was called to serve on the original Church Home Teaching Committee, which was chaired by President Lee and managed by Elder Marion G. Romney. Then in 1967, with the dissolution of the committee, I was called to serve as one of the original Regional Representatives of the Council of the Twelve, so my association with President Lee remained uninterrupted.

In the winter of 1968–69, President Lee invited me, as a Regional Representative of the Twelve, to help him divide the Lansing and Detroit stakes and create two new stakes, the Mid-Michigan and the Dearborn stakes. We had a very unusual experience in choosing a patriarch for one of the new stakes. We had interviewed most of the stake priesthood leaders and had invited their recommendations with respect to a patriarch. Without exception these leaders put one particular man first, saying that he was the most spiritual man in the stake. It was natural for us to have the feeling that we had found the servant whom the Lord had chosen for this holy calling. When he was invited to meet with us, President Lee asked me to lead out in the interview. (Although it is the responsibility of the Twelve to choose a patriarch, President Lee had graciously invited me to assist in this matter, and upon the direction of President Lee, we had taken turns in conducting the interviews.) At the conclusion of this particular interview, the brother under consideration was thanked and was excused without any suggestion that he was being considered for the office of patriarch.

As soon as he left the room, President Lee asked, "How do you feel about him, John?"

I thoughtfully responded, "I think he is a fine man, but I am well aware of the revelation appointing the Twelve to choose and to ordain patriarchs 'as they shall be designated unto them by revelation.' " (See D&C 107:38.)

President Lee responded, "Yes, I know, but you are a representative of the Twelve and are also a patriarch, John, and I want your feeling about this man for a patriarch."

There was no hedging. I spoke frankly, "It is my feeling that he is not the man for the position."

President Lee quickly said, "I have the same feeling." He continued, "We'll have to start over in finding a patriarch, and we know where to start."

Even as he was speaking he was kneeling. I joined him. He led in prayer. It was an unusual prayer. It didn't seem like President Lee was praying to some faraway person. It was more like a consultation with someone there in the room. He talked about the many recommendations that we had received respecting the choice of a patriarch and our feelings with respect to the matter. Then he said, "Father, wilt thou make known to us the man *thou hast chosen* as patriarch?"

The simplicity and faith with which he made the request were soul-stirring. It would hardly have surprised me if we had heard the patriarch's name. As I have thought about it since, I have often compared it with the choice of an Apostle to take the place of Judas after his transgression and fall from the apostleship that had been conferred upon him. Addressing the assembled disciples of Jesus Christ (there were about 120 present on the occasion), Peter set forth the qualifications of one who would be ordained to the apostleship and serve as a witness of Jesus Christ and his resurrection. Two men were found who fulfilled the specified requirements: Joseph called Barsabas, surnamed Justus, and Matthias. The record said the disciples "prayed, and said, Thou, Lord, which knowest the hearts of all men, shew whether of these two *thou hast chosen.* . . . And they gave forth their lots; and the lot fell upon Matthias; and he was numbered with the eleven apostles." (Acts 1:24, 26; italics added.)

President Lee and I arose from our knees after prayer and searched further for the man whom God had chosen for patriarch. After each interview, President Lee would ask, "How do you feel about him, John?" In every case we had the same feeling. When the chosen man left the room, we knew we had found him, and President Lee asked him to wait a little while. I said I felt that he would be a good patriarch. President Lee said, "He is the man whom the Lord has chosen."

The next night, as we traveled by train to Chicago in a winter storm that grounded all aircraft, we talked at length of the experience and of the opinions of the many brethren who had unanimously recommended another man for patriarch. We both felt that the brother whom they recommended was a fine Latter-day Saint. President Lee summed it all up by saying that the Lord gives revelation to men to discharge the duties he has placed upon them. It was not the duty or the privilege of the stake leaders to choose the patriarch. This assignment had been given by revelation to the Twelve, and after sincere prayer, the Lord revealed to one of the Twelve the man whom He had chosen as patriarch.

A few months after this experience, Jasmine and I were called to preside over the California Mission with headquarters in Los Angeles. I was set apart for this mission by President Lee, assisted by Richard L. Evans; and Jasmine was set apart for her mission by Richard L. Evans, assisted by President Lee. The blessings were recorded and copies were sent to us in Los Angeles. Elder Lee gave me an extraordinarily beautiful, significant, and prophetic blessing in which he said, among other words, "When this mission shall have been concluded, the way ahead of you shall be as an open road. Put aside all worry and anxiety for the future because the Lord will help you map that future. You may be certain that the faith that has led you thus to enter his great service will be fully justified in the years that lie ahead of you."

These promises were miraculously fulfilled. After three busy, challenging years as president of the California Mission and just a few weeks before our release, the "open road" came into view when President Lee and his wife, Joan, visited us at the California Mission home. They spent a night and two days with us. Within a few minutes after they arrived, when we were standing in the guest room, President Lee turned to me and, putting his hand on my shoulder, said, "John, you have been called to preside over the Salt Lake Temple, and," referring to Sister Edmunds, he continued, "your sweet Jasmine is to be called as the temple matron."

Before our mission was completed, Elder Lee had become the prophet, seer, and revelator and the President of The Church of Jesus Christ of Latter-day Saints. On 2 August 1972, he again laid his hands upon my head and set me apart as president of the Salt Lake Temple and conferred upon me the sacred sealing authority. Now, again, I was closely associated with President Lee and turned to him often for counsel and direction.

President Lee came each Monday to the Salt Lake Temple to instruct and inspire the newly called full-time missionaries. It was customary for these missionaries to spend a week in the Salt Lake mission home before going to their fields of labor. On Monday morning of each week, these missionaries had the privilege of going through two endowment sessions in the Salt Lake Temple. Between these two sessions, they were invited to the solemn assembly room to have their questions answered and to receive instructions regarding the temple ceremonies from the prophet, Harold B. Lee. Sister Edmunds and I frequently attended these meetings.

On one such occasion, a missionary asked President Lee this intriguing question, "President Lee, would you tell us where it was that the Savior appeared in the Salt Lake Temple?" The elder was probably referring to the Savior's recorded appearance to President Lorenzo Snow.

President Lee obviously considered this question for a few moments and then replied, "Son, where in your home has your father not been?"

The elder answered, "My father has been everywhere in our home!"

The President then said, "Well, this is the house of the Lord, and he's been everywhere in it and knows it much better than we do."

This and other experiences kept each missionary group thrilled as they listened to and learned from the prophet of the Lord in the Salt Lake Temple.

Those years in the Salt Lake Temple gave me many opportunities to counsel frequently with President Lee and to receive direction and inspiration from him. My last conference with him occurred only a few days before his death, when I spent an hour and a half with him in his temple dressing room, discussing temple ordinances and procedures. The memory of this experience will always remain a precious one to me.

Jasmine and I last saw President Lee, accompanied by Sister Lee, as they went through an endowment session on a December evening in 1973, just before the temple closed for the Christmas holidays. He so commended us for our temple service that we left his presence with a warm, loving, dedicated spirit that we shall always remember.

We have often talked about President Lee and of his particular gift of making people feel that they were somehow special. We always felt that we had become a little better because of having been in his presence. When President Lee used that rare gift of making people feel important, it caused them to strive to reach the potential he could see in them and spelled the difference between success and failure in helping them become their best selves. Unnumbered are the souls who will bless President Lee for providing this motivation in their lives.

25

Ruth Hardy Funk
Former Young Women General President

Ruth, Come Walk with Me

It has been a joy to review the deep river of President Harold B. Lee's profound influence that swells through my life, not unlike the mighty Nile of Egypt that overflows its banks and gives nourishment, life, and enrichment to whatever it touches. It is difficult, actually impossible, to enumerate the endless incidents and associations with him that have changed my life. I will share but a few events that have been stepping-stones beside this river.

This first example came as a telephone call on Monday, 18 June 1962, following the conclusion of a glorious June conference. Brother George I. Cannon and I had been the coproducers of a new musical play, *Papa and the Playhouse*, which commemorated the one hundredth anniversary of the famous old playhouse, the Salt Lake Theater. It had been a thrilling experience, exhausting and most fulfilling, doing the work I love so much: praising our Heavenly Father through music. The conversation went like this:

"Hello, Ruth. This is Elder Marion G. Romney. You must be pleased with the outcome of the recently held June conference."

Of course I responded with great excitement as to the events which had preceded this phone call. As usual, Elder Romney got right to the point, "Well, Ruth, we're changing your assignment. We are calling you to serve on the Correlation Committee of the Church."

I responded in a rather direct and spontaneous way by asking, "What in the world is correlation, President Romney? How can you do this to me? You know how I love serving on the General Music Committee of the MIA, and I've done it for twelve years."

Ignoring my pleas and sensing the tears in my voice, Elder Romney responded, "Ruth, I am not asking you. I'm telling you." How foolish of me to question a calling from the Lord. He went on, "You will report for an orientation meeting called by President Harold B. Lee, the chairman, on next Wednesday. There you will hear all about the Correlation Committee's work."

Little did I know how dramatically this telephone call would change my life. It was a call that would provide an opportunity to work with and be taught by one of the greatest souls and prophets our Father in Heaven has ever sent to this earth.

We convened at the appointed hour. I was surprised to recognize many of those who were in attendance, including three Apostles of the Church, several former mission presidents, stake presidents, executive directors of major departments of the Church, and professors from Brigham Young University and the Church Educational System. I knew then that this was no ordinary meeting.

President Lee presided and conducted the meeting. After a general greeting and a bit of humor, he explained to us the work and purpose of the Correlation Committee. In almost a visionary manner, he described the situation of the world today, the decadence, the challenges, and the tragedies that were eroding the values and lives of the children of God. He described how the Church will go forth unto every corner of the world. With this anticipated growth of the gospel of Jesus Christ here on the earth, he described the urgent need for a powerful, well-organized and correlated foundation that must be based upon the supremacy of the family and the importance of the home. He spoke of the priesthood of God in a manner I had never heard nor understood before. He called it an all-encompassing power from our Heavenly Father, which will guide the affairs of men and would become the core that will provide the power to motivate the expansion of the kingdom of God here on earth.

He explained also to us the need for the examination and evaluation of the curriculum that had been developed in the Church from its very beginning, identifying the basic principles of the gospel upon which our Heavenly Father has founded his kingdom here on earth and of the needs of his children.

As he spoke, a luminous radiance seemed to emanate from his countenance, almost surrounding his entire being. I had never had such an experience before, and I've never had one since. I knew this was no ordinary man who had been called by the Lord to correlate and orchestrate all the elements of the gospel. It overwhelmed and awed me that I might be a small part of what he envisioned in that first meeting. It was an hour of great inspiration and revelation during which he articulated specifically where the Church was then and where it was to go.

Next President Lee identified the structure and organization that would implement the work of correlation. The organization would be divided into three segments: a committee attending to the peculiar needs for children, another committee for youth, and a third for adults. Much to my surprise, I was assigned to the adult area, which would be headed by President Romney.

President Lee stressed the confidentiality of the work. He stressed the sacredness of what was to take place, the commitment that had to supersede anything that any of us had been engaged in before, and the integrity of the project that would emerge. He blessed us that we would have the strength and the power to put our lives in order and that we would be able to serve our Heavenly Father in this capacity.

As it is stated in Doctrine and Covenants section 4, I knew that "a marvelous work is about to come forth among the children of men" (verse 4) as a supportive foundation to the restored gospel of Jesus Christ. How I yearned and prayed that I might be worthy of such a calling. No longer would the word *correlation* be a cold, academic term. It had taken upon itself an entity of tremendous sacredness and worth.

The correlation work did go forth. For me, it continued for the next eleven years. I will not attempt to describe the specifics of the unfolding of this program since that was beautifully developed in the splendid biography of President Lee's life entitled *Harold B. Lee, Prophet and Seer.* The principles developed during this dynamic period appeared throughout President Lee's utterances and administration as long as he lived, and they will continue to provide the substance for the mighty work that will in the future go forth on the face of this earth.

As program after program was developed, made ready for presentation, most often the statement was made, "We will put it in the top drawer ready for the time of its implementation." How wonderful it has been for me to have lived these additional decades to see program after program being lifted out of this top drawer, polished, published, and implemented as the growth of the Church and the vision of this prophet is being fulfilled.

One of the most significant creations developed and put in place was the assignment in leadership of the Regional Representatives of the Twelve. Seminars for Regional Representatives were held the day before the formal opening of each biannual general conference. At that time, all the General Authorities, general auxiliary presidencies, and the Regional Representatives gathered together to be given the "state of the Church" address and the specific guidelines of the work that would be emphasized and the changes that were to be made. As chairman of the Correlation Committee, President Lee gave these keynote addresses at the seminars from their inception — at first while he was President of the Quorum of the Twelve, later while he was First Counselor in the First Presidency, and finally, when he was President of the Church.

The first session was held on Thursday, 28 September 1967, in the Seventeenth Ward in Salt Lake City. Preparations for this historic event were made by the Leadership Committee, composed of Elder Thomas S. Monson, chairman, and Neal A.

Maxwell and Wendell J. Ashton. As cochair of the Adult Correlation Committee, I was asked to be responsible for the physical arrangements for this occasion, including the provision for the refreshment breaks, the luncheon, the flowers, and most particularly, the dinner, which was to be held in the evening in the Hotel Utah's Lafayette Ballroom.

An incident of momentous significance took place that day, one that continues to change my life. President Lee gave the keynote address. I was sitting in the foyer of the chapel, listening to the profound orientation given to the sixty-nine newly called Regional Representatives of the Council of the Twelve and to all the general leaders of the Church. It was an inspiring and revealing moment in the Lord's timetable. Following his address and the singing of a hymn, President Lee walked out of the chapel and into the foyer. Seeing him approach I stood up, and as he took my arm, he said, "Ruth, come walk with me."

We then walked through the halls of the Seventeenth Ward, as President Lee, in his most inspiring manner, talked about the women of the Church, the youth of the Church and the tremendous need to activate the magnificent priesthood power in their behalf. He talked of empowering the women and the youth to know the tremendous blessings that are available to them and of the need for the youth to govern themselves and lift and bless the lives of one another, of taking upon themselves the accountability for the serving of others. He spoke of some of the enormous forthcoming challenges, particularly those involving women. The choices must be made, for there was danger that the sacredness and prominence of the home and the nurturing of families was eroding away. I listened. I was taught. What a sacred privilege! Little did I know how these prophetic musings and utterances would aid me in the responsibilities that would soon come to me. I was being prepared and taught, while walking with a prophet.

This same pattern continued at subsequent seminars held in the Seventeenth Ward. Almost anticipating them, I was ready to ask questions and received excellent guidance relative to the youth of the Church. It helped me greatly in my work on the Adult Correlation Committee as we sought for improved ways by which parents and leaders might better prepare their youth for this glorious, but challenging, era in which they live.

My calling as president of the Young Women organization also came with a telephone call. I was the chorale director at East High School in Salt Lake City. Having more than five hundred students a day, I loved my work, loved the young people, and loved the profound influence of music that softens the hearts and makes more beautiful the lives of all who embrace the arts. I had enjoyed this opportunity immensely.

On Friday, 27 October 1972 the telephone rang in my office, and as usual, a student answered to take the message and note a number so I could call back. However, this time it was my husband, and the call was urgent. When I answered the phone, Mark said, "Sweetheart, are you sitting down?" "No", I answered, with much anxiety. I asked what had happened. He responded that Brother Arthur Haycock had asked us to meet with President Lee immediately following school at 4:00 P.M. All I could do was weep. He kept asking, "Are you there? Are you there?" Yes, I was there, but the Spirit bore witness to me that this was not a usual call. I was dissolved in tears.

We arrived at President Lee's office and were ushered into his presence. He seated us in the two chairs in front of his desk. President Lee then turned to Mark. He described to him the tremendous challenges of the youth in the world today and particularly those of the youth of The Church of Jesus Christ of Latter-day Saints. He spoke about the changes that must take place to fortify and strengthen these young people. He spoke about the necessity to strengthen the family and the parents, and the process whereby young people are nurtured and made ready to serve in the kingdom of God. Not once during this long discourse did he look at me but directed all his instruction to Mark.

After they had exchanged these observations, still without even a look at me, President Lee said, "Brother Funk, I would like your permission to call your wife as the president of the Aaronic Priesthood MIA—Young Women organization of the Church." Continuing on, they discussed the position, what it would mean to our family, and my love for the youth. They spoke as though I were not there, for neither one had looked at me, even once. Finally, after Mark had described some of the situations in our home, of his business, of our health, of his deep affection for me, Mark reached out, took my hand, and looked into my eyes for the first time and said, "We accept, President Lee."

Oh, how wise and profound and necessary it was that this calling should come to me through him who stands as the patriarch of our home. His support and understanding for this calling has been, was, and continues to be of infinite worth to me.

I had served on the general board for some twelve years, plus eleven additional years on the Correlation Committee. Always there had been a feeling in my heart of concern for the welfare of my family and of Mark's attitude on my being away from home so much. With this calling coming to us (not just me), I was taught truly the magnifying power of the priesthood, of the tremendous support of a priesthood bearer in our home, and of that power from God that blesses all of his children in an orderly, prescribed process and pattern. I was taught the order of the priesthood by this prophet that changed my life.

Later, my husband wrote a letter of appreciation for our calling to President Lee and received a warm, sensitive reply in which the President of the Church said:

> When I called you and Ruth into my office, I did so realizing that this was to be as much of a call for you as it was for Ruth and that I wanted you to feel that your approval and your support were most vital to the welfare of the program that Ruth is now to guide as the new president, along with her counselors.
>
> If there was in your thoughts a feeling of reservation at the time I met you in my office, I was not aware of it, although I fully appreciate your concerns that there would be some financial problems as well as family problems. But for you to tell me that these things have now been resolved and that the compensations are much greater than the deprivations is indeed another testimony as to how the Lord blesses those who serve him and keep his commandments.
>
> Particularly was I impressed by your closing statement that the motivation for this letter came as the Spirit of the Lord touched you as it did me in the closing message of the recent general conference. I must say to you that what I said had to be

something beyond me personally, and my hope is that it may have reached out to others who received similar witness as you received that afternoon.

At the conclusion of our calling interview, President Lee advised me to consider prayerfully the selection of my counselors. He suggested that as soon as I knew, I should advise him, and he would proceed with the organization of the general presidency of the Aaronic Priesthood MIA–Young Women. We left with this blessing, love, and encouragement, driving home in humbled silence as we contemplated the portentous events that had just transpired.

A few minutes before arriving home, I realized that I didn't ask President Lee whom I should consider as my counselors. Certainly he must have some candidates in mind. Mark reassured me that a telephone call would be appropriate, so I called him immediately. His response was, "The Lord has called you, Ruth, through me, his prophet. Now having been called, you will be the one to receive the revelation as to who will serve at your side. I know you will be blessed, and it will be made evident to you at the appropriate time who should serve with you. Be assured; the Lord will bless you."

Within a few days, the Lord did reveal to me in a rather dramatic way those who would serve as my counselors. They were Sister Hortense H. Child (Smith) and Sister Ardeth G. Kapp. Here again, my husband was a major part of this supplication to the Lord, and I will ever be grateful for the continued and loving help he and the Lord gave me through many blessings that sustained me.

I had been taught the true order of the priesthood, the patriarchal order. Some women might say it would surely be sufficient for the presiding Church authority to make the call. How little do they understand the tremendous magnification of having been called in such a manner as to include my eternal companion. For this profound lesson I shall be ever grateful.

I often stand before the noble portrait of my friend, which hung in my office during my term as president of the Young Women organization and which now occupies a most prominent place in our home; and I continue to draw deeply from his wisdom, his love, his encouragement, and his teachings. His divine inspiration and revelation guides me in seeking more surely the blessings and opportunities in the kingdom of God. How much better I now understand the love of my Heavenly Father and that of his Son, Jesus Christ.

Yes, President Harold B. Lee was, and is, a prophet of God, a seer and a revelator, and he changed my life in marvelous and unforgettable ways, for which I will be forever grateful.

26

L. Ray Gardiner
Member of President Lee's Ward

I Remember Best His Humble, Unpretentious Friendliness

My contacts with President Harold B. Lee were so power-fully impressive that I made several diary entries to describe them in November 1973. I recorded the historic, un-usual testimony of President Lee at our November fast and testi-mony meeting. Then, I recorded a further conversation with him on the following Sunday, because I believed that it demon-strated a special attribute of his remarkable character.

This was our stake conference Sunday. The Emigration Stake holds its stake conferences in the Assembly Hall on Temple Square. Some of our children sang in the children's Pri-mary chorus and sat in the choir seats at the Assembly Hall. Others of our children sat with me, located fairly close to the front of the hall.

Later, on this same Sunday afternoon, I attended with our children the Federal Heights Ward sacrament meeting. By coin-cidence, we entered the chapel directly behind President Lee. When he saw us, he turned around, and with a pleasant smile, took me by the arm and said, "Ray, how are you?" Then, turning to the girls he said, "I saw your daddy watching over you at conference this morning."

I mentioned to President Lee that I was impressed by the testimony that he had borne at last week's testimony meeting concerning the reality of Satan and that I had recorded it in my family journal. He replied, as best as I could recall, since two days had passed before my journal entry, "Well, I felt I had to say that. I did not want to be too dramatic, but I wanted, without giving the details of the event that caused me to say what I said, to stress that message. I did not want the Lord someday to say to me, 'Why did you fail to tell the people, to warn them?' "

The attribute of character that I wish to emphasize is President Lee's humble, unpretentious friendliness. I was most flattered that he would call me by my first name, indeed, flattered that he really knew me by name. He had always been friendly and affable. I had observed him on many occasions in our ward, and he always had a genuine, sincere smile and greeting for everyone.

He had that smile for me on occasions in the past; but although I knew his greeting on those occasions was a genuine greeting to one whom he recognized as a member of the ward, it was not until this meeting that I realized that he knew Ray Gardiner by name.

While speaking of his friendliness, I remember an occasion, perhaps a half dozen years before he was President of the Church, when I was leaving the main waiting room of the Salt Lake City Airport en route to the concourse to board a plane. President Lee and other Church officials were coming from the same concourse I was entering. He caught my eye and I his, and I still remember the warm and personal smile he gave in greeting. At that time he did not know me. I have seen other notables of celebrity status under similar circumstances. Without disparaging them, for they were busy men with much on their minds and certainly could not be expected to greet every soul that crossed their path in this hectic world—especially, for example, at a busy place like an airport—but they were not ready with the same warm smile and the warmth in their eyes that, when looking at you, made you feel as if they were greeting someone they knew well. I think that is the key. Even though President Lee's greeting was but a smile and a nod of the head in acknowledgment of recognition of one's presence, on that occasion, in greeting me, a stranger, he seemed as if he knew me. As we passed in the crowd, he was saying hello to one whom he knew and respected.

I came to see him often in our ward, and he always had the same warmth of personality. I think it came from his eyes. They were warm and soft but with a sparkle of knowing friendliness, and when he looked at me, he peered at me with eyes communicating with a known friend, not with a stranger. That was the impression I had in the airport years ago and that is the impression I still had when I was no longer a stranger.

Another impressive incident of personal contact with President Lee was recorded in our family journal. My wife's brother, Gilbert, was visiting with us from Wisconsin. He is a physician and was in Utah to attend some medical meetings. On a Sunday we attended church together, and when we were entering the side door to the ward meetinghouse, leading from the west parking lot, President Lee was also entering. He stopped and held the door for several of the Saints and also for us to enter. I insisted that I should hold the door for him, but he would not have this.

After we had entered and as we were going up the stairs, I said, "President Lee, you should not hold the door for us, but we should hold it for you."

He replied, "You know what the scripture says . . ."

At this point, there came to my mind the scripture that states, "And whosoever will be chief among you, let him be your servant" (Matthew 20:27).

President Lee paused very briefly, not stating that scripture, but said instead, "It is better to be a door holder."

He had a big smile on his face, and Gilbert and I chuckled too, at his adroit reply. I am certain that he refrained from quoting that scripture because in his modest way he would not want to equate himself with "the Greatest of all."

On another occasion in 1973, I had been in the junior Sunday School to see one of our children perform, and as I was coming up the stairs and passing the doorway leading from the west parking lot, I noticed President and Sister Lee arriving in their car. President Lee was driving. Sunday School was in progress already, and no one else was around. The car stopped at the sidewalk, and Sister Lee began to exit. I ran out to assist her. As I opened the car door, she leaned toward President Lee, and he gave her a sweet, affectionate kiss. He looked at me and smiled, saying, "Today is our wedding anniversary." He explained that he was late for a meeting and would not be at Sunday School and then thanked me for helping Sister Lee.

I have found that there are many advantages and blessings in living in the Federal Heights Ward, but one of the greatest was this choice opportunity for our family to frequently see and observe President Lee and enjoy a relatively close association with him. These expressions are not new, and greater and nobler thoughts have been stated by more important people. But they come from me as an ordinary citizen of the kingdom allowed to live in President Lee's own ward and serve as a corroborating viewpoint of his personal warmth with people and his humble, unpretentious friendliness.

27

Joseph Clifford Gibby
Former Young Student of Harold B. Lee's

Memories of a Student in Oxford, Idaho

The most marvelous and greatest experience of my lifetime was when I stood in the solemn assembly in the Salt Lake Tabernacle on 6 October 1972 and raised my arm to the square to sustain President Harold B. Lee as the prophet, seer, and revelator, and President of The Church of Jesus Christ of Latter-day Saints. Afterward, I sat there almost entranced, gazing up at my dear schoolteacher, and my mind took me back to that little schoolroom in Oxford, Idaho, where we spent so many wonderful hours together.

In our association in 1920, when I was twelve years old and Harold B. Lee was twenty-one years old, he made a place in my heart through his love and understanding that caused me to regard him, next to my own dear father, as the best friend I had on this earth. That same feeling has remained with me for over sixty years.

He encouraged my art ability and, because of his interest in my drawings, I decided then to follow art as a livelihood, which is what I did during my entire working career. He gave me courage to face the challenge. He was my harbor lighthouse.

I remember so well the *Pageant of the Nations*, which Harold B. Lee wrote for the students to perform during the winter of 1920 at the Oxford District School. He assigned each student a part and asked the parents to make all the costumes. I was a Chinaman, and he gave me the name of Hi Lung Chee. Ina Anderson was my student-partner or female counterpart, perhaps my wife for the play. When the pageant performance hour arrived, we all marched out on the stage, and I was to sing:

> My name is Hi Lung Chee. I came from Lang Chow Aye.
> I like Amelica so much, I always want to stay.
> Washee, washee, pound, and lubbie; Standing arr day at my tubbee;
> Washee, washee, pound, and lubbie; I'm a very nice young man!

I was to sing those words to the tune of "Mine Eyes Have Seen the Glory of the Coming of the Lord," but it didn't come off too well. I started the tune too high and couldn't reach the top note. So, I began again in a lower key, but that was not any better. Then a miracle happened. Just at the point of utter discouragement, despair, and almost tears, before I could start over again, I heard the pitch for me on the piano. My teacher, Harold Lee, had gone over to the piano and sounded the right note. He could never have known how grateful I was for his rescue. I completed my rendition and marched proudly to my place with the other performers and felt not the slightest degree of embarrassment. But how different that experience might have turned out without his sensitive and timely assistance to avoid a student failure.

Yes, I loved to attend Harold B. Lee's religion class after school, too. I enjoyed being with him wherever he was, in Sunday School and the other meetings, where he always took such an active part in teaching and in the musical presentations.

I also remember how he took care of my sprained knee when, during a basketball game, I was thrown into one of those steam radiators we had around the wall of the gym. There was no doctor to attend to my needs, but my teacher knew just what to do for a badly sprained knee. He bandaged it up, and I recovered in a week or so with no lasting ill results.

I shall always cherish these fine boyhood memories in Oxford, Idaho. They have stayed with me my entire lifetime, as fresh as the days they happened. I liked to draw for him, and I enjoyed writing the themes he assigned. He encouraged me in both of these areas, and it set my course in life. Over the years I found that the lessons I learned in Harold B. Lee's classroom were instrumental to helping me succeed in my life's work, both in the field of art and in writing.

My positive early exposure to the Church through Harold B. Lee and others has led to a lifetime of Church experience. I have served a stake mission and been a district president, a member of a bishopric, and an active, ardent genealogist, having spent thousands of hours in research in this country and in Great Brittain. I am a forty-year veteran of Scouting and hold the Silver Beaver Award. I have painted murals for two of our temples in Los Angeles and in Switzerland.

My college textbook on the subject of *Technical Illustration, Procedure and Practice* is widely used throughout the world. The illustration industry has been generous in referring to me as the "grandfather of technical illustration." I retired from teaching after thirty-one years as a college professor and instructor in commercial art and technical illustration.

I mentioned these lifetime accomplishments to President Lee in a letter of congratulations to him when he was sustained as President of the Church. I wanted him to see what came out of his early, youthful teaching endeavors in a tiny Idaho town and give him a report on the life of one of his students who didn't care a bit for arithmetic. On 17 November 1972, President Lee graciously acknowledged my letter and wrote:

> Your heartwarming letter took me back to those early days when you and I were much younger and I had the privilege of growing up with a group of wonderful boys and girls who, like yourself, have distinction in their chosen fields. Thank you for recalling those incidents of so long ago.
>
> Beyond that, I cherish your expressions of loyalty and faith and encouragement, as I now move into a chapter of my life

that only by the help of the Lord can I accomplish that which the Lord has for me to do.

I felt compelled to write my letter to President Lee, not to boast but to inform him what his example and teaching had done for me. I also wanted to express the joy I felt that my favorite teacher and my dearest friend became the President of Christ's church on earth. I still take pride and find much happiness in these glorious reflections.

28

Diana Bird Holt
An Accident Victim

He Has Kept
a Light Burning
in My Life

In April of 1968 I was in a very serious accident that has caused no end of trouble. What was once a very busy and active life in the pep club at Highland High School—playing tennis, water and snow skiing, swimming, and dating—came to a screeching halt when the car I was in slid on snow and rammed into a mountain, throwing me through the window. My head and neck took the force of the blow. Since that time I have been in chronic pain and spent over two years of days and nights in the hospital, endured five major surgeries on my spine, been through treatment at two pain clinics, and spent hundreds of thousands of hours horizontally coping with intractable pain. Nerves and muscles have been damaged beyond repair. Further disc deterioration and paralysis have threatened my lifestyle. In the matter of a moment, my life changed from activity and fun to pain and bed rest.

Later, in 1968, after spending weeks in and out of the hospital, I went through a period of time when I was sleeping for extended lengths of time, such as from Monday night until Wednesday afternoon, or from Saturday afternoon until Tuesday, when the clouds would finally leave my senses and life would slowly come back into focus.

After one of these episodes, I was with my daddy, who was sitting on my bed. He had given me some pain medication and was talking quietly to me. His voice was so comforting and encouraging, yet I was very concerned. I was afraid to go to sleep because I thought that I possibly wouldn't awaken until the next day or never. I poured my heart out to Daddy and explained my fears. Daddy said, "You need a special blessing. Is it all right if we set that up for you?"

A phone call was made to reach Elder Harold B. Lee through the Goates family, to whom we are related by marriage. Only a brief explanation was made, "Diana is very ill and needs a blessing. Could that be possible in the near future?" Nothing was said about the accident, the great pain, or the hospitalization, just that I was very ill and needed a special blessing. President Lee said he would begin fasting that moment and my parents were to bring me to his office the next day.

As Mother and Daddy prepared me and dressed me for the outing, I remember thinking that it was crazy to go to all this work and more pain to go out for a blessing, no matter who was giving it. Daddy and Mother were very gentle and kind that day. They both stayed home from work to be with me. We have a special bond of friendship that nothing will ever break. Daddy has hugged and loved the pain away more times than I could ever count. He is always there for me.

The weather was nice the day of the blessing. I only opened my eyes once, but I do remember sunshine and warmth, as Daddy and Mother and my Aunt Leah Wood made our way to Elder Lee's office. Daddy propped me up in a large wing-back chair, and President Lee asked Daddy if he would like to join with him in this blessing. Daddy told him that he held the Aaronic Priesthood and President Lee asked him to be seated in such a sweet, gentle manner that precluded any possibility of hurt or embarrassment.

President Lee came around in front of me and took my hands in his, saying, "Diana, the Lord has a very important message for you today, and I feel privileged to be his mouth-piece."

He then went around behind me and gently placed his hands upon my head. I recall being somewhat embarrassed because not all of my hair had grown back since they shaved off much of my hair for the surgery after the accident.

The very first words in the blessing took me completely by surprise and shocked a silence into the room that was deafen-ing, "Diana Bird, at the time of the accident, the Lord saw fit to place his finger down upon your life and save it, for you have not yet completed what you've been sent to earth to do."

I looked up and saw shock on the faces of Mother, Daddy, and Aunt Leah. It was as if President Lee could sense this trauma, and he allowed us time to absorb the great impact of that mighty sentence. At exactly that moment, the three of us realized that I should have been killed in the accident. We also understood that this man, this mortal, had received divine inspi-ration during the blessing because he had no previous knowl-edge of the accident or the damages. Then he continued with several encouraging promises, a few of which I will cite because they have truly helped to raise me above the tides when the undertow of pain seemed to be drowning my desire to live and endure another day.

President Lee promised me that I knew the pain and suffer-ing I would be asked to endure in this life, and yet, when the day came for my arrival here on earth, I rejoiced. He said I had a guardian angel whom I knew and who would, on many occa-sions, intercede for me when I had a close encounter with death. (This has happened on three occasions already, and I have no doubt about this promise.)

He told me that I would be a mighty instrument in the Lord's hands, that I would have many opportunities to speak to groups on a large scale, and that my experiences would become power-ful teaching tools. I have been blessed with many opportunities to teach, and I have never turned down an offer with the exception of two times when I was hospitalized for surgery. I have spoken to youth groups; to groups of the Relief Society; at elders', bishops', and leadership meetings; and at stake camp firesides. I have taught the care of chronically or terminally ill people to all of these groups and spoken at a tri-stake youth conference in Dallas, Texas.

Speaking to the Latter-day Saint Student Association at the University of Arizona was one of the most rewarding experiences of my life. Two months later they awarded me with the Elect Lady of the Year Award, and somehow it covered a multitude of days that were spent feeling nonproductive and unnecessary. It made the pains, experiences, and trials seem worthwhile and important.

President Lee blessed me with patience and a kind heart and told me that my pain would enhance my ability to give strength to others in their time of need. During the two years that I was a hospice family advocate counselor, I used my knowledge and experience to comfort others, and it brought many hours of calm reassurance to my troubled heart. Also, working in the hospital emergency room allowed me to share my knowledge in a positive way and gain greater perspective myself. It's hard to have pity for oneself when others are in more serious condition. Those hours of service brought a deeper relief than any shot or pill ever could have. It was an opportunity to serve instead of being served all the time.

President Lee said that I would be blessed with a husband who would be a strong priesthood holder, who would help me during my struggles, and that I would live to raise a good family. Those blessings have been fulfilled in wonderful ways.

I am clinging to one more promise that has not yet come to pass. President Lee told me, "There will come a day when you won't be able to remember the last time you were in pain."

These promises and blessings are the primary source of my strength from which I have drawn comfort a thousand, maybe two thousand, times over the years. Nothing could persuade me not to believe that these words and the other ten or so minutes of the blessing were directed from the Lord. President Lee never knew what an effect that blessing has had on my life. He died before I could tell him how much the blessing encouraged me each day, even hour by hour, to hang on.

How can I express how much that blessing has meant to me over the years? I hope everyone can read between the lines and see the difference it has made in my life. I am not bitter; I am sweet in spirit. I am no longer angry or afraid. I'm like clay in the Master's hands. I do not ask for miracles; just for the strength and peace of mind during the roughest times. My Heavenly Father blessed me that autumn day to meet a man of great faith who had an overwhelming desire to comfort a frightened little girl. The blessing President Lee gave me has kept a light burning within me for, oh, such a long, long time.

This is such a private experience that I have never before written it, but I am willing to share it now in the hope that it will bring faith, hope, and confidence to others to believe in their priesthood blessings. Each day, when my eyes become accustomed to the light, I have a sense of wonder and awe at the miracle of life. My being able to celebrate it for these extended years is due in large measure to this special blessing I received from President Harold B. Lee. My gratitude knows no bounds.

29

C. Dennis Smith
Bishop

I Have Tried
to Be Like Him

For most of us in the Church a certain leader becomes espe-cially dear to us in our lives. I had close ties to President Harold B. Lee, and that relationship provided many special blessings in my young life. My wife grew up as a member of the Church in Salt Lake City, and she too had a number of instances where her life was profoundly touched by President Lee.

My favorite Harold B. Lee story provided me with the assur-ance that he knew well the Lord of whom he testified frequently. It was an experience Elder Lee told concerning an assignment that Elder Stephen L Richards gave him to deliver a radio address at Easter.* This was one of his first assignments after being called to the Council of the Twelve Apostles. Since the topic was on the challenging theme of the life and mission of Jesus Christ, Elder Lee locked himself in a room in the Church

---

*See Richard O. Cowan, *The Church in the Twentieth Century* (Salt Lake City: Bookcraft, 1985), p. 341.

Administration Building and began reading the story of the life of the Savior. He related how he almost felt as though he were living the events and reading them simultaneously. He comprehended with a reality that he had never before experienced. I have never forgotten this story.

We had requested Elder Lee to perform our temple marriage in 1959, but unfortunately he was out of the state on assignment and could not render this service for us. However, he did come into our lives in a most significant manner just a few years later.

It was a bitter cold day in Rochester, New York, where we were living in 1964. My wife was surprised to see me walking up the sidewalk towards our house in the middle of the day. When I greeted my wife I told her that I had received some rather bad news. I had been annoyed with a bothersome cough and, seeking some relief, I obtained a chest X-ray. The results showed some unusual tumors lying around my chest activity. When I reported this finding at my employment, I was told to go home and to contact a good physician and proceed with what would be necessary to check out these ominous reports. My wife is a graduate nurse, so she knew immediately that this was a serious situation.

I remember sitting in our kitchen in the home on Needham Street holding on my lap our two youngest children. I looked up at my wife and said: "I need to receive a priesthood blessing, and though I know in my heart that it is impossible and really not necessary, how I wish I could call on Elder Harold B. Lee."

Within two days we had made arrangements to be checked by a fine physician, and now we were turning our thoughts to receiving a blessing through the priesthood. During that next day we were informed that some of the Brethren were coming from Salt Lake City to direct the division of the Eastern States Mission. We inquired as to who was assigned. You can imagine our feelings of elation when we learned that one of these Brethren would be Elder Harold B. Lee. After his arrival we made our special request of Elder Lee, and he asked us to come to his motel room later that night when his business was completed so that he could talk with us.

At 10:00 P.M. we met with Elder Lee and the other Brethren in his motel room. We had the X-rays with us, and he asked to see them. I remember how he held them up to the light as we pointed out the tumors to him. He made no comment at that time. Then we spent some time visiting about our past mutual associations. He had known my mother well and had spoken at her funeral. My brother, Wallie Smith, had lived with his wife in a basement apartment the Lees rented to them when they lived on Connor Street in Salt Lake City. We talked of our children and also of my new calling as the bishop of the Rochester Ward.

Elder Lee asked the other men in the room—Elder Franklin D. Richards, a General Authority, and President Wilburn C. West, president of the Eastern States Mission—to join him in giving the blessing. My wife stood a short distance away. I do not now recall all the exact words of that blessing, but I do remember vividly the feeling and general spirit of the experience. The most impressive remembrance I have, however, was the manner in which President Lee presented all the facts to the Lord in extreme detail. It was as though he were a lawyer pleading a case in a courtroom. My wife and I remember him saying, "In order to make a fair assessment, we need to present all the facts."

The other powerful impression which has stayed with me through the years is the ease with which Brother Lee talked to the Lord. We almost felt as though he were conversing with someone who was in the room with us; I knew it was someone with whom he spoke often and intimately.

At the conclusion of the ordinance we were both promised we would have the strength to endure whatever would come. Elder Lee assured us that he felt great blessings would come into our lives soon. I remember a wonderful feeling of peace as we left that night. Elder Lee took my wife's hand and said to her, "Write me and let me know what happens."

There were some hard, anxious moments in the days that followed, but my wife and I have both reflected many times on the peace we felt from the time of that blessing.

The day of surgery was scheduled. The members of our ward held a special fast on that day, and we felt their love and support. The operation revealed over twenty large tumors. The laboratory examinations showed them to be a type of tumor not easily recognized and difficult to classify; finally, however, it was concluded that they were benign. My health returned rapidly and I regained full strength.

Within a few short months of our blessing from President Lee we learned that my wife was expecting another baby. We named this baby Michael Smith, and he grew up to be an All-American basketball player for Brigham Young University. Two more sons were to join us later, Mark and Steven, and along with them and the first two children, Clark and Shauna, we moved to southern California, where we received many more blessings.

Before leaving Rochester, my wife did as Elder Lee requested — she wrote of the successful outcome of my health threat and then added:

> As for my husband and me, one word describes our feelings now — rededication — to each other, to the Lord, and to our part in building up his kingdom upon this earth. My husband asked me to mention in this letter to you that the bishop who returns to the people of his ward is a more humble, compassionate, and dedicated servant than ever before. It has taken this experience, though frightening as it has been, to bring me to the full realization of how precious life itself is and how glorious is this gospel which unites a love like ours for all time and eternity.

Elder Lee must have appreciated our letter, for he quoted it in his general conference sermon of 4 April 1964. Then he added: "Through their surmounting sickness, heartaches, and disappointments, their experiences had resulted in better fruit. They had proved their fruit by their works. By their fruits, the Lord has proved them. Life and service have taken on an altogether different meaning."

This story has a happy ending. Not all stories end this way, and we have shared some of those times as well. We are too well-founded in the gospel to doubt that at times the Lord will deal with his children differently.

The true value of our experience is what we have learned by it. Since my blessing by Elder Lee I have adopted his style in giving priesthood blessings and ordinations. I have also found in myself a desire to converse with the Lord in prayer, as Elder

Lee did, as though I were talking to someone I truly knew intimately. And then, I frequently remember my favorite Harold B. Lee story of how he prepared himself for the sermon on the life of the Savior, and I keep learning and reminding myself of the importance of truly becoming worthy and ready to participate in spiritual experiences. Besides the obvious health blessings I received, the lessons from the life of President Lee continue to be internalized in my life, a life which was changed by his loving service.

30

Elliott D. Landau
Family Therapist

Testimony—
In the Heart or
in the Head?

It was a very special evening to be with the President of the Twelve Apostles, back in my hometown of New York City, and to have him turn to me and say, "Elliott, these are your people. You speak to them. I'll introduce you."

For months Elder Harold B. Lee had had a scheduled engagement at the Eastern States Mission Home. He was to address a group of businessmen concerning the Mormon Church and tell them of its origins in their state and its many programs for the family.

I had been baptized by Golden L. Berrett, with President Lee being witness for that ordinance, on Temple Square in Salt Lake City. Confirmation by Elder Mark E. Petersen of the Council of the Twelve followed on that same afternoon.

As a college professor, I often traveled to my publisher, Prentice-Hall, in New Jersey to consult about how the next book was progressing or to review progress on past projects.

When President Lee and I discovered that we were both going back to New York at the same time, he suggested that we go together. Since we each had our own tickets, he instructed his secretary to arrange for side-by-side seating. She called to say that our problem was that President Lee was in the first class section and I was in the coach portion of the plane. Later on in the day she called to say that he had moved his seat to be with me in the coach section.

It was in those seats that I first became acquainted with the "Book of Lee." Both of us were reading our scriptures until I glanced at his volume and noticed that there were pages there not present in mine—lots of them. Thinking I had the wrong volume or that his was in error or something, I asked him what the additional carefully typed pages were in his volume. He smiled broadly, even chuckled, as he said, "You know, Elliott, I have always carried and read the scriptures wherever I was, and I have delighted always in what the presidents of the Church have said about certain parts of scriptures. So for many years I have selected certain commentary on the scriptures by past prophets. I had my secretary type them on paper the exact size of my own scripture set and pull back on the binding and insert these latter-day commentaries just behind the appropriate original scriptures. Today they make quite an additional volume, which I sometimes jokingly call the Book of Lee."

Once in New York City, alone with each other in the top floor apartment of the Eastern States Mission Home where visiting Church leaders were housed, President Lee asked me to speak in his place at the program that night. I was taken aback and promptly asked for a priesthood blessing to support me on that occasion. He immediately responded with a blessing, one which I can never forget. Part of it stated, "I bless you to speak to the people in and out of the Church without notes and only by the spirit of inspiration. And you will know what to say by intently studying your audience where there will always be one or more who will, by the Spirit, prompt you in what to say. Speak with and of the Spirit, and you will never need a text."

I cannot tell how often this blessing served me and still does. That night I used the blessing fully.

I spoke to those men who had assembled to hear the man who would, in just a few years, become the President of The Church of Jesus Christ of Latter-day Saints. I spoke without notes, without fear, and without text, not knowing even my theme. I knew I needed to explain how modern-day revelation and how the Book of Mormon could be believed by a scientist and scholar who insisted, before he ever joined the Church, that he must read every anti-Mormon text at the University of Utah library, even as Ann Widtsoe Wallace, the librarian, looked on in dismay at my attempts to become closer to the Church by reading what everyone had said against it.

I know not what I said, but I will never forget what I concluded with and how President Lee so loved it that it nearly became his standard theme whenever he spoke about the gospel.

I was carried along in my talk by the Holy Spirit. Suddenly I realized that somehow I had to make some sense of this Jewish man's quest and eventual belief. I closed, bearing testimony and saying, "All that I know is that which I cannot understand with my head, I can know in my heart."

President Lee took that inspired statement and translated it to his holy purposes for explaining the miracle of testimony. His version, which he used constantly in his sermonizing, was, "When your heart tells you something that your mind does not know, it is the Holy Ghost bearing witness to your soul."

31

Robert J. Martin
Former Mission President

"He Looked
and Acted
Like God"

How I wish my vocabulary was broad enough to express the love and admiration I shall always have for President Harold B. Lee. No one individual has touched my life so profoundly as he. No one person taught me so much in such a short time.

It all began when President Lee called me to be the president of the South Davis Stake. He later reminded me, and did so with great firmness whenever I questioned my calling, that the Lord had called me, not him. I was reminded that I should never forget that fact, and I have not.

My call was extended at 6:20 P.M. on 24 January 1970. President Lee asked that I go home for my wife and return in twenty minutes with her and also bring the names of those I would like as my counselors in the stake presidency, as well as six names to be called as high councilors. I remarked that I didn't feel I was capable of doing this in such a short time. A very wise prophet said, "The Lord will make known the names of the men that are to serve with you." This came to pass in a very sacred manner. It was an experience that is so precious that it has been rarely shared with others.

President Lee set me apart with the assistance of our Regional Representative, Elder L. Brent Goates. Great and wonderful blessings were pronounced and promised to me by President Lee. Many of these blessings came to pass during those years of service. Others became a part of my life in the three years I presided over the Hawaii Honolulu Mission.

President Lee took time to personally set apart all those who had been sustained. I am certain that he knew of my inadequacy. As he set apart my counselors and the high councilors, he used their blessings to teach me their responsibilities while I stood in the circle with President Lee and Elder Goates.

This was the very weekend that the First Presidency of the Church had been reorganized with Elder Lee being named as First Counselor to President Joseph Fielding Smith. Despite the momentous events of that Saturday morning, President Lee insisted on keeping his assignment to divide the South Davis Stake. It was the last such assignment in his lifetime to appoint new stake leaders. But his pressing new responsibilities didn't keep him from spending several hours with me during that weekend. I shall never forget leaving the old stake center, when he put his arm around me and said these comforting words, "It is now all yours, president. Be assured that the Lord will bless you."

I am also most grateful for several personal visits I had with President Lee. Many of these were at his own request. He would call and ask me to come and just visit upon occasion. He would have me sit at his side, and we conversed about many different facets of life.

The last such visit was but two or three days before his sudden passing. He had telephoned me and asked if I could come and visit with him. Needless to say, the trip from my office in North Salt Lake to the Church Administration Building took little time. We visited for well over an hour. I remarked that he appeared to be very tired. His response verified my observation. I consider that as one of the better hours of my entire life.

Perhaps the greatest tribute that I can pay President Lee came from the lips of my daughter, Janice. She was sixteen years of age at the time. She said, "Dad, if I had to choose a person who looked and acted like God, it would be President Lee."

My answer to her verified her lofty thoughts. I later shared that statement with the President, and he responded to my letter saying that it humbled him very much for anyone to place him in that high position. He added that he hoped and prayed that he would never betray the confidence our sweet Janice placed in him.

I have gained a great love and respect for each of the prophets I have met personally and also those whose lives I have studied. I say without any hesitation that my greatest love was and still is for President Lee. Other than my own father, I have never loved or respected any man as much as I did President Lee. I loved and respected him as a Church leader, but I also loved and respected him as a cherished friend. I still find myself thinking at times how this would have been done by him or just plainly asking, "What would President Lee have done?"

I sincerely hope and pray that I might be strong enough to live the remainder of my life in such a manner as to be worthy to again be at his side in the beautiful world to come.

32

Steven R. Pogue
Former Missionary

He Made a Difference
in My Study
of the Scriptures

In October 1973 I received a call to serve for two years in the England East Mission. I had spent much of my life in the Church drifting in and out of activity and had recently determined that a mission would be a good way for me to show to myself and the Lord that this time around I really intended to stay with it.

Upon receiving my call, I was particularly impressed with the fact that it was in the form of a personal letter signed by the prophet, President Harold B. Lee. I felt that since the call had come from the Lord's prophet, it was the word of the Lord, and that bolstered my confidence in my ability to carry out my errand from the Lord.

On the first of December, I and 224 other missionaries reported for training in the old missionary home in Salt Lake City. In those days, the missionaries who were going to English-speaking missions spent only five days in training before departing for the field. But what a glorious five days they were! We

were spiritually fed and nurtured in a way that I had never experienced. The General Authorities of the Church came daily to
address us and give us guidance and strength for the work that
lay ahead of us.

The highlight of this feast of testimony, though, came on the
day when we were favored to attend endowment sessions in the
Salt Lake Temple. After having gloried in the sanctity of the
Lord's holy house, we were privileged to spend some time with
President Harold B. Lee in the upper priesthood room of the
temple. We were told that he would answer any questions we
might have in our minds as we embarked in the service of the
Lord.

What a rare opportunity to gather with the Lord's chosen
servant in the holy temple and have him address our concerns.
We were all looking forward to it with great excitement. I marveled that, in governing the affairs of the whole Church, he had
time to come and spend with us in the temple. This made me
feel again that our work was indeed considered an important
one.

As we gathered in that great hall in the heights of the temple,
I could feel the anticipation in the air. I had never been near a
prophet before and had little idea what to expect. We rose to our
feet as the President entered and sat as he stood before our eager
throng.

I don't know what the others thought, but I was rather sup-
posing that upon receiving our questions, President Lee would
assume a prophetic stance, hand on forehead, and give forth
revelations from the Lord in answer to our earnest queries.
Indeed, some of the questions posed by the missionaries
seemed to me most complex and mysterious. I waited to see
what new information the prophet would impart.

Somewhat to my surprise, what I saw was not a Moses on
the mountain but a kindly, familiar teacher. Almost before each
questioner had finished asking, President Lee was turning to a
pertinent passage in the scriptures before him. He used no
index, but simply leafed through the sacred works as though he
had written them himself. Each time, he taught us from holy
writ, choosing passages that I could see were as familiar to him

as his own name. In a friendly, fatherly way, he opened up to our understanding scriptures that I had never known before.

I marveled greatly at this. Never did he reply, "Hmm, that's a new one on me. I'll have to check with the Lord." He simply told us what the Lord had already said long before.

That was when a realization came to me that I had never really had before. I recognized that the Lord is not going to give new revelations on a subject when he has already told us about it and we have it before us in our scriptures. While I am sure President Lee had many great revelations, he did not need any that day to address our concerns. He simply had to be intimately familiar with the ones the Lord already had given. It was plain as day that the prophet had done his homework and had been so doing for many years.

Up to that time, I had never been particularly diligent in gospel study. I had a strong testimony from childhood, but I had the attitude that if I knew the scriptures were true, I didn't really have to know what was in them. That attitude was changed that day, as I sat at the feet of one who already had devoted a great part of his life to knowing what was in them. I determined then and there that I was going to know the word of the Lord so that I, too, could use them as comfortably as had our beloved president.

We departed enriched and filled and made our ways to our various missions. We were the last class of missionaries through the missionary home before it closed down for the Christmas holidays. It was a scant three weeks later when I was serving in my first area in Norwich, England, that our district leaders came to see us. They informed us that President Lee had passed away the day after Christmas. As we pondered this news, I was grateful that I had had the opportunity to learn a great lesson from this wonderful man, as he taught his last group of missionaries in what had proven to be the last days of his mortal life. He had made a real difference in the way I looked at the study of the scriptures.

As I look back now, I cannot recall any of the questions the missionaries asked President Lee in the temple that day, nor any of his answers. What I gained from that session was a powerful example and a zeal for knowing the mind and will of the Lord. Though tempered by time, that enthusiasm for learning and the memory of that example have never been diminished in the years that have passed since then. I shall always hold in fond remembrance the lesson he taught me and the fact that he had enough interest in the missionaries to be there to teach it. Though we were never acquainted, nor even so much as shook hands, he changed my life for the better.

33

Gerald B. Quinn
Former Mission President

The Most Inspiring, Uplifting Experience of My Life

I was called to serve as the stake president of the Antelope Valley Stake (later named the California Palmdale Stake) by Elder Ezra Taft Benson on my thirty-sixth birthday, 13 May 1972.

In October of that year, I was considering an impending employment change and came to Salt Lake City to receive counsel from Elder Mark E. Petersen. While at the Church Administration Building, I thought to myself that it would be a tremendous spiritual lift if I could just meet the prophet, President Harold B. Lee. I had no idea as to whether or not this was possible, but I inquired anyway of his secretary. I was asked to sit in a reception area. After several minutes, I was escorted into President Lee's office area and saw the prophet standing at his office door to greet me. My only expectation was to shake his hand and meet him in person.

I will never forget his greeting to me as he said, "President Quinn, young man, come into my office so that I might become better acquainted with you." As we entered his office, I started to seat myself in front of his desk, but he stated, "No, come around here beside me so I can converse better with you." I was directed to sit in a chair next to his, behind his desk.

He asked me several questions about myself and was most gracious and kind. He then related several faith-promoting incidents to me, and this one I will never forget. He asked me if as a stake president I had ever felt any doubt about individuals I had called to Church positions and if my selections had, in fact, been sustained by the Lord. I indicated that I had such doubts on occasions. Then President Lee related the following event that took place in his life after being called as President of the Church:

> The first major calling for which I had to make a decision after President Smith's death was to fill the vacancy in the Quorum of the Twelve caused by the calling of Elder Romney to the First Presidency. After much fasting and prayer, I felt I was certain as to whom the Lord wanted, that being Elder Bruce R. McConkie. Even then, however, I felt I needed additional confirmation from the Lord on this important calling.
>
> An area conference was held during the summer of 1972 in Mexico City, and a number of the General Authorities attended this conference, including Bruce R. McConkie, who was then serving as one of the Seven Presidents of the First Quorum of Seventies. As the General Authorities were being sustained in the conference, only eleven names of Apostles were read, inasmuch as Elder Romney had been elevated. Elder McConkie at that moment heard his name read as the twelfth Apostle, even though it hadn't actually been read. He tried to put such thoughts out of his mind, but the Holy Spirit told him again that he would be called to fill the vacancy in the Quorum of the Twelve. Elder McConkie also heard this same message from the Spirit after returning to his home.
>
> When I requested Elder McConkie to come to my office where I called him to be an Apostle, he related this incident to me. This gave me additional confirmation from the Lord as to Elder McConkie being selected as an Apostle. It was comforting to me to receive this added confirmation that the proper selection had been made.

As a stake and mission president, and now as a bishop, when calling individuals to Church positions, this example of

President Lee always comes to my mind. It is humbling to me to realize that even a prophet sought assurance from time to time regarding the inspiration behind his appointments. It has made me more fervently seek for the Lord's counsel and look for spiritual guidance in callings made by me.

That day President Lee visited with me for approximately twenty-five minutes. It was the most inspiring and uplifting experience of my entire life.

About six weeks later, I had another memorable experience involving President Lee. Following our stake conference, which was held the last weekend of November 1972, I had a problem that needed the attention of a General Authority. I telephoned the office of the Quorum of the Twelve, and after explaining the problem in our stake, my call was transferred for an answer to the office of the First Presidency. After I had explained the situation to the secretary, President Lee came on the line and discussed the matter with me.

After resolving the problem at hand, he inquired of me about my family and their health. I had just admitted my son Robbie, then just three years old, to the Children's Hospital of Los Angeles. He had been diagnosed as having acute leukemia. I was, in fact, making my phone call that day from the hospital. I told him everything was fine, not wanting to bother him with our personal problem. He seemed to sense, however, that there was a problem and inquired of me again about my family. I then explained to him about Robbie's condition.

President Lee then stated that the First Presidency and the Quorum of the Twelve would be in meeting the next day in the Salt Lake Temple and that he would see that Robbie's name would be especially mentioned in their prayer circle.

That was such a comfort to my wife, Libby, and me. When I told her about the conversation with President Lee, we both wept in thankfulness for such a kind, perceptive, loving prophet, who cared about our personal circumstances.

Robbie received a complete remission of his disease one month after the miraculous prayer circle of the Apostles in the temple. He went off all medication after he was six years of age. He grew in perfect health and strength. He was baptized at eight years of age, played Little League baseball, enjoyed his Scouting days, and became a good student and a very spiritual boy. He had a perfectly normal boyhood, with never another problem with his health, moving through the ranks of the Aaronic Priesthood, engaging in cross-country running and golf, and becoming the president of his high school student body. He earned a scholarship to enter BYU—Hawaii before his anticipated call into the mission field.

President Harold B. Lee certainly had an unforgettable influence on the Quinn family. My sacred, private visit with President Lee in his office is still the most inspiring experience of my life. He was the kindest man I have ever met.

34

Glenna L. Reese
Former Tabernacle Choir Member

He Wrote His Record upon My Heart and Life

At the time of President Harold B. Lee's last general conference (October 1973), I was a member of the Tabernacle Choir. During the closing session of conference, I was feeling happy and in high spirits. It had been a wonderful conference, but I was a little tired, for singing in the choir was strenuous and required much concentration. Therefore, I was looking forward to a wonderful closing session and then going home to rest.

Because for many years I worked daily as a secretary to General Authorities, I may have come to take for granted the very special spirit that surrounds them, and while conference was inspiring as always, I felt no unusual "spiritual tinglings." My feelings, however, soon changed as it became without a doubt the most profoundly moving, spiritual conference I have ever attended.

I sensed nothing remarkably out of the ordinary until President Lee began his final remarks, and then the spiritual atmosphere became so intense that people in the congregation, including those around me in the Tabernacle Choir, suddenly began to weep as he spoke. By the time President Lee finished his sermon, people were sobbing openly, yet I can't recall that President Lee actually said anything more extraordinary than usual. All his addresses were uplifting, and when possible, he always shared with the Saints his personal spiritual experiences, thus strengthening our testimonies.

When Brother Wilford W. Kirton came to the stand to pronounce the benediction, he could barely speak due to his tears. I was sitting one or two rows directly behind him and marveled at the effect the outpouring of the Spirit had upon Brother Kirton and upon all of us present.

It was an extremely moving experience! Tears were streaming down my face, yet I did not really know why. I looked at my friends in the choir, and they, too, had tears streaming from their eyes. I was somewhat confused as to why we were all suddenly weeping, and then I realized that this was a direct and distinct manifestation of the power and strength of the Spirit of the Lord that was present with President Lee as he spoke. Little did we know that this would be the last conference speech we would ever hear from our beloved President Lee. People all around me were not crying just a little bit, but were openly sobbing. I then remembered reading in a Church publication that when the Spirit is present and especially strong, there is no way for mortal man to express or handle this intense feeling other than through tears.

Although I never had more personal conversations with him, other than to say hello, President Lee was, to me, the most Christlike man in whose presence I had ever been. I believe he affected my spirituality and my life more than any other Church leader I have been ever privileged to see or hear.

When he was sustained as President of the Church, President Lee stated, "The only true record that will ever be made of my service in my new calling will be the record that I may have written in the hearts and lives of those with whom I have served and labored, within and without the Church" (in Conference Report, Oct. 1972, p. 19; or *Ensign*, Nov. 1972, p. 24).

I can testify that President Lee did, indeed, write upon the record of my heart and life.

When I returned to my home after conference, I found my parents also visibly moved. They had been watching the conference proceedings on television and were profoundly affected. My mother remarked to me, wiping tears from her eyes, "I don't know what was going on during that closing sermon of President Lee's, but suddenly the most overpowering desire to weep came over me, and I just sat there and cried as he spoke."

I assured my mother that this feeling also had been felt strongly by many who were present in the Tabernacle. As a family, we earmarked this particular conference session and speech of President Lee's as one of the most spiritual experiences of our lives. We shall never forget the extraordinary feelings we experienced on that blessed day as President Lee closed his last general conference sermon accompanied by this holy manifestation of the Spirit.

35

Paul E. Reimann
Former Missionary

He Became a Prophet When Ordained an Apostle

On 16 January 1836, the Prophet Joseph Smith stated that the authority of the Twelve Apostles is next to the Presidency and that the Quorum of the Twelve Apostles are subject to no one except the First Presidency, namely, "myself, . . . Sidney Rigdon, and Frederick G. Williams, who are now my Counselors; and where I am not, there is no First Presidency over the Twelve" (*History of the Church*, 2:374).

Since that time, when a man has been ordained an Apostle, he is given all the keys of the holy priesthood, but those keys of authority to preside over the Church remain inchoate, or dormant, until and unless he becomes the senior Apostle. He does, however, as an Apostle, exercise immediately all the powers of a prophet.

I was personally acquainted with President Harold B. Lee when he was president of the Pioneer Stake, and along with many others, I was very fond of him. In 1940 I was a member of a group of young lawyers who wanted to have him nominated for the position of governor of Utah. He graciously declined and stated that he had dedicated his life to the service of the Lord. At that time I was convinced that someday he would become one of the Twelve Apostles. When he was called to be an Apostle, my wife, Maybeth, and I were very happy. At that time I believed that someday he would become President of the Church.

Elder Harold B. Lee was called to the apostleship on 6 April 1941. Not long thereafter, he telephoned me at my office and told me he wanted me to do some special research for him involving Church history. He asked me how long it would take me to do it. I estimated two weeks. He told me he had to have it within three days! When I said I did not believe I could possible obtain that information for him within three days, he said to me, "Paul, if you will go into your inner office and close the door so you will be alone, and kneel down and ask the Lord to guide you, he will guide you and inspire you so that you will have that information for me in three days."

His statement reminded me of Naaman, the leper, who hesitated when he received the message from the prophet Elisha to dip himself in the Jordan River seven times.

I did exactly as Elder Lee had counseled me to do. After praying alone, as I arose from my knees, I felt the instant inspiration. Instead of proceeding as I ordinarily would do as a lawyer, I was inspired to go immediately to the Utah Historical Society. Arriving there, I was impressed to go to a volume that was not published by, or for, the Church. I walked to the very stack where the volume was located and took it out and found, within seconds, the information Elder Lee had requested. My steps could not have been in a more direct path if I had been given a detailed map on where to find this material.

In fulfillment of the promise of Elder Harold B. Lee, a prophet of God, I was able to write up that information and present it to him at his office within two days instead of three.

This experience has given me indisputable evidence that Elder Lee became a prophet when he was ordained an Apostle of the Lord.

36

John M. Russon
Former Temple President

My Mentor and Dear Friend

One of the most influential persons in my life was President Harold B. Lee, a most remarkable servant of the Lord. He became a spiritual giant in my eyes when he was called to the apostleship during the depression years and became the ''father'' of the Church welfare plan.

As a young bishop and subsequently as a stake president, vice-chairman, and eventually chairman of a welfare region, I shall always remember the regular visits of Elders Lee and Marion G. Romney, as they taught us the basic principles of this magnificent program and inspired us with the vision of its potential for all Saints.

When he stayed in our home while assigned to our stake conferences during my thirteen-year tenure as stake president, he became a favorite of the family, and soon my wife and I were always known as John and Mary to him.

Mary had successfully given birth to our first seven children, but the next two only lived a matter of hours. When Mary was expecting again, she sought a blessing at the hands of her favorite General Authority and was promised in Elder Lee's blessing that she would deliver a healthy child. Just before time for delivery, complications developed with uremic poisoning, and the doctor informed me that he was unable to detect a fetal heart beat and was afraid that it would be a stillbirth. But, thirty minutes later he emerged from the delivery room with the joyful announcement that we had a healthy nine and one-half pound boy, whose shoulders were so broad his arm had to be broken to effect delivery.

In 1962 I was called to preside over the Swiss Mission. This meant a return for me to Leimenstrasse 49 in Basel, which served as mission headquarters when I was a young missionary in the Swiss-German Mission from 1931 to 1933. We had only been on our mission three months when we received a phone call from the Swiss Temple. It was Elder Lee asking me to meet him and Walter Stover in Zollikofen and drive them to Zurich that afternoon. He had been devastated by the death of his dear wife, Fern, only a few weeks before, and I had never seen him so sad and discouraged. Brother Stover was a real strength and support to him.

In Zurich that evening, Elder Lee was at his best, however, in strengthening the new presidency and high council and encouraging them to invite the mission president to the council meetings and to take advantage of his (my) experience as a bishop and stake president. The next morning was Thanksgiving, and we drove back to Basel for a choice dinner with the staff at mission headquarters. Sister Russon and the children were overjoyed to see Elder Lee, and it was a special time for all of us. Visits to four groups of our district missionaries later that day in Basel and Zurich resulted in wise counsel to this "green" mission president and his missionaries. He left us inspired and strengthened for the challenges ahead.

Our next meeting occurred nearly one year later on 4 November 1963. Mary and I, with the children, were attending the servicemen's conference at Berchtesgaden, Germany. We had arrived the evening before and had driven to Chiemsee the next morning before the start of the conference to visit Ludwig

II's famous castle on Herren Island. Imagine our pleasure and surprise to find Elder Lee and his new bride, Joan (Freda Joan Jensen), with our mission president, Elder Theodore Burton, and his wife, Minnie. They were also visiting the castle en route to the conference. What a difference the year had made in revitalizing the spirit and attitude of Elder Lee. He was again at his dynamic and inspiring best. We invited the Lees to come to Zurich for a day or two after the conference to be our guests at the new mission home on the Dolder.

We were so pleased that they came. We took them to dinner at the Hotel Alexander, about fifteen miles southeast of Zurich on the shore of the Lake of Zurich. The bond between us was developed further, and we became very fond of his dear wife, Joan.

Upon our return to California, we had brief encounters while I served as a member of the General Welfare Committee of the Church for two years.

Then, the memorable years came when the Regional Representatives of the Twelve were initiated at the general conference of October 1967. Elder Lee had long advocated the regional concept in welfare work, and now he was broadening it for all Church administration. The Brethren looked to Brother Lee to spearhead the program. Under his wise and fatherly direction, all of us who were called looked forward to the training seminars held at general conference time and occasionally more often. It was a time of trial and error while we were learning our roles in effectively helping the stake and mission presidents achieve their objectives. During the seven years that I served, Elder Lee became the president of the Quorum of the Twelve at the passing of President David O. McKay, and then the President of the Church when President Joseph Fielding Smith was called home. Through all of these transitions, he was our mentor and constant inspiration.

Early during this period, my life's companion, Mary, was stricken with congestive heart failure, which claimed her life on 11 March 1970. One of the first persons from whom I heard after her passing was President Lee. He wrote a warm, tender, intimate letter of consolation, which I keep among my most treasured possessions.

A few weeks later, during the Regional Representatives' seminar at general conference, he paid a special tribute to Mary and me in the context of the "Johns and Marys" of former times. How grateful I was for his feeling and loving concern. Six months later, when we were again together at conference, he called me aside and offered me some fatherly counsel with regard to the importance of choosing another companion for the future, which I did shortly after the following April general conference. My union with Lyn Redding met with his complete approval.

Then, the stunning news of his sudden passing on 26 December 1973 left us all in a state of shock, because he had presided over the Church for only eighteen months. In the wisdom of our Heavenly Father, President Lee was needed more urgently on the other side of the veil. One of my dearest friends had been called home, and I shall be forever grateful for the trust and confidence of this great man of God.

37

John Schreiner
Professor of Finance

An Unforgettable Lesson on Delegation

In the early 1960s when I was living and studying in Boston, the Boston Stake was privileged to have a visit from Elder Harold B. Lee, then a member of the Council of the Twelve Apostles. His instruction to the leadership of that stake on that occasion changed my life for good. I have never forgotten his sage teachings, and I have often borrowed upon them in my professional and Church assignments. In doing so, I find them to be ageless and always appropriate and needed.

After the conference, I made written notes of one particular lesson on the subject of delegation, as taught by Elder Lee. As nearly as I could recompose his words immediately after they were given, I kept his matchless lesson on delegation:

> Some years ago, I was preparing for an assignment to visit a stake conference in southern California. Looking over the file for that stake I was impressed greatly by one particular fact. The stake president had been serving for nineteen years and during that time had served with twenty-four counselors!

This disturbed me greatly. Was there a problem? Was he unable to work well with counselors? Why would so many, so often, need to be released? This was an unusually high turnover of counselors, yet the president, himself, had continued to serve for so many years. I asked for further data on the subject.

The records confirmed that indeed there had been that number of counselors. It showed also that of the twenty-two counselors who had been released over the years, nineteen had themselves been subsequently called as stake presidents. This shed new light on the matter and reversed my frame of reference. Perhaps it was the case that this stake president worked unusually well with counselors so that he was, in fact, developing them, helping them grow in spiritual stature so that they themselves acquired the capacity to be called as stake presidents.

Needless to say, it was with a good deal of anticipation that I traveled to that stake conference in California. With the ever-growing need in the Church for the development of leaders at every level, I was curious to meet a stake president, who, somehow, had been of influence in the development of so many future stake presidents. What was he like? What was his personality? What was his administrative style, his spiritual strength?

On Saturday afternoon, we held the usual meetings with various groups of stake and ward leaders. As we walked to supper before the evening conference session, I caught up with one of the stake high councilors and casually inquired, "Tell me, what is it like to work with your stake president and serve on his high council?"

The high councilor squared his shoulders and responded with obvious pride, "What is it like to work with President Cannon? Why, I can tell you in a sentence. He wouldn't breathe if he could get somebody else to do it for him."

I have never been able to forget that response—"He wouldn't breathe if he could get somebody else to do it for him." I have tried to remember and teach Elder Lee's summary lesson on this subject.

He told us that here was a president who cared about his brethren. He cared enough to give them opportunities to grow. He gave them leeway. He shared the limelight of his office with them. And with what results? Elder Lee said they felt his love, his warmth, his strength, his caring. They were willing—even excited—to work on his team and to receive his coaching and encouragement. He believed in delegation, but that didn't mean dumping. It didn't mean shucking off the tough projects. It didn't mean putting himself on a pedestal and standing "above it all." It meant being sensitive and seeking inspiration in giving out assignments. We were told that assignments should never be given just to get a job done, but should also be carefully matched with the needs of the doer. It meant being a good shepherd: guiding, encouraging, loving, counseling, challenging, letting go, and then following up, praising, and teaching.

Elder Lee then turned to the leadership of the Boston Stake and said that this example was not confined to just stake presidents. Its meaning applied equally to all Church leaders, including bishops, elders quorum presidents, and Sunday School leaders. "Choose," he said, "with great reliance on prayer and inspiration, the best, the strongest counselors you can find. Don't be afraid if they have some rough edges. Be forgiving if their past has been rocky. Look for their strengths, not weaknesses. Look for what they can do and what they may become—bishops, stake presidents, and, who knows, even Apostles, of tomorrow."

And finally, he taught us to then let them, or allow them, to serve. We were to let them do everything for us, even breathe for us, as it were, if they were willing to do so. In that way, we would be teaching them with love.

In concluding his lesson, Elder Lee assured us that such practices were vitally needed in the kingdom. He believed that the Lord is hoping that each leader will practice the loving teaching and preparation of his associates through the abundant use of delegation.

I have found that these principles fit just as perfectly in my instruction of management in the graduate school of business as they do in my Church applications. I therefore have come to cherish this brilliant insight from a prophet of God who long ago came to Boston and left us changed, never to be the same again, through the inspiration of his lesson on delegation.

38

Rex A. Skidmore
Former Regional Representative

Changing Teaching in the Church and in My Life

My recollections of President Harold B. Lee are intense, spiritual, beautiful, and inspiring. He was not only a magnificent prophet and teacher but he also personally influenced my life for good in many ways. One experience with him was particularly significant to me and benefited the entire Church—the establishment of the teacher development program.

In October 1968, I was interviewed by Elder Thomas S. Monson of the Council of the Twelve, who informed me that I would be released as stake president to head a committee designed to improve and enrich teaching in the Church. The General Authorities, particularly because of the creative leadership of President Lee, had decided to innovate a priesthood-sponsored program Churchwide for teacher development. The beginnings of this endeavor originated with President Lee, deriving from his practical experiences in teaching and leadership and his deep concern about all Church members learning more about gospel principles and applying them in daily living.

President Lee interviewed me, gave me his blessings, and said we should always remember the following:

There are many wonderful teachers in the Church, also many good teachers, but there are also some poor ones. Every teacher, no matter how effective, can become a better teacher. It is so important in teaching that we have a goal of changing lives for good, not just entertaining class members. Hopefully, each person—child, youth, or adult—who leaves a Latter-day Saint class will be a different person, whose life will be fuller and more meaningful because of that lesson. Teaching, in a practical, applied sense, should bring worthwhile changes in the behavior of class members, particularly changes in spiritual behavior.

Armed with such lofty concepts and inspired by President Lee's vision of how the entire Church membership could be benefitted through improved teaching, our committee set out to fulfill its momentous charge. Finally, on 4 June 1970, we presented plans for teacher development to the General Authorities in the upper room of the Salt Lake Temple. President Joseph Fielding Smith presided at this meeting, and President Harold B. Lee conducted. After a twenty-minute discussion, the teacher development proposal was unanimously approved for implementation throughout the worldwide Church.

The wisdom, practical experiences, deep spirituality, and inventive genius of President Lee had once again brought forth a new emphasis to the Church, one that could benefit all members and others, directly or indirectly. The influence for good that President Lee had, and still has, to bless the Church members with increased knowledge and meaningful actions seem immeasurable. His spiritual greatness and goodness is seen in Church teaching today almost as a trademark on how we learn, worship, love, and live.

President Lee's teaching contributions have not only been profound and enduring for the Church, but have also made significant changes in my own professional life as a college professor. His insightful understanding of the dynamics of the teaching and learning processes was brilliant. On many occasions he explained to me, by precept and example, that effective teaching results in helping persons to know, to feel, and to do. All three of these aspects are important, but the third is particularly significant. He explained that we may know much about Church doctrines and even have deep feelings of testimony in our hearts, but if we stop there and do little or nothing about what we know and feel, we are just "treading water." As a result of his guidance, I adjusted my own teaching with university students and in Church positions to be much more practical, more related to actual changes in behavior for good.

I shared many additional experiences with President Lee that influenced my life and are cherished by me. When he set me apart as a Regional Representative, 12 December 1970, he gave me a blessing that I shall always remember. As he placed his hands on my head and began to talk, I experienced a penetrating sensation I had never felt before. I received a spiritual witness that he was a prophet of God, which was inspiring for me.

President Lee helped me to become more positive in my relationships with my family, teaching associates, students, and neighbors. His example of being positive was superb. When he would meet me on the street or on the university campus at graduation exercises, he would always make comments to build me as a person. I was never in his presence but what I felt an increased desire to love more and serve better, through sharing appreciation and caring.

Another influence of President Lee on my life was his helping me to develop and increase my faith. His conference messages and his personal contacts were always faith promoting. On the front of his Christmas card for 1973 was a beautiful colored picture of Christ in the Garden of Gethsemane. Inside, his words of greeting recognized the turbulent times in which we lived; then he suggested:

> Remember . . . His divine promise to all who faithfully put their trust in Him:
> "Peace I leave with you, my peace I give unto you: not as the world giveth, give I unto you. Let not your heart be troubled, neither let it be afraid." (John 14:27.)

President Lee often emphasized the importance of the family as the basic unit in the kingdom of God. On one visit to our quarterly conference, when I was stake president, he admonished our leaders to put our families in top priority. I shall never forget his specific admonition, "Ordinarily, if you have to make a choice between your stake calling and your family, remember your family comes first."

It is clearly apparent that President Harold B. Lee changed my life for good in many ways. His influences upon me have been profound and rewarding. I'll always cherish the blessings I received from close association with this wonderful prophet of God.

39

Richard B. Sonne
Former Temple President

He Answered
All My Questions

I greatly admired and loved President Harold B. Lee. He meant a great deal to me. There were several occasions when he and I had an opportunity to communicate and visit, and some of the memories I have of those moments are very precious to me.

He came to my aid when I was bishop of the Palo Alto Ward, located near San Francisco. This was in 1949. We had a tragedy occur among the ward members when a good, active member killed his wife and committed suicide in front of their three children. Unknown to me, he had been under treatment for war-acquired malarial fever at the Veterans Administration Hospital. Apparently the disease had affected his mind.

When I heard about the tragedy, I placed a telephone call to Elder Lee, who was attending a stake conference in California. When I told him of the tragedy, he was upset; he could hardly speak. He had known this couple very well, and only weeks before, they had tended his grandson when he had been in our city visiting with his daughter and her husband.

I indicated that I had two or three questions to ask him, and he promptly replied that inasmuch as I was an ordained bishop that I had the power of discernment and should use it in this situation.

This tragedy happened on a Saturday, and I had talked to President Lee early on that Saturday evening. On Sunday morning he telephoned me, and his first words to me were that he did not sleep a wink the night before because he was so concerned about having let me down. He said to me, "Richard, you talk to me just as long as you want and ask just as many questions as you would like."

I then proceeded to ask him many questions, such as could the deceased be dressed in temple clothing? What type of service should we have? Should a General Authority be asked to speak? He answered all questions entirely to my satisfaction. Then he asked if I was going to be in Salt Lake City in the near future. I told him that I was arranging a trip to the Middle West and would probably stop off in Utah for a few days. Accordingly, I made an appointment to visit with him at his home on a Saturday in June 1949.

At President Lee's home he related to me two or three wonderful experiences. He told me about when he was a stake president, before he was called to be a General Authority. He had been called to administer to a young woman who was possessed of an evil spirit. He told me how frightened he was when he saw the situation. After the administration, the sister calmed down and became relaxed and rational. He felt that this experience was a test for him.

President Lee then indicated that he thought the tragedy in my ward was a test to me and to the members of the Palo Alto Ward. He indicated that he did not see how Satan could have done much more to disrupt our work unless a personal tragedy would have come to affect my own family. After a visit with him of about an hour or more, I left his home very much humbled upon hearing his wonderful testimony. This experience will remain with me throughout my life.

I had other communications with President Lee, particularly when my father, Alma Sonne, became ill and was unable to perform his service as a General Authority. On one occasion my sister took Father to President Lee, who gave him a special blessing. When I heard of this, I wrote and thanked him for his thoughtfulness in taking time from his busy schedule to visit a few moments with Father. Shortly thereafter I received a reply from him in which he again expressed his love and appreciation for me and for Father, and indicated how happy he was with my assignments in the Church. This letter is placed with my treasures, and on occasion I refer to it as a reminder of my happy association with President Lee.

40

Asael T. Sorensen
Former Regional Representative

Blessings from Traveling with a Prophet

My wife and I had a most unusual experience in being permitted to travel intimately over many weeks with one of the living Apostles of the Lord.

In July of 1959, we were recalled to South America by the First Presidency. I had previously served as president of the Brazilian Mission. When President David O. McKay put his arm around me, he said, "The Lord wants you to return to Brazil." We were informed that we would have the privilege of returning to Brazil by ship in the company of Elder Harold B. Lee and his sweet wife, Fern Tanner Lee. What a wonderful experience it was to be with them aboard the *Brazil*, a Moore-McCormack passenger liner.

One of our last meetings with Elder Lee on board the ship before we arrived in Rio de Janeiro was a fast and testimony meeting. Elder Lee offered the benediction on the meeting and also on our travels. Also, because we had expressed our concern about finding a suitable mission home that would be adequate for our needs as headquarters for the new Brazil South Mission, he prayed that "in a most remarkable manner," the Lord would lead us to a mission home that would serve as both our living quarters and a mission office.

We left him in Rio with President and Sister Wm. Grant Bangerter. Elder and Sister Lee were to tour with them in their mission for ten days before continuing to Curitiba, where the new mission headquarters would be located. It was at that time that the Brazilian Mission was divided for the first time. The new mission in the south was to be known as the Brazil South Mission.

Before we arrived in Curitiba, a residence had been selected for us that was unsuitable. It was far out from the city and had a small bridge crossing a drainage ditch over which all must traverse to enter the home. Because we had young children, we felt it would be a dangerous location. Besides, it was also situated on the airport road, a busy thoroughfare in and out of the city. So we made it a matter of prayer, and within two days, it was indeed "in a most remarkable manner" that we had located the ideal mission home.

We found it on the very day that the owners were preparing to place it on the market to be sold to settle an estate. It was a beautiful, well-constructed building, enclosed within an attractive rock wall. The cost was approximately $55,000. It had adequate space in an extensive, large wing adjoining the mission home for offices. This wing had a separate entrance for people to enter, which preserved the privacy of the family residence. This made it most desirable. It was referred to as the "Castelo Branco," or "White Castle," and that was the only information missionaries and others needed to know when asking for directions.

This acquisition made it possible for us to completely set up our offices with a staff, desks, and typewriters and to have everything organized and in full operation by the time Elder and Sister Lee arrived. They were amazed at how quickly this had been accomplished. We reminded Elder Lee that we felt certain that it was through the inspiration which had come to him from the Lord that this facility had been made available to us "in a most remarkable manner."

As we traveled with Elder and Sister Lee, this same spirit of inspiration and revelation accompanied him. The sermons he gave were filled with wise counsel and instructions, which had been carefully recorded by my wife in shorthand. After Elder Lee left us, we read through those notes and found much direct instruction from the Lord through Elder Lee as to how we should proceed in each area of the mission that we had visited. Through following that inspiration, the mission prospered and enlarged. Thus we give much of the credit to Elder Lee for being in tune with the Lord so that we could, through him, find the path to success on our mission.

During a final missionary meeting held with Elder and Sister Lee in the city of Porto Alegre in the state of Rio Grande do Sul, Elder Lee was inspired to share his beautiful, inspiring testimony. He mentioned that testimonies were of a sacred nature and should only be shared with those who could appreciate sacred truths. During the entire course of that meeting, the Spirit of the Lord was so strongly felt that Elder Lee quietly stated that the veil that separates us from the spirit world was almost entirely withdrawn. One of the most inspiring stories he told us was of his childhood experience on the farm in Idaho where he first heard the voice of the Lord. He said, "I had just parted the wires to crawl through when I heard a voice as distinctly as a person could speak, command, 'Harold, don't go near that lumber over there!' " Having been cautioned not to enter the blown down sheds, where injury might have come to him, he listened and obeyed and ran from an unknown danger.

At Iguacu Falls we were with the Lees and with Elder and Sister Bangerter for a meeting concerning the division of the Brazilian Mission. On the way, Sister Lee developed a problem with the retina of her eye. It was apparently agitated because of the rough taxi ride from the Asuncion Airport to the hotel. The ride was especially rough because small logs had been laid across the macadam road to alleviate its swampy condition. At that time the roads had not been blacktopped. This probably was the cause of the retina becoming disengaged from her eye, with a resultant optical hemorrhage. She seemed seriously affected. Yet, she was confident that she would be all right if her husband would give her a special priesthood blessing, which he did. We again saw a demonstration of the power of his gift of healing through the priesthood and the faith of Sister Lee in the administration. Soon she was again able to join with the others in our activities.

It was such a delight to travel with Elder and Sister Lee. They were wonderful traveling companions. They were so interested in each of our children, which of course endeared them to all of us. Sister Lee was one of the warmest, most gracious sisters whom we have ever known, one to whom living the gospel came so naturally. We have felt so close to her that we have saved her letters to us over these many years. In a letter from President Lee in the early 1970s, he told us that we had become like family to them.

Our prayer is that, through our testimony and that of others, the Church membership may come to understand that President Harold B. Lee was truly a great man and a devoted servant of the Lord, an exemplary prophet and seer.

41

Betty B. Stohl
Associate Director of Church Hosting

He Awakened in Me
a Desire to Gain
a Testimony

I didn't realize it at the time, but I was being taught by a future prophet of the Lord. I did know that I was listening to the teachings of an uncommon man, one whose words taught me to listen to and read everything he said in later life. He was my seminary teacher during my junior year in high school. He was Harold B. Lee.

I discovered in a later conversation with him that early in the depression years of 1931 and 1932, Harold B. Lee was selling Bible books and teaching high school seminary classes to supplement a meager income.

I have difficulty remembering the course of study he taught in the upstairs room of an old home adjoining the newly constructed South High School in Salt Lake City. It is much easier, though, to remember the handsome man with dark, wavy hair and a commanding appearance.

Since no credit was given for the seminary course, and no released time, we attended seminary before school started each morning. Very few students ever missed his early morning class. He kept us spellbound with lessons about life, illustrating them with actual examples. These were the teachings we were fortunate to hear before he published his book *Youth and the Church*. His sincerity and knowledge provided a foundation for me to use later in teaching many youth classes over the years.

We were silly, noisy high school kids, yet he had a firm control over us. His penetrating voice commanded respect as he talked to us of the importance of ourselves and the value of self-respect.

One bit of advice he constantly gave was, "Make the right choices." He stressed ideals. He would ask what kinds of friends, books, and pleasures we were choosing. He told us that life had deeper values than satisfying our desires of the moment.

Another statement he made I have never forgotten. He taught us, "You learn to do by doing." This counsel pointed out that by serving the Church and the community we will gain confidence and self-respect. I always have tried to remember his words and teachings.

Harold B. Lee was the first person to awaken in me a desire to gain a testimony of the truthfulness of the Church. When he said, "The greatest goal in life is to gain a testimony of the gospel," his words burned within me. I knew I had to begin to search for the way to gain my own witness. I now have an unshakable testimony, which is one of my greatest treasures.

I loved Harold B. Lee as our eleventh President and prophet, but never more than on that day long ago when he took away the treats my friends and I had sneaked into the seminary classroom. After class he asked us to share them with him. As we ate the goodies, he encouraged us to enjoy each other and life in general.

He was not only my favorite teacher, but he was also a worthy ideal to follow. During my time with him in class the seeds of a deep love of the gospel of Jesus Christ were planted and nourished.

Since those days of my youth, President Lee has continued to be a source of spiritual strength to me. My dear husband, Clark, had been hospitalized into the fifth week for multiple cancer surgeries, during which period President and Sister Lee were in almost daily contact with us. We reached a crisis one night when another operation due to complications was scheduled the next day. Late that night a knock came on the hospital door to arouse me from my somber depression. It was President and Sister Lee coming unannounced to extend their love. After a warm greeting, President Lee said, "I would like to give Clark a blessing." On that occasion I witnessed his closeness to the Lord as he exercised his apostolic priesthood in behalf of my desperately ill husband. He promised my husband that he would live to complete his work upon the earth, and Clark was spared for many more long years of service. Then President Lee turned his compassion to me by giving me a priesthood blessing. Although I had not slept for many nights due to my great anguish for Clark, and despite the fact that this was the night before his crucial cancer surgery, I had a wonderful night's rest after the blessing from President Lee. I felt assured that we were in the Lord's hands.

Elder Lee also set apart our only son as a missionary, which was the beginning for him of a splendid career of Church service, including a term as bishop. Elder Lee's influence has been upon our entire family, and it still remains to this day. I have used his book *Youth and the Church* in teaching the youth in our wards and stakes and with our own children.

I shall be grateful forever for the way I have loved President Harold B. Lee and been able to enjoy his pervasive spiritual and caring influence upon me throughout my life.

42

Walter Stover
Former Member of the
General Church Welfare Committee

Memories of My Dearest Friend

I was acquainted with President Harold B. Lee ever since I arrived in the United States in 1926. I lived on Montrose Avenue, in the Fourth Ward of Pioneer Stake. Our bishop was Phileon F. Perschon. Harold B. Lee was the stake president. At age thirty-one, he was then the youngest stake president in the Church. I greatly admired and respected him for his outstanding leadership ability as a stake president.

In 1929 the Great Depression hit our beloved country, and in 1936 the Church security plan (predecessor to the Church welfare program) was organized by President Heber J. Grant. After serving as the first managing director of the welfare plan, Elder Lee was called in 1941 to be a member of the Quorum of the Twelve Apostles. He was twenty years younger than the next youngest Apostle when he was called.

His special calling as a member of the Twelve Apostles was to head the welfare program because his Pioneer Stake had become the cradle for the development of a Churchwide welfare plan. From the very beginning, I became engaged in the welfare program and had many occasions to meet and counsel with President Lee.

At the close of World War II, I was called to serve as a mission president in my native country of Germany. Under the direction of President George Albert Smith and Harold B. Lee, more than one hundred carloads of food, clothing, and vitamins were sent to me to help the starving members of the Church in supplementing their meager rations of food. President Ezra Taft Benson was then the European Mission President, with headquarters in London, England. Later, Elder Alma Sonne became the European Mission President.

Most of the members of the Church in East Germany had lost their homes and all their belongings. They were destitute, hungry, and cold. They were driven from their homes by the invading Russian armies and had nothing but the clothing on their backs. More than twenty branches of the Church were abandoned. Cities were destroyed and reduced to rubble. If it had not been for the Church welfare program, many of the Saints would have perished.

After serving more than five years, I returned from my mission in 1951 and accepted a calling by President David O. McKay to become a member of the General Church Welfare Committee. In this capacity, I attended stake conferences nearly every week, accompanying the General Authorities of the Church. I was always happy when I was assigned to be with President Harold B. Lee.

As members of the General Welfare Committee, we were instructed each week by J. Reuben Clark, Jr., of the First Presidency, along with Presidents Henry D. Moyle, Harold B. Lee, and Marion G. Romney. I was assigned also to serve on the finance committee of the General Church Welfare Committee, which held weekly meetings. For twenty years I was a member of the temple clothing advisory committee of Beehive Clothing. Under President Lee's direction, we met monthly with the Relief Society General Presidency, who were in charge of the distribution of temple clothing. President Lee and I were the committee in charge of production. In all these associations, frequent and intimate, I was greatly inspired with the prophetic wisdom of Harold B. Lee.

When his beloved wife, Fern, passed away on 24 September 1962, President Lee and I were assigned to go to Germany, Austria, and Switzerland for four weeks to hold many conferences. At that time President Lee was in deep sorrow from the loss of his beloved eternal companion, and I saw him weep on many occasions. It was very difficult for me to cheer him up. Despite his grief, we held many extra meetings with missionaries and Church servicemen stationed in various cities of Germany. On most of these occasions, I translated for Elder Lee.

In Berlin, he was so depressed one night that he had to go to his hotel room and turn the conference over to me to conduct.

After we had held the conference in Stuttgart, Germany, we prepared for our return to the United States. We were to fly to Frankfurt the next day because that is the point of origin for overseas departures. The night before our departure, President Lee said to me, "Walter, we had better fly to Frankfurt tonight; I know that our connection from Stuttgart to Frankfurt will be canceled in the morning, and we will be stranded in Stuttgart and miss our flight from Frankfurt to New York City." True to his prediction, when we were at the airport in Frankfurt, it was announced over the public address system that the flight from Stuttgart, which we would have taken, had been canceled. I didn't say a word, but President Lee just looked at me knowingly as we watched the flights out of Frankfurt. I knew that he was a prophet of God.

In New York City we stayed at the headquarters of the Eastern States Mission. President Lee and I shared the same bedroom. I did not want to go to sleep because I snore, and I was afraid it would disturb him. I managed for a long time to stay awake, and in so doing I soon found out that President Lee did a little snoring himself.

If I were gifted as a writer, I could fill an entire book about my dearest friend, President Harold B. Lee. We exchanged small gifts for Christmas. He visited with me in my home, and I visited with him in his home. I may have been one of the last visitors to talk with President Lee on Christmas Eve in his home between

6:30 and 7:00 P.M. I found him subdued in spirit, and he told me that he had just listened to the taped recording of the solemn assembly general conference when he was sustained as President of the Church. He talked of the great progress the Church was enjoying at that time and of the marvelous work that lay ahead. I had no insight that anything was physically wrong with President Lee and no suggestion that he would pass away just two days later. I saw no sign of illness. I am inclined to believe that the Lord just needed him for a special purpose that we cannot yet understand.

These are just a few of the precious memories I have of my dearest friend, President Harold B. Lee.

43

J. Clifford Wallace
U.S. Appellate Court Judge

My Most
Influential Teacher

Life seems to me to be one continuous educational process. During that schooling, there have been many leaders and teachers, within and outside the Church, who have had an impact upon me. Some of those influences have been so profound that I can now see how they changed my life.

Church administration is an area of special importance to me, not only as a result of administrative callings, that have come to me, but equally due to an interest in administration generally. When I reflect upon those who have taught me most in this area, one especially stands out: President Harold B. Lee.

My contacts with him were not extensive, but the experiences were exceptional. One or two will serve as examples.

When the first group of Regional Representatives (then called Regional Representatives of the Twelve) was called, none of us had a clear perspective of our duties. During the first years, we struggled to identify our responsibilities and how we were to interact with the stakes to which we were assigned. Our principal teacher at our semiannual seminars was Elder Lee. As I look back, it is astonishing how much we were taught. He seemed to have a clear understanding of what we needed to learn to carry out our responsibilities in this newly created office. Principles were identified, illustrations were used to help us understand, and motivation was provided.

The how-to-do came less freely. What I failed to understand then is that a good leader instructs only as far as experience allows and inspiration dictates. Elder Lee was critically aware of this principle. After one of his instruction periods, he allowed us to ask questions. Mine was on target: the lack of clarity of what we were to do was specifically identified, and my question was precise. His response added little to the original instruction. Because of my many years as a trial lawyer, I knew how to re-ask questions following a less than responsive answer. I did so. His unruffled response gave me no additional enlightenment. After the session, one of the Twelve, in a very kind and charitable way, suggested that it is inappropriate to cross-examine members of the Council of the Twelve.

It was only on reflection that I realized he was teaching me that changing administrative concepts mature slowly; that, as more experience is gained, inspiration directs how to proceed. Recognizing my limitation of not seeing the whole picture when the first few pieces of the puzzle are placed on the table has assisted me as I have tackled new administrative needs within and outside the Church.

But perhaps his most profound effect on my life was his personal interaction. One event is typical.

When he was assigned to a conference in the stake where I presided, I already had a commitment to lecture on a Saturday morning to members of the bar in Palm Springs, California. He encouraged me to keep the appointment but arranged his flight plans so that his plane landed in Palm Springs where I boarded. From the time that I took a seat next to him until I left him at his plane at the San Diego Airport Sunday afternoon, I was exposed to one continuous leadership training experience.

Because of his vast experience and reputation, there were many areas of Church government and administration that I wanted to explore. In each instance, when I asked a specific question, he did not answer directly. Instead, he carefully raised questions and guided my thinking. In doing so, he taught me the principle or principles involved so I could answer the question myself. Of course, it took longer, but I not only had the answer, I also had been taught how to find the answer and how to decide.

His genius in teaching priesthood leaders was equally apparent as he conducted leadership meetings. He made each moment a teaching experience in which principles were identified and learned in such a way that each listener understood and was a better prepared leader.

Men with great wisdom and inspiration can tell us how to accomplish a task, and that task will ordinarily be done quickly and correctly. But the master teacher takes the time to teach us so that we may learn for ourselves how to do it. In either instance, the task is done, but in the latter the doer is left better prepared to accomplish effectively on his own. President Lee had the gift and the interest to teach correct Church administration principles so that we could be better administrators ourselves. I shall always be grateful for his kindly and effective teaching to me, which has greatly benefited my leadership in both Church and professional endeavors.

44

Harriet E. Jensen Woolsey
Former Missionary

Early Signs
of His Greatness

When I read the biography *Harold B. Lee, Prophet and Seer,* I recalled the many memories I have of him while we served simultaneously in the Western States Mission in Denver, Colorado. He was three years older than me, lacking twenty-five days.

When I arrived in the mission field on 6 September 1922, Elder Lee was president of the Denver Conference and serving as assistant to the mission president, John M. Knight. He also played the piano and organ for all the Church meetings and for the elders conferences. He took care of the housecleaning of the chapel and kept it sparkling from top to bottom. He was respected and loved by all the missionaries and members of that mission.

I lived with three other sister missionaries (Sisters Olsen, Nielsen, Hubbard) across the street from the mission and church house. We cooked our meals at the church, so we would see and mingle with Elder Lee every morning. We also helped him on Saturdays to prepare the meetinghouse for Sunday services.

One experience concerning his leadership I have never forgotten. There was a big fashion show promotion in downtown Denver that offered an enticement to us. So instead of going to choir practice, Sister Johnson and I went to see the show. The next morning at breakfast Elder Lee said, "Where were you two last night?" We answered honestly that we went to the fashion show. Elder Lee looked piercingly at us and stated, "Don't let it happen again." As I looked at him, I wished the floor would swallow me up. His look said more than words and made me feel like I had committed a huge crime. Later we came to appreciate and respect the high standards that he held for all of us.

On one occasion, a member of the Reorganized Church of Jesus Christ of Latter Day Saints wanted to debate one of our missionaries on the Book of Mormon. Since Elder Lee was our most accomplished authority on the scriptures, he was asked, and agreed, to accept the challenge. In the debate Elder Lee so soundly defeated everything this man said that the man became frustrated and angry and abruptly marched out of the building. I don't think anybody in that mission, among elders or members, had a comprehension of the Book of Mormon equal to Elder Lee.

Another similar incident has remained in my memory. When our elders were invited to explain Mormon doctrine over the pulpit of another church, again it was Elder Lee who was chosen to be our spokesman. He gave such an inspiring and faith-promoting sermon that his audience was captivated and respectful, and no one interrupted his presentation.

It was while Elder Lee was speaking that night that I saw a hallowed light encircle his head. The light was much brighter around his head than was the surrounding light, and it was mingled with several beautiful colors. His head was framed in a half circle from the top of one shoulder to the other. I was so impressed with this manifestation that when we were outside after the meeting I said to him, "Elder Lee, you are going to someday be the President of the Church." His reply was, "Sister, I won't be worthy enough to be the President." But from that day on, I was convinced that he would become our prophet.

Another reason for my closeness with Elder Lee is that we came home together on the train with President Knight, from Denver to Salt Lake City, at the close of our missions in December 1922.

Our association continued after our missions. I saw Elder Lee when I lived on West Temple Street between Fourth and Fifth South in Salt Lake City. I talked with him many times when he was courting his future wife, Fern Tanner, who was one of our sister missionaries in Denver. When he was selling the Master Library (Bible books), I bought a set from him.

One day he told me about what a difficult time his wife had giving birth to their two little girls and how disappointed they were that they could not have more children. I felt so badly for him. On another visit to my home, when he was selling books, he was just glad to rest for a moment in a big chair. After he left, I found five silver dollars in the chair. He returned the next day to reclaim them, explaining to me how much those dollars meant to him to take care of his little family in the early days of their marriage.

I also saw him when he taught school and was the principal of the Woodrow Wilson School in Salt Lake County. We lived just through a vacant field north of the school, and a nephew of mine lived next door. This boy, Leslie, was late to come back into the classroom after recess one day. When the teacher told him to march to the rear of the line of children entering the room, he ran instead to the front. When she insisted that he follow directions, Leslie kicked her and ran home. In thirty minutes a knock came on their door. I was present and witnessed the scene.

Harold B. Lee, the school principal, was at the door, asking, "Leslie, why did you kick the teacher when she told you to go to the back?" Leslie hid behind his dad and would not answer. Harold told Leslie that he wanted him back at school in twenty minutes to apologize to his teacher. At first his dad said he wouldn't go back, but the principal said firmly as he left, "You'd better come!'' A few minutes after Harold had left, I watched Leslie and his dad go across the vacant field to the school. Later, his dad returned and said Leslie was in school, having made amends as he had been guided to do.

I saw Harold B. Lee installed as the president of the Pioneer Stake when he was only thirty-one years of age, but I knew, better than most, that his capacity was far beyond his years. When a vacancy came in the Council of the Twelve, I knew Harold B. Lee would be chosen to fill it. My home teacher asked me, "Who do you think will be added to the Quorum of the Twelve?" I said, "Elder Lee will be named." I was right, too, for in the general conference of April 1941, he was called to the apostleship.

I am so thankful I had the privilege of meeting and knowing a future President of the Church, Harold B. Lee. From our youthful days together, I have always admired this wonderful man, husband, father, and a true prophet of our Lord and Savior, Jesus Christ. It has always been a goal in my life to seek to do all I can to be worthy of a place in the celestial kingdom and there be able to meet and be again with Elder Lee. He has greatly strengthened my testimony of Christ and his true Church on earth.

45

Buddy Youngreen
Author-playwright

Unifying the
Joseph Smith Family

Throughout 1972 and 1973, I enjoyed a close association
with President Harold B. Lee. He encouraged me in my
efforts to unite the family of Joseph Smith, Sr. This work began
with President Lee's blessing at Nauvoo, Illinois, in August of
1972, and at Independence, Missouri, in August of 1973, within
the framework of the Joseph Smith, Sr., Family Organization.

I have served as the chief officer of this organization since its
inception. There have been nine family reunions during the past
fifteen years, and it has been my privilege to confirm members
of three generations of the Prophet Joseph Smith's direct
descendants into the Church. During this time, I have been
privileged to baptize the first male descendant of Joseph Smith
III and to ordain to the Melchizedek Priesthood the first recipient in the Prophet's direct line. Serving in the family organization has given me many opportunities to demonstrate my love
for the Lord, the Prophet Joseph Smith, and for President
Harold B. Lee.

On 21 May 1973, I and my family enjoyed family home evening with President Lee and his family. It was a sweet experience with a modern-day prophet of God. Before the evening ended, President Lee clasped my hand for a moment and looked, as it were, into my soul. He told me, a convert to the Church, that the Lord had raised me up to bring the family of the Prophet Joseph together. Immediately I received a confirmation of the Spirit that what he had said was true.

I first met President Lee on 20 March 1972, when he was serving as First Counselor to President Joseph Fielding Smith. My appointment with him had been arranged by my business associate and friend Joseph Beesley. I came to President Lee to share with him my plan to stage a reunion for Joseph Smith's family under the auspices of a Joseph Smith, Sr., family organization that would include descendants of Joseph's brothers and sisters as well as his own. I proposed having the reunion in Nauvoo that coming summer.

My longtime friend, Dr. Clinton F. Larson, had suggested in 1971, because of my deep concern about the divided Smith family, that perhaps I should stage a gigantic family reunion for all the descendants of Joseph Smith, Sr., and bring them back together again. He told me that because I had worked with temperamental actors, as producer and director, that I ought to be able to handle the divisions within the Smith family. Knowing that to be true, I decided to bring about a Smith family reunion.

President Lee listened very attentively as I told him I had contacted the president of the Reorganized Church, W. Wallace Smith, a grandson of the Prophet Joseph, and had secured his pledge of support for such a gathering. I told President Lee how I had received also the support of many other descendants of Joseph, Sr., and his wife, Lucy Mack Smith.

Recognizing the significance of such a reunion, President Lee cited section 128 of the Doctrine and Covenants and then spoke of his personal conviction of the importance of creating a "welding link" among the brothers and sisters of the Prophet Joseph Smith. He related many of his own experiences with members of the Reorganized Church and told me that President

J. Reuben Clark had said that we would need to love the Prophet Joseph's family into the Church.

After pledging his support, President Lee asked if I needed any financial assistance for the proposed reunion. I told him I hadn't thought about that, but surely there would be. President Lee set up an appointment for me the next day with Elder Mark E. Petersen of the Council of the Twelve and told me that Elder Petersen would be my financial liaison with the Church; on all other matters, I was to report directly to President Lee.

On 6 April 1972, I rushed to Church headquarters to show President Lee the first copy of thousands of letters that would be mailed across the country announcing the first Joseph Smith, Sr., Family Reunion to be held that next August. It didn't occur to me that President Lee might be too busy to see me during general conference. When I was ushered into President Lee's office, he was talking with his wife. He rose to greet me and said, "Joan, this is the young man I've been telling you about." I handed him the newsletter, and after he had read it, he said, "This is wonderful . . . really wonderful." Then he added, "Is there anything else I can do for you at present?"

I said, "Oh yes, President. Would you be the one to tell President Joseph Fielding Smith that we're going to have this reunion?"

He smiled and said, "Why, Brother Youngreen, where do you think your financing has come from? President Smith has already approved your project."

On Monday, 12 June 1972, my wife and I accompanied our friend, Gracia Denning, to the Church Administration Building to meet President Lee. Gracia had joined the Church in 1956. She was the first descendant of Joseph Smith, Jr., to go through the temple; and her son Paul was the first Aaronic Priesthood holder in the Prophet's line. We came to President Lee to get permission to perform temple ordinances in behalf of the families of Joseph and Emma Smith. There are restrictions pertaining to performing such work in the lines of a President of the Church. President Lee graciously arranged clearance for the temple work, which was Gracia's lineal right to accomplish.

On Wednesday, 14 June 1972, a little after 4:00 P.M., Gracia knelt at the alter as proxy for the Prophet's wife, Emma Hale;

and my wife and I knelt as proxies for her parents. Willard R. Smith, brother to President Joseph Fielding Smith, performed the sealing ordinance that would unite them in the eternities. It was a special time for Gracia, for my wife and me, and for Emma and her parents. In that sealing room in the Salt Lake Temple, we felt to praise God for this privilege, and we rejoiced that President Lee had made the occasion possible.

In July of 1972, following the passing of President Joseph Fielding Smith, Harold B. Lee became President of the Church. During President Lee's eighteen-month service in this office, I had opportunity to visit with him at least once a month. I was always welcomed warmly and cheerfully. President Lee made me feel that my service had glorious purpose and that my visits were always significant.

On 14 August, my wife and I had a long visit with President Lee before our departure to Nauvoo, for the long-awaited Joseph Smith, Sr., Family Reunion. President Lee enjoyed our being with him. He listened carefully to the details of the 17–18 August gathering. Then, he told us of his profound feelings on becoming the eleventh President of the Church. He noted that he had been a General Authority for many years and had been consistently going to the Tabernacle for conferences and meetings but that last night he had had an unusual experience there. He was to address a youth conference. Outside the Tabernacle, before the conference meeting, everyone seemed eager to touch him. He said that before that time, no one had ever tried to touch him. "I stopped, and pondered why it was that this change had taken place. I thought, I am the same man I've always been." But now, the mantle of the President had fallen on him. As he began his address, he told the young people of his experience and then told them that he did not mind their revering the office he held or the mantle he wore, but that they should always remember that he, President Lee, was not the head of this Church. The head of the Church was Jesus Christ. "I simply preside over his Church at the present time," he had said.

President Lee told us that at President Smith's passing he had felt heavily his responsibility for the members of the Church, and he wondered how he could meet it. That night when he and his wife knelt to pray, he saw in vision the millions of members of the Church, and he felt in his heart an overwhelming love for each one of them. He felt this was a sign and a direction to him.

As my wife and I said farewell to him, he told me again that I was the right person to work with the Smith family. I told him that I had hoped he might attend the reunion, but he declined, saying it would be better to keep the reunion a family matter. He told us the presiding quorums of the church would be praying for the success of our project.

After the reunion was over, I submitted a written report to President Lee. I felt the reunion had been a most successful and historic meeting. Between 250 and 300 descendants of Lucy Mack and Joseph Smith, Sr., were in attendance, including two grandchildren of Patriarch Hyrum Smith, two grandchildren of the Prophet Joseph Smith, and four grandchildren of the restored gospel's first missionary, Samuel Harrison Smith. These three brothers had given their lives for the gospel in 1844.

In my report to President Lee, I told him I had given his best wishes to W. Wallace Smith, president of the Reorganized Church of Jesus Christ of Latter Day Saints. I had told him, "President Lee sends his warmest personal regards." President Wallace Smith replied, "I'm sure that President Lee is sincere in his wish." As I was conducting the last session of the reunion, during the singing of the closing song, "God Be with You Till We Meet Again," I distinctly heard a voice in my mind say, "Joseph is here." At first this startled me. Then I thought, "Of course, where else would he be?"

At the close of the reunion, a presiding patriarch of the Reorganized Church, Lynn E. Smith, suggested to the assembled family that since his great-grandparents, Joseph and Emma Smith, had adopted twins, the family should adopt my wife and me. Everyone wholeheartedly agreed. From that time, we have officially belonged to the family of Joseph Smith, Sr., and I have served as the chief officer of the family organization.

The reunion concluded with the family's voting to meet again the following August, and biennially every other August thereafter. The joy of being together made everyone feel wonderful. All of us laughed, wept, sang, ate, and prayed together. Because so many miraculous events had led up to bringing the divided family together, I told President Lee that the reunion was indeed the work of God. President Lee replied that he was sure that the Prophet Joseph Smith had gone to the Savior in behalf of his family and that the Savior had sanctioned and assisted our efforts.

On 23 January 1973, I had another visit with President Lee. After some conversation, President Lee took a letter from his top desk drawer. He said, "I received this letter not long ago. I'm sure it will be of interest to you." The letter was from President W. Wallace Smith of the Reorganized Church of Jesus Christ of Latter Day Saints. The first part of the letter contained a thank you for President Lee's personalized Christmas card and expressed warm season's greetings to President Lee. It concluded with an invitation to President Lee to meet him in the future to discuss the development of RLDS-owned historical properties in light of LDS interest in the same properties.

When President Lee finished reading the letter, he put it down and looked up at me. "You know, Buddy," he said, "it is a marvelous thing that we are beginning to enjoy this kind of communication. This is a breakthrough. The Prophet Joseph himself, from the spirit world, is at work on his family." President Lee stated that the family reunion had made this possible. Sitting back in his chair, he mused aloud, "You know, I wonder what would happen if I took my wife and traveled to Independence. Who knows what might be accomplished during such a meeting?"

As I left his office, I told President Lee that the next Joseph Smith, Sr., Family Reunion was scheduled for Independence, Missouri, in August of 1973. President Lee again said how pleased he was for the good public relations that were now developing between the two churches. He added his blessing to my efforts. In time, he said, the whole Smith family will come to realize the intent and purpose of genealogical work. I was admonished to keep a record of the Smith family activities so that in time they might have insight as to the way the Lord had brought them together and the eternal purposes of that development. As I left his office, he said, "Drop in and see me anytime, Brother Youngreen."

It was perhaps a kind of culmination of all these events that I and my family were invited to family home evening with President Lee and his family on 21 May. That evening, we spent an unforgettable few hours with the living prophet. President Lee said to me during the course of our conversation, "The best thing about you, Buddy, is that you are a no-Buddy (nobody)." Sensing that my self-esteem perhaps might suffer from this, President Lee explained that my leadership of the Smith reunions was a precarious position. Should I make mistakes, they would simply be my mistakes. But were he or President Smith to make mistakes, these mistakes would reflect on their offices in the organizations they represented. "You are the man to do it, Buddy. Think what our chances in our official positions would be. Continue as you are doing, and rely upon your feelings from the Lord. It is wonderful that you are not a member of the Smith family. It would have been impossible for a family member to accomplish what you, an outsider, have done." Then he turned to my wife, "Buddy is what his name implies—a buddy. He belongs to both families, and that is important!"

The second Joseph Smith, Sr., Family Reunion was held 16–18 August 1973, in Independence, Missouri. After the reunion, I reported to President Lee, commenting on the power of the Spirit, which had accompanied and surrounded the project, and I thanked him once again for his support and encouragement.

It was Tuesday, 2 August 1973, just after the second Smith family reunion, when I and three descendants of Joseph and Emma Smith came to President Lee's office for a visit. Those descendants were Gracia Denning, my Church friend; her mother, Lorena Normandeau; and her mother's sister, Elizabeth Hahn. Lorena and Elizabeth were not yet members of the Church. President Lee welcomed them graciously. He was most kind. As we were leaving, Gracia's Aunt Elizabeth told President Lee, "This is the best time I have ever had in my whole life." There was a powerful spirit present. President Lee gently took Joseph Smith's great-granddaughter's hand and looked deep into her eyes, "In other words," he said, "as Agrippa said to Paul, 'Almost thou persuadest me'?" (See Acts 26:28.) In time, it was as the prophet of God replied, for Lorena Normandeau joined the Church in 1979, and Elizabeth Hahn in 1986.

On 18 October 1973, my wife and I accompanied another descendant of Joseph Smith to meet President Lee. Her name was Donna Lee Smith, and she had just joined the Church. Her grandfather, Israel A. Smith, had been president of the Reorganized Church from 1946 until his death in 1958. He had been followed in that office by his brother, W. Wallace Smith. President Lee commended Donna for joining the Church. He told her, "Our cousins of the Reorganized Church do not have to give up any truths. We simply offer them the fulness of the gospel of Jesus Christ." President Lee continued, "We are hopeful of cultivating a friendliness, which in part is being accomplished by the family reunions." He expressed a hope that the old barriers might be broken down and through "tact, persuasion, much prayer and fasting, we may achieve great results as we look towards the future." President Lee told Donna that there was "great rejoicing in the realms where the Prophet Joseph is, to know that members of his direct descendants are now coming into the Church."

On 30 Novemeber 1973, I introduced Michael A. Kennedy to President Lee. Michael was a third great-grandson of the Prophet Joseph Smith. He had joined the Church the preceding April. When I ordained him an elder in 1974, he became the first descendant of Joseph and Emma Smith to hold the Melchizedek Priesthood. His ordination fulfilled a prophecy made in 1886 by President George Q. Cannon, First Counselor to President John Taylor, "Just as sure as God lives, just as sure as God has made promises, so sure will some one of Joseph Smith's posterity rise up and be numbered with this Church, and bear the everlasting Priesthood that Joseph himself held" (*Journal of Discourses,* 25:367).

The last time I saw President Lee, he was with his wife, Joan, in the Church Administration Building. It was 4 December 1973. He said, "Hello, Buddy, do you need to see me?"

I replied, "No, President. I really only need to see your secretary, Brother Haycock." I knew that Brother Haycock would report to President Lee any matters that the President needed to know.

President Lee changed my life. He gave positive direction to my desire to be a friend to the family of the Prophet Joseph Smith. He took time to get to know me and my family. He cared about what I was trying to accomplish. He shared my vision of a united Smith family and used his influence to help bring it about. Each time I visited with him, I was strengthened. Each time he counseled me, I was edified. Each time I left his office, I was filled with a desire to do more.

Following our last meeting, I received a Christmas card from him. It quoted the divine promise found in John 14:27: "Peace I leave with you, my peace I give unto you: not as the world giveth, give I unto you. Let not your heart be troubled, neither let it be afraid." This promise sustained me the day after Christmas when I heard of President Lee's death. It gave me peace during his funeral. It comforts me today, many years later, when I recall my precious association with him and how it has changed my life.

President Harold B. Lee, like the Prophet Joseph Smith, and like our Savior Jesus Christ, is still alive today. Even yet, I feel his influence reaching out to me from the spirit world as he continues to make a difference in my life.

46

Elaine A. Cannon
Former Young Women General President

He Taught Us
the Vision of
Eternal Families

At many crossroads of my life, a dear friend and prophet has
stood nearby to provide his steadying guidance. He was
President Harold B. Lee.

My heart fills to overflowing as I think of his gracious, kind,
and patient interest in us, and for his prophetic indication of my
major calling. He shared his wisdom with us during several
years of preparation for correlation in the Church. We also had
the constant blessing of living in his home ward. Every Sunday
we took renewed hope and inspiration from just looking at him,
shaking his hand, and feeling his powerful spirit.

I hold precious in my diary innumerable stories and memorable anecdotes which flowed as he took time to teach me
through his own experiences.

Back in the 1960s I had a conversation with President Lee
that indicated again how much the Lord worked through him to
benefit the membership of the Church. The period of rebellion
on university campuses was demanding on LDS students. President Lee already had preached that since it was impossible for

every LDS student to attend a Church college or university, an enhancement of the university experience should be provided for those on other campuses. Under these conditions the Latter-day Saint Student Association was formed. I was called to represent the women on that governing committee at Church headquarters.

One day as I was talking with President Lee about my specific assignment to establish a collegiate organization after the pattern of the national fraternal system on university campuses, I said to him: "I am amazed that this assignment has been made. I was a member of a national sorority during my university days, and, while it had been a choice experience for me, I wasn't sure that a true Greek-letter society was in line with the thinking of the General Authorities."

President Lee was firm in his answer: "The Brethren are serious about this call, Elaine."

I replied, "All right, but I just wanted to be certain I understand. I have been called to write initiation ceremony, charters, creeds, and constitutions; and to design coat-of-arms and purposes for a sorority like those of the Pan-Hellenic system, only with a Church slant?"

He immediately expressed his concurrence and encouragement. President Lee was a practical, family-oriented man. What was good for his beloved family was good for the whole Church. He explained further: "Whatever it takes to provide an alternative to what the world offers, we want for our youth. Elaine, I have a grandson starting at the university soon. He has several brothers and a sister coming along. I want this boy to have a well-rounded college experience, but I want him to be an example. If fraternity life is an option he wants, then he should be able to have that kind of experience, with Church guidance."

From that conversation we moved forward under the immediate leadership of Elder Paul H. Dunn. We gathered our committees to establish the LDS Student Association with the unique groups of Sigma Gamma Chi, an LDS fraternity for college-aged men, and Lambda Delta Sigma, a sorority for college-aged women. Interestingly, some years later President Lee's eldest grandson became a national officer of the governing body of Sigma Gamma Chi.

Another unforgettable sharing moment occurred in the parking lot of the Federal Heights Ward soon after President Lee had returned from the area conference in Munich, Germany, in August 1973. A record-breaking number of Saints from many nations had attended the conference. On such a grand scale, it had been costly and complicated to arrange for translation of the proceedings into several languages. Although the translation situation was difficult, the Spirit of the Lord had prevailed.

"I worried to some extent about being translated correctly," said Elder Lee.

"Like Enoch?" I laughed.

President Lee chuckled, too, and then said: "Not exactly, but in good humor I told the European Saints that if they wanted to understand me and the gospel they were going to have to learn to speak English first. There was a lot of laughter at that statement. But you know, Elaine, I have been startled at the response to my little joke."

"What happened?" I asked.

"Why, they took me literally! By the time I returned home there was a message waiting for me. Disregarding cost and inconvenience there has been a mass registration for English classes and tutoring."

"How amazing!" I observed.

"Yes, isn't it? But I have learned a lesson," President Lee explained.

"*You* have learned a lesson?" I marveled. "What lesson did you learn?"

"I learned," said President Lee, "that the President of this Church has to be careful what he tells the people to do, because they're likely to do it."

Time showed that this counsel given in some jest became a blessing to the scattered Saints from many nations. Many have learned English and have increased their capacity for service because of it. Being obedient to inspired direction from the prophet brings many blessings—even when that direction is given in good humor.

Closest to my heart, however, is this choice remembrance. Through the generations it seems that everything changes, but nothing of real value changes. President Lee helped our family

understand this through the part he played in the marriage ceremonies of our daughter and me, thirty years apart.

One person can help change and bless many lives. It
requires that person to be a remarkable individual committed to
the Lord's work of bringing to pass the immortality and eternal
life of man. In addition to this commitment, such a person must
be responsive to the particular situation at a given time, and
alert to unique individual needs. With such qualities a person
can then be effective in helping others. Harold B. Lee was such a
person for us, and he helped us catch the vision of eternal families.

My earliest memory of him was when I was introduced to
"Brother Lee" in my parents' home on Capitol Hill in Salt Lake
City, Utah. At the time I was serving the members of a study
group my parents were entertaining. Brother Lee was a guest
with a presentation to make. I recall still his dark hair—a thick,
wiry pompadour—that crowned his kind face. He had a gentle
manner and did not joke or tease me as adults often do with
their friends' children. He treated me with gentle respect. This
was so pleasant for me. I felt grown up and of worth in his presence.

When the mantle of apostleship fell on his shoulders some
years later, I was warmed at the enhancement that came to this
good friend of my father's and noted how responsive he was to
the gifts of the Spirit. I had not watched this metamorphosis
before. I'd known Apostles in our Salt Lake Stake, but to see the
"before and after," if you will, was a lesson in God's power and
in the light that fills a strong, principled man who lives God's
will and does his service.

It was 1943 before I was again conscious of Harold B. Lee.
World War II was upon us. It stepped up the pace of growing up
and heightened our sense of vulnerability.

My friends and I were earnest and somewhat threatened, full
of ideals but lacking hope for fulfillment. We spoke of hydrogen
bombs and of the world coming to an end. We watched the
departing missionaries turn into a parade of servicemen, leaving
us dateless. As young women we used to comfort each other

about never marrying, never having children—our dreams dashed by a moustached man in a faraway country, who seemed to us to be in league with the adversary.

In 1943 I was a senior at the University of Utah, president of both Chi Omega sorority and the University of Utah Associated Women Students. I would graduate in June, and I had just accepted a position as society and woman's editor of the *Deseret News*, to begin on 29 March 1943. I was busy!

Most important, I was engaged to Jim Cannon. Jim had graduated from the University of Utah and had filled a mission in Hawaii for the Church. When he returned home he went into military service and at that late date in the war was facing immediate overseas duty. But there was one hitch—he didn't have a proper uniform! He was 6'6" and too tall for the standard G.I. (government-issue) soldier's uniform. Special orders took weeks to be filled, so meanwhile he was given temporary duty at the induction center in Salt Lake City, just a breath from his home. We felt that we might not have a future, but we had now! Financed by Jim's $100-per-month private's pay and the $375 per month I would make as an editor, we knew that heaven was with us for whatever there was left of life. Such was the doomsday attitude of our age group, and we decided to grab what time we had and be married.

We selected 25 March, between quarters at the end of test week. Jim was able to obtain a three-day pass, and I didn't start work and my final classes until the next Monday. Life may be fleeting, we said, but we would taste of love in spite of the war.

Jim's father was Elder Sylvester Q. Cannon of the Council of the Twelve Apostles, and we had asked him to perform our ceremony in the Salt Lake Temple. When the time came, we were greatly disappointed that he was too ill to be a part of our marriage. Instead, his new colleague, Elder Harold B. Lee of the Council of the Twelve, was invited to perform the ceremony.

Of course, this was the first temple wedding I had seen and I didn't know what to expect. It made an impact upon my life— not just the fact of being married, but what was taught me on that occasion.

In the years since, I have attended thousands of weddings. My position as society editor and other opportunities in the community have meant that I have been to weddings in cathedrals, synagogues, country clubs, and Protestant churches. I've been to grand Greek Orthodox ceremonies, and to simple weddings in private homes, in gardens, in the top of the mountains, and at beaches. And I have been back to the temples countless times for the weddings of friends and loved ones. In every case there was a beautiful bride, breathless and wondering. There was a nervous, excited groom. There were loving, tender parents. There was a sincere officiator of ceremonies. There were promises made. God was mentioned.

But what takes place in the House of the Lord makes all the difference. The Spirit of God is present. People are spiritually prepared. It is the incredible bonus to the joy in any wedding.

But for us, there was more. When President Lee performed the ceremony for me, and then for our youngest daughter thirty years later, he provided a gift of priceless value to our family. These special blessings came because of his style, his emphasis, and his prophetic vision.

On my wedding day, Elder Lee isolated Jim and me from our loved ones waiting in the sealing room. He talked with just the two of us in the celestial room for some time, teaching us sacred truths. He commanded us, if you will, to live our lives in accordance with the holy purposes for which we came to earth. He was specific. He was personal.

We who were clean living but caught up in the worries of war years, in the frantic scramble to grab what we could of life, were being cautioned to live life deliberately and purposefully, with choices based upon long-range views; to live patiently and wait for the Lord's timetable to unfold. We were counseled to prepare and to be prayerful, to live not by carnal influences but by the Spirit.

The eternities were opened unto us. There was a reason why we stood in holy places and why we would kneel at sacred altars. Elder Lee told us we were different. We had a work to do and must be ready for it—let the world seek, feel, choose, and live as it would, notwithstanding. We had "miles to go before we'd sleep; we had promises to keep.'' This is but a part of what he said to us under these remarkable and unusual circumstances.

It was wonderful! Slowly now we were realizing really why it was that we were marrying. It was something far more than to satisfy legal boundaries for the expression of quick love before inevitable separation.

After the talk Elder Lee led us up the steps into the sealing room, and before our loved family and friends he united us in the new and everlasting covenant of marriage, for time and for all eternity.

What, then, was war?

For many years afterwards we sent flowers to President Lee on *our* wedding anniversary with a note and a report of our progress, since he had asked us to keep in contact with him. He felt a part of our union, and always has.

Then, thirty years and six children later, we asked President Lee to perform the temple ceremony for our youngest daughter. Again, with Harold B. Lee in charge, the experience was unusual.

As I greeted him at the temple he said to me these tender words: "These days I don't have time to perform many wedding ceremonies and certainly not dressed as I am in my white temple suit, but I wanted to show you that you are family to me."

It is customary for the officiator to give a few remarks about marriage in counsel to the bride and groom before the sealing ceremony is performed. That had been the case in every temple wedding ceremony I had attended over the years, except our own. Now, in the case of our daughter, it was different again.

President Lee came into the room and stood at the head of the altar, inviting the couple to take their places at the altar at once! He then performed the sealing ceremony. They were then asked to return to their seats as man and wife. The couple was married, he said; now they could relax and keep their minds on his important message.

He spoke reverently, with a magnificent outpouring of the Spirit; he spoke about covenants and never-ending life and love. He spoke of the particular portion of service in the kingdom of

God on earth that was assigned to these two choice people, as directed by the Holy Spirit. And so it has come to pass.

We've talked many times over the years as a family about these high-water mark memories. It wasn't just that Harold B. Lee was an agent of God in the good work of blessing individuals. He was conscious of individual needs and satisfied those particular yearnings. His teachings were specific for the unique and choice people involved and the certain situations which existed. Harold B. Lee taught us as the Holy Spirit moved him.

Modified as our lives are by war, by circumstances, by age, and by personal gifts, this one man helped us to understand that God's plan spans the generations—His promises and purposes are forever.

47

George W. Cornell
Associated Press Religion Specialist

Remembering a Brother

He always came bearing little dolls. They were beautiful things in costumes or native dress of various cultures and periods. Every time Harold B. Lee visited New York City in those days, he brought with him one of those lovely little dolls of shimmering apparel and sunny eyes.

It was an oddly sentimental counterpoint to his trips from Salt Lake City to New York, formally for purposes of business and church matters. He was on the board of directors of the Union Pacific Railroad and the Equitable Life Assurance Society of New York, and each board held monthly meetings in New York City. But somewhere in those satchels of official papers, he seemed always also to have included one of those little creatures of childhood magic, the vividly lifelike, dainty "dollies."

He would extract them proudly, saying, "This is something for our wonderful little girl." Or, when feasible, he would present the doll directly to her, my daughter, Marion Emma. I recall in one case he gave her a frisky, little Dutch doll in bonnet and wooden shoes, carrying a wooden pail. Emmy proceeded to pepper him with questions about it, and he, attentively matching her serious interest, described details of Dutch dress and customs. It was a tender scene I won't forget—the Apostle and little girl off in a world of their own.

She was about six then, and their affair had gone on ever since she was baptized as an infant in the Episcopal Church. Brother Lee, as we called him, had by then become a close personal friend of my family, and I had the audacity to ask him to serve as Emmy's godfather. That's a rather serious responsibility in the Episcopal Church, imposing the obligation of sharing in the spiritual nurture of the child. Furthermore, if something should happen to the parents, the godparent inherited the duty of seeing to the child's upbringing in the faith.

I telephoned Brother Lee about it, outlining the significance of it, and asked him if he'd be willing to take on that role. There was a pause, and then he said, "Yes, George. I'd be honored to do it."

"That's great," I said. "I really appreciate that." Then, rather impulsively, I added, "That means, you know, that if I die, you have to raise her as an Episcopalian. Is that okay with you?"

This was sensitive ground, I knew, considering Brother Lee's high office in The Church of Jesus Christ of Latter-day Saints, his total commitment to it, and its supplemental concepts distinguishing it from those of the Episcopal Church. Nevertheless, wanting us to be entirely clear on our pact of such seriousness, I had pressed that brash question—was it okay under those circumstances?

He answered, "Yes, I understand."

Thus was sealed that unusual, private ecumenical tie between us. I generally kept it private, assuming that Brother Lee had dared a somewhat unconventional undertaking. In view of the Mormon belief that only their church holds the full, renewed truth, some of his colleagues might have found it objectionable that he had pledged, if need be, to bring up his goddaughter in the Episcopal heritage.

At the time, he had been one of his church's Council of the Twelve Apostles and in charge of that church's immense welfare operations, as well as other activities. In those upper echelons of ecclesiastical politics, whatever the denomination, divergencies from official policy, even if only on an intimate, personal matter, can have repercussions. Consequently, my assumption was that Brother Lee had taken something of a risky step in his greathearted commitment to my family and our daughter.

Perhaps he knew something few of us do, that giving a hand to others is the first principle of practicing Christianity, regardless of organizational technicalities. In any case, as I saw it, Brother Lee had put his status on the line in behalf of a friend.

Our relationship had a dual quality to it. As the religion specialist for the Associated Press, I have schooled myself in maintaining an objective, impartial attitude toward religious sources of any stripe; and that, on a professional level, was the nature of my working relationship with Brother Lee. Interviews with him never dodged the hard questions. But apart from that, in a separate, personal category, was our genuine, individual caring for each other.

In that dimension, we could sound off as we pleased, arguing sometimes about religious matters as I love to do; he in his careful, thoughtful way pointing out the qualifying realities; both of us, I think, enjoying it, knowing without it ever having to be said, that this was confidential talk. He spent a couple of evenings at our Manhattan apartment, once bringing with him a fellow Council member, Spencer W. Kimball. Also, I and occasionally my wife, Jo Ann, had dinner with him at the Church's Eastern States Mission Home, or at Manhattan restaurants, usually with a few other Church personnel present.

Those Mormon dinners out were a healthy break in my routine: no coffee or other stimulants, no smoking, and those marvelous chocolates at the end, with those tall, cool glasses of water. But it was on those evenings at our Stuyvesant Town apartment where we would really "let down our hair." It was mainly Jo Ann who would needle Brother Lee about the Church's ban at the time on blacks holding the priesthood. He would delve into the problem, the in-built Church obstacles, but then he would say it was going to change when God willed it. He always attached that qualification, but nevertheless, he said repeatedly that the barrier would be removed. It awaited God's signal, he said, but at the same time he knew it was coming.

When he became President of the Church, I kept expecting, on the basis of those private conversations, that one day the conviction in his heart about the matter would materialize in a "revelation" to the Church. I remain convinced that it would have happened under his presidency if his time in office had not been cut so short by his death. Of course, the change did come not long afterward in the presidency of Spencer W. Kimball.

Besides their comembership on the highest councils of the Church, Lee and Kimball were quite personally fond of each other and mutually appreciated each other's companionship, something that was quite obvious that evening when they both were in our home. They were as interested in each other's ideas as in ours. God gets his message across through various channels and on various levels in ways beyond our reckoning, and I've often wondered if Jo Ann's persistent twitting of Brother Lee about the racial issue somehow had something to do with the ultimate word working its way through him via Kimball. In any case, those personal times with Brother Lee, mostly apart from any such substantial matters, are sweet memories to me.

Once, too, he visited me while I was in the hospital for a stomach ailment, bringing me some books to read, not all about Mormons either. One of them was a Zane Grey novel. He knew I loved the Old West. And he thoughtfully didn't linger in long conversation, something patients don't need. But his taking the trouble to come gave me a lift.

Did he ever, as Mormons are supposed to do, try to convert me? Never overtly, or directly, but in roundabout ways, such as his stories about other people who had made the switch; and once, having a demonstration of those felt-board talks put on for me, I could tell he would have liked for me to do so. Sometimes, even though he never directly suggested it, I nevertheless would kid him about his circuitous intentions. He would neither deny it nor admit it, just smile, and go on to something else.

But on that score of switching, I wasn't a good prospect. I've knocked about in all kinds of religious circles and have a deep respect, appreciation, and even a sense of identification with many of them, including Mormons; but I also find the particular church niche I'm in quite sufficient, however poorly I absorb its enlivening fare.

Essentially in our friendship, however, Brother Lee wasn't out to bring me into his fold. As I say, the idea was never even broached directly. We liked each other as we were. He gave me lots of good advice, often about family matters on which he was a specialist in home Christian education, supplying me with materials on how to do it. I've regretted I didn't use all of the techniques more conscientiously, but in any case, I've always been grateful for his efforts and his influence.

After his death, his widow and Jo Ann held many a long, evening telephone conversation about him, and occasionally Mrs. Lee and I talked, too. Mainly, however, those long, mutually comforting conversations were between the two women about a man who was gone from our environment. Doubtless to them, however, and certainly to me, the stamp of Brother Lee was not gone from our lives. He left a strong and lasting imprint and spread big chunks of love in those little dolls he toted to brighten the world of a child.

48

Leo D. Jensen
Temple Worker

He Treated Me as the Savior Would Have

In January 1934, my parents moved into a Mormon community, a type of neighborhood I hadn't experienced before, where everyone was a member of The Church of Jesus Christ of Latter-day Saints. I made friends with the boys my age very easily, but they were always trying to get me to go to their church. I was dead set against that and made up my mind that there was no way they were ever going to get me to go with them to church. As a result, I was alone practically all day on Sundays and again on Tuesday evenings while they all went to their Mutual Improvement Association and Scouting meetings.

This situation continued all through spring and summer, until school started again in the fall. I walked to South High School in Salt Lake City with older fellows because I was a couple of years ahead of those my age, having skipped two grades by special promotion. These new older friends were more persuasive than the younger fellows had been, and after a month, I yielded and said that I would go to their YMMIA meeting that night. I had a wonderful time playing the games and participating in the activities of the evening.

After Mutual was over, we walked to the front of the church building. We were having fun and just talking when one of my friends said, "Let's go swipe some apples." "Oh, boy," I thought. I was all for that. After all, I had swiped apples many more times than I had ever been to church.

We walked some distance down Eighth West Street before the others ducked into a yard. I followed them to the back of a house where we found a huge apple tree. En route we had seen the family having their dinner through the big window in the back of the house. The others began picking apples, but I climbed right to the top where the big, juicy apples were hanging.

It wasn't long before the owner of the tree came outside and made his way directly to the big tree not far from the Jordan River. I thought that I was so high up the tree he wouldn't see me. I heard him say rather loudly to my friends, "I don't mind you taking an apple to eat. You don't have to steal them, but why have you taken so many? You have three or four in each pocket. You can't possibly eat them all, and you'll just waste them."

Then, he looked up toward the top of the tree and said, "Come on down. I know you're up there."

I climbed down and jumped to the ground. He took one look at me, and his eyes went as big as saucers. He exclaimed, "Just look at this fellow!" His amazement was justified because I had tied the pant legs of my bib overalls to my ankles and had filled both pant legs with the apples. Then those dark eyes stared directly at me, "Now, what are you going to do with all those apples?"

"I will take them home, I guess."

"What are you going to tell your mother when she asks you where you got them?"

"I will tell her someone gave them to me."

He looked me piercingly in the eyes again and said, "Well, just so you won't have to lie to your mother, you may have them. I give you my permission to take them home."

I couldn't believe that a man could be so nice and forgiving as he was. As we were going back to the street, I asked my friends, "What's the matter with that man? He didn't kick our pants or box our ears or anything like that. Who is he?"

One of the fellows answered, "He is our stake president." Well, at that point in my life I didn't know a stake president from a deacon, so I asked another question, "What's his name?"

They answered, "Harold B. Lee."

That is how I met a man I'll never forget. Although this experience happened many years ago, I am still trying to be like him. I'm not always successful, but I think I'm doing better every year.

President Lee later became the prophet and President of the Church. He taught us that we shouldn't do anything that we don't think the Savior would do if he were here among us. As I have thought about this memorable experience, I think that if the Savior had owned that apple tree he probably would have said the same words to us boys that President Lee said. He knew it was more important to teach boys not to lie to their mothers than to have them give the apples back to him.

Not many months after this experience, I joined the Church. My service as an adult in the Church has included work in the stake mission presidency and the ward bishopric and as an ordinance worker in the Jordan River Temple.

I have always treasured this providential meeting with President Lee. The experience illustrates to me how President Lee treated some mischievous boys with the same love that the Savior would have given to us under like conditions. If all of us would treat others the same way as the Savior would, then we would always be living his commandments.

49

Paul H. Dunn
Member of the First Quorum of the Seventy

Choice Memories
of a Prophet

My personal acquaintance with President Harold B. Lee
began in 1953 when he attended a special meeting of our
seminary students in Southern California. As a coordinator of
seminary work, I sat on the stand with him and Elder Henry D.
Moyle. That was as close as I had ever been to him physically,
and he impressed me as a compassionate person who was sensitive to his audience and who didn't seem so hurried or harassed
that he couldn't take a minute to sincerely greet and visit with a
new friend. So often, leaders seem to hustle their associates here
and there because of administrative chores that must be taken
care of prior to a meeting. It is rare for a person to take the time
to study your soul and spirit for a moment, as President Lee did
with me on that occasion.

Always, but particularly since 1964 when I was called as a
General Authority of the Church, I have felt great awe, respect,
and love for all the Brethren. But somehow my feelings for President Harold B. Lee have been very special. Looking back, I

realize that my respect and reverence for him and the delight of being in his company were a reflection of an earlier time, the 1950s, when I was a seminary coordinator and later an institute director in southern California. During those years, all full-time Church education teachers were invited to five-week special summer training sessions at Brigham Young University, and President Lee was the teacher for the course. Along with several hundred others, I was a student under his direction every day during the class periods. It was at this time that I began to appreciate the depth of his spirit, the understanding he had of the gospel, and his sensitive feelings for people.

In 1965, after having been in Salt Lake City a year as a new General Authority and having had the personal thrill of associating closely in a spiritual environment with men for whom I had such admiration, I was given my first assignment to travel with Elder Lee. We were to tour the missions of the South Pacific and, in conjunction with that work, to attend a number of stake conferences in the area. I thought it quite a contrast, a new, inexperienced General Authority paired with a wise, seasoned senior Apostle of the Lord, both going together on this lengthy trip, and I felt it would be a great learning experience for me.

Our first stop was Honolulu, where we had a stake conference, a chapel dedication, and other administrative business. While there our course of events gave me a rare and choice opportunity to gain great insight into Elder Lee's true character and personality. Previously, while flying to the island, he had said to me, "I hope we get to Honolulu on schedule, because Sister Moody, the wife of one of the stake presidents there, is very ill and not expected to live, and I would like to call on her before anything serious occurs." Well, our plane was two hours late, and when we arrived we learned that Sister Moody had passed away. This was a great shock to President Lee, and he was noticeably disturbed that he had arrived too late to see her. It was then I learned that he and his first wife, Fern, had been close personal friends with the Moodys for years. Now President Lee made the necessary inquiries and paid his respects to President Moody, who asked him if he would speak at Sister Moody's funeral. President Lee, of course, consented to do so.

Two nights later I assisted him at a chapel dedication. During the proceedings another close friend, Patriarch Arthur Kapewaokeae Parker, Sr., was called upon to speak. Patriarch Parker was Hawaiian, the only full-blooded native Hawaiian in the Church at that time who had been called as a patriarch. He had been ordained by President Lee some years earlier, was an extremely spiritual leader, and possessed a tremendous spirit and a stature like that of pioneer stock. As he was bearing his testimony, with arm upraised, he suddenly fell backward behind the pulpit right at our feet, having died from a heart attack. Imagine the shock and the impact on President Lee, as well as on the rest of us!

I'll never forget the lesson Elder Lee taught me on that occasion and how he handled sudden emotional pressure. Certainly as disturbed as anyone in the vast audience, he very calmly leaned over, took me by the arm, and said, "Now, don't move, Paul, because the people will follow our example. If we show panic and emotion the audience will do the same."

Then, after the situation had been handled in an orderly way and the patriarch's body had been removed, President Lee wisely and cooly and with great spirituality and respect proceeded with the meeting, and we performed that which we had come to do. Of course, the emotional impact of the evening's experience on him was even greater because of Sister Moody's death two days earlier.

The next day was Sister Moody's funeral, a very delicate assignment for President Lee, partly because of the two couples' close friendship and partly, I am sure, because of the remembrance of his own wife's passing. During the short time we had been on the island and since he had accepted the responsibility of speaking at the funeral, he had commented to me several times about his concerns, saying, "I just hope I can do what I know I should do at the service because of what I have learned from my own suffering."

I have attended many, many funerals in my life, but I have never heard given any comfort, spiritual counsel, direction, or especially impact—real personal impact—that has equaled the message delivered by President Lee that day. Of course, as he so faithfully did whenever he talked, he taught. That was one of the marks of his genius. Whether giving a blessing or counseling or talking as a father, he was always teaching the gospel. This day he focused his remarks on President Moody and the family and gave powerful counsel—delicate, intimate, and personal. As I look back on this experience years later, I realize that the words he said that day, he himself would have to follow the very next day.

I was awakened in my hotel room the following morning by a telephone call from President Lee in an adjoining room. He informed me that his daughter Maurine was seriously ill in a Provo Hospital with complications resulting from pregnancy. Rushing quickly to his room, I received instruction to get him the first reservation possible for a flight home and that he would be terminating his part of our lengthy tour. In the few moments it took me to fulfill the assignment and return to his room with the confirmation of his flight, he had received word that Maurine had passed away.

In sharing this traumatic experience of the sudden loss of a daughter, I saw the tender, fatherly side of President Harold B. Lee. We knelt in prayer, and while it was one of the most heart-rending experiences I have ever had, it was also one of my most spiritual blessings. I learned how a man, greatly pressured already with his apostolic calling, reacts in tragedy—how he, destined to be the prophet, meets crisis. Certainly no one escapes heartache, even prophets, and surely the Lord permitted this great loss to come to him. President Lee was struck down by it, as any father would be in the loss of a cherished daughter. But I witnessed that even in that terrible moment, the adversary still didn't have control. It was one of the greatest lessons of my life to be there and learn from the wrenching experience he was going through.

At another time and another place, I had a reaffirmation of a fact I already knew, that President Lee had a deep compassion for people, was very sensitive to them, and had a rare genius for identifying with them. On the occasion in question, which happened to be a General Authority social function, one of the ladies present slipped on the waxed floor and fell. She went down hard! Almost before anyone else in the group could begin to react, President Lee, witnessing the accident, was by her side giving comfort and assistance of every kind possible. It was an act that so typified him in his great concern for people, and I have seen him react unhesitatingly in the same way in a number of other situations because of that concern. He didn't have to think about it; he just did it. His natural reflex was to move instinctively to assist someone in need.

Among the many strengths of President Lee was his unwavering, uncompromising approach to what the Lord has taught and commanded. He believed the Lord's counsel sincerely. It was so refreshing to see him frequently reaffirm that the Lord simply meant what he said. Nephi had reminded his brothers that "the Lord giveth no commandments unto the children of men, save he shall prepare a way for them that they may accomplish the thing which he commandeth them" (1 Nephi 3:7). President Lee believed this with all his heart. He had that simple faith and understanding and testimony that asserts, "If the Lord says it, he expects us to do it." So, whether counseling the priesthood or the auxiliaries, the General Authorities or priesthood leaders or the people in the stakes, he took the Lord's commandments at face value.

From my observation as I went around the Church during his presidency, there was a feeling of, "We know where we are going. We are in troubled times, and the world concerns us, but President Harold B. Lee is unwavering. What he says is of the Lord." While we have felt that way with all Presidents of the Church, it seems that this spirit was so apparent under his leadership, so specific. We didn't wonder, "Well, do we or don't we?" There was no hesitation; we knew we must follow. People liked that. The Saints always want to know where they stand, even if they might not like the circumstances.

Consider the situation of the transgressor. There has been a tendency on the part of some of our local ecclesiastical leaders to spank the sinner's hands and say, "Now, don't do that again." That may be a needed and appropriate method to use in some cases, but sometimes, in trying to maintain good relationships, no action is taken at all. One of the things I appreciated so much in President Lee's leadership was his teaching that priesthood leaders need to act. The action taken, of course, is a matter between the Lord and His servant. I believe President Lee gave leaders that assertive feeling, which was refreshing and vital to the times.

During President Lee's administration, the First Council of the Seventy (that group consisting of seven presiding Seventies who functioned together as a presidency prior to the present organization of the First Quorum of the Seventy with its greater number of members) was given the assignment by the First Presidency to study section 107 of the Doctrine and Covenants for a thorough, comprehensive, and more complete understanding of its instruction. Then, as asked, the Council would make recommendations to the First Presidency for the better implementation of the revelation. In section 107 the Lord outlines quite specifically the functioning of the Church quorums, including the Seventies' duties as they relate to the Quorum of the Twelve. Doctrine and Covenant 107:38 outlines, "It is the duty of the traveling high council to call upon the seventy, when they need assistance, to fill the several calls for preaching and administering the gospel, instead of any other."

President Lee brought this scriptural concept into sharp focus. He more ably defined what this revelation in the Doctrine and Covenants teaches. He felt that the priesthood role was to delegate more and more responsibility to Church and family leaders. There is a natural tendency in all organizations to hold power at the top. President Lee had a genius for delegating, and he did that through the Quorum of the Twelve, the First Council of the Seventy, and on through the priesthood line to the individual. His talks to special groups of seventies, to the then-called missionary representatives of the Twelve, and to mission presidents, all showed that he was as much a missionary as any of the leaders before him, but he worked through priesthood channels of the Church to accomplish the task. This is not to say that in traveling through the world he wasn't a good ambassador. He was a great ambassador, but he continually taught how the priesthood, properly used, can bless the people.

One aspect of President Lee's work was his contribution toward the internationalization of the Church. It was very common in the middle 1960s to pick up a lesson manual or a handbook and find that it tended to have a western United States orientation. Any attempt to translate one of the typical lesson manuals into Japanese or other languages and then to teach the lessons to the youth in Osaka or other foreign areas met with frustration. The lessons simply didn't fit. As chairman of the Priesthood Correlation Committee from its inception, President Lee helped develop teaching materials which gave an international flavor and which included all nations and cultures rather than just Utah or the Intermountain West. In his correlation efforts we received an outward expression of what President Lee himself felt and believed and taught for many years. We moved under his direction from a feeling that to be a good Latter-day Saint one had to live in Utah or in the United States; along with President McKay, he broadened the view that we were a worldwide church. I have appreciated President Lee's teachings, as at the Munich Germany Area Conference and elsewhere, where he said such things as, "You do count; you are important; build Zion where you are." That message came across forcefully in his leadership.

One of the many things I respected and admired so much in President Lee was his ability to sift through much conversation and discussion, especially in committee meetings, and get to the very kernel of an issue after everyone else had finished talking. He had the genius for going right to the heart of the matter. He asked the penetrating question at just the right moment. His timing was superb. In a simple statement of inquiry, he could bring all the discussion back into focus. Considering the tremendous amount of material that must be covered in order to direct the work of the Church and the countless man-hours involved to do it all, this ability of discernment, of being so able to separate the wheat from the chaff, was invaluable and so practical. It was a thrill for me to participate in these experiences with him.

After watching President Lee use his leadership power for many years, and after actually being able to work with him on many occasions, and after much personal and ecclesiastical counsel from him in these various settings, I began to feel almost the same kind of kinship and personal relationship with him as with my own father, and I felt that I knew him well. Then, in 1973, the mantle of presidency fell upon him. He became the new prophet of the Church, and I saw a different dimension of the man. I had seen Harold B. Lee, Apostle; Harold B. Lee, the man; Harold B. Lee, the father. I had sat with him in committees and in the temple, had flown on planes with him, and had been counseled by him, yet when the mantle fell upon him, I received a genuine testimony that he was somehow different. He looked the same, his mannerisms were the same, but he now had an air of confidence, a new spirit that gave me the assurance that he was truly a prophet. I believe that that perspective is vital for a General Authority to acquire. As I go out and take greetings from the President of the Church to the people in the stakes and missions, it is important that this is not just a mechanical act; I must receive that witness so that I can in all sincerity bring his message to others. And I *received* that witness. President Lee was not the same Harold B. Lee of earlier years. As he spoke and testified, there was a clear ring in the mind that was easily understood by all. I don't mean to suggest that as an Apostle he didn't have that power to bear witness of the Lord. He did, of course, but it came through with a greater force after he became President of the Church.

To me, one of the finest accomplishments of his presidential labors was his moving out among the people wherever he went. He would go many extra miles to meet with the members. This was particularly important because it followed a period when President David O. McKay had been somewhat restricted and President Joseph Fielding Smith had presided only briefly. It is impossible for the President of the Church to shake hands with every member of the Church, but President Lee moved quickly to close the gap. He went to conferences in England, Mexico, and Germany. Between these tours he attended scores of youth conferences, which had a very positive effect on the young people of the Church. They found it easy to shake hands with him and feel his love and warmth for them. He took time out of a very busy life to go to them. And it was not only what he said *to* them but also what he did *for* them. The youth of the Church are very discerning. Words about what they ought to be are commonplace, but President Lee went to those young people personally. Those in all areas of the Church will never forget their day with the prophet. It caused renewed testimony, devotion, and dedication to enter their lives.

Others will concur with me that President Lee had power to engage in Pentecostal experiences on some occasions. I had such an experience while I was managing director of the Latter-day Saint Student Association of the Church in 1966. We had approval from the First Presidency to hold a series of special temple meetings with returned missionaries. They were special meetings not associated with temple endowments. At one meeting, Elder Lee was our keynote speaker in the Salt Lake Temple. I had the sacred privilege of conducting that meeting. This was surely one of the three or four most spiritual experiences of my life. And the returned missionaries who were in attendance would surely agree with me. Elder Lee literally threw away whatever script he might have prepared and taught us by the Spirit. We got about as close to heaven as one can on earth. I saw Elder Lee in a completely different light as he spoke and bore witness to us that night in the Salt Lake Temple.

It isn't often that one reaches that pinnacle spiritually. I've had some great experiences in my life—great sacrament meetings, great testimony meetings, great mission tours—but this meeting in the temple reached a new plateau. Nobody wanted to move. There was a special spirit there and we knew it. There was no question about it. Doubts were gone. We knew. It was a choice, never-to-be-forgotten experience.

I have had memorable and choice moments with this great man, President Harold B. Lee, privately, with my family, and with others. Each of those moments are and will always be cherished by me; they are invaluable to me as insights into a masterful character, as examples to follow, as depths to ponder, and as reminders of superb learning experiences. I consider that I have been taught by a master teacher in President Lee. And some of my most vivid memories of him are those as he taught. He was always teaching. He might tell a story seemingly to carry on a conversation but actually to teach. I have stood in circles with him as he blessed and ordained, and, while all these occasions were spiritual ones, they were teaching moments as well. In my mind he was always the teacher.

I will ever be grateful for my association with him. I love him; I honor him; I trust him and leave my witness with all who would hear that he truly was and is a man of God, a man of the greatest spiritual stature.

50

James E. Faust
Member of the Quorum of the Twelve

A Call
Never to
Be Forgotten

I became acquainted with President Harold B. Lee when he was a member of the Twelve and was officing at the Church Administration Building in Salt Lake City, with a common reception room with President Henry D. Moyle, also of the Twelve. President Moyle had been our neighbor and stake president in Cottonwood, and I had grown up with his older children.

President Lee ordained me a bishop and seven years later called me to the stake presidency. At the time of my call to the bishopric, he emphasized that from that time forward I was not only to avoid evil but the very appearance of evil. When I was a member of the Utah legislature, I had some contact with President Lee and President Moyle and also had infrequent contacts with President Lee over the years thereafter. He was always very approachable, friendly, kind, and supportive.

I was called to the Church Leadership Committee under the chairmanship of Elder Thomas S. Monson of the Quorum of the

Twelve. President Lee was the chairman of correlation and had overall supervision. Neal Maxwell and I were a team, and Wendell Ashton and Hugh Pinnock were also a team. Brother Maxwell and I had concern for the training of the Regional Representatives, which brought us into frequent contact with President Lee because he was our general overseer. We did considerable planning, programming, and writing, which he ultimately had to approve.

I was serving in this capacity when I was called as an Assistant to the Twelve. Without question, this was the most supernal experience I ever had with President Lee. This was 5 October 1972. The day I was called was on the Friday before general conference, during the Regional Representatives seminar. I had been calling people to the service of the Lord for over twenty years in the bishopric and stake presidency, but I felt that no one was ever called with more kindness, love, consideration, and power than I was. President Lee indicated that he wanted to see me in the bishop's office in the 17th Ward meetinghouse during the break. When he had finished giving the keynote address, he motioned for me to follow him, which I did.

He took me into the bishop's office and stood all the time while he delivered my call. He commended me for my past service, spoke some wonderfully kind words about my wife, Ruth, and then said that I should change my life because the Lord had called me to become an Assistant to the Twelve Apostles and that the Brethren had approved the appointment yesterday. He told me I could tell Ruth and my family. I had experienced some previous whisperings of this call some days before. Without question, this was the most movingly spiritual experience I had had in my life up to that time. As he finished, President Lee embraced me and kissed me. I felt that the expression of President Lee was shrouded with love as he called me to the work.

I was immediately placed as managing director of the Melchizedek Priesthood MIA, which was the introduction of the new singles program into the Church. President Lee was President of the Church for only a short time, but all during that time he treated me with great love and kindness. His door was always open to me, and he was very gracious.

51

Theodore M. Burton
Member of the First Quorum of the Seventy

Two Remarkable
Healings

As a young man, I returned home from Europe where I had
been working for the United States government to attend
the Purdue University in West Lafayette, Indiana. When I ran
out of funds, I had to cease my university studies and accepted a
job teaching chemistry, physics, and mathematics at Carbon
College in Price, Utah. At the end of that school year, 1941–42, I
returned to Purdue University in the hope of completing the
research work leading to a degree of doctor of philosophy in
chemistry. However, in June 1942, I became seriously ill with
appendicitis and was operated on for that condition. The surgeon who did the operation was careless, and as a result, an
infection began that nearly destroyed my life.

It was wartime, and my doctor was inducted in the U.S.
armed forces. Then began a parade of doctors who cared for me
for a week or so at a time, and then each one in turn also was
replaced. The incision ruptured; and as the infection increased,
empyema set in, my diaphragm ruptured, and the infection took
over the whole body cavity. That was in the days before anti-

biotics, and even sulfa drugs were new and in such great demand for the military services that they were forbidden for use by civilians. Operation followed operation as attempts were made to locate the source of infection and drain away the fluid. My wife in Salt Lake City was sent for to come prepared to take my body back home for burial. My brothers came with her and blessed me that I would recover. The mission president also came by and blessed me, but I only lost further weight and became more seriously ill.

During that September, Elder Harold B. Lee was in the Midwest on a mission tour. At the same time, his former counselor in the Pioneer Stake presidency, where I had grown up as a boy, Charles S. Hyde, then serving as our stake patriarch, was in Chicago auditing the mission accounts. Elder Lee said to him, "Charlie, I understand that Theodore T. Burton's son, young Theodore, is down in Indiana fighting for his life. I feel impressed that we should go down and give him a blessing."

Brother Hyde approved of the idea, and they had the mission president drive them to Lafayette, Indiana, a distance of ninety miles, just to give me a blessing.

In the meantime my lung had collapsed. I could scarcely breathe, and I was filled with pain. I had lost weight until I was merely "skin and bones." The doctors had decided upon one final operation to remove more ribs and by entering my chest cavity, to see if they could flush out the infection. They had prepared for the operation, and I had been wheeled out into the hall on a gurney to take me to the operating room. As they did so, we saw those three great men walking down the hall toward us. They stopped, and Brother Lee and Brother Hyde gave my wife, Minnie, a hug, for they had known her many years. They asked the orderly to wheel me back into my room. Since the surgeons were waiting, they had to hurry their actions. The floor nurse, who was a Catholic nun, was with us at that time, too.

Brother Hyde anointed me with consecrated oil. Then those three men placed their hands on my head, and Elder Lee, as mouth, sealed the anointing and gave me a blessing. I don't remember all he said, but one idea stays in my memory. He did not bless me to get well as the others had done. He *commanded* me to get well and said that my work on earth was not yet finished. He *commanded* my spirit to take over the healing process and, through me, blessed the doctors who were about to operate that they would know what to do to restore me to health.

The orderly wheeled me to the operating room for the surgery. Until Elder Lee gave me that blessing, I had not cared whether I lived or died. I was just worn out with all the pain and suffering.

The doctors dared not give me a general anesthetic because I was too far gone to tolerate that. They did give me several local injections, but all that failed to deaden the pain much (I suppose because I already was too full of natural poisons for the medicine to take effect). With an orderly at each arm and a nurse holding each foot and leg, they made the incision. Then, with an instrument that looked like a bolt cutter, they cut away two ribs. I can still hear in my mind the bones crunch as they were cut away. They found and drained away a large quantity of fluid, then wheeled me back to my room where I fainted away.

In the meantime, after the brethren left, the Catholic sister came back to comfort Minnie, but chided her for bringing in the "priests" to give me the last rites so soon. She said, "I believe he can live until tomorrow, perhaps for another day, but now he knows he is going to die and all hope is gone."

Minnie told her that I had not been anointed to die but that I had been anointed to live. She told the sister that one of those men was an Apostle of the Lord, Jesus Christ, and that he had blessed me to live. The sister replied, "My dear, it is well to have faith, but you must face up to reality. He cannot live, and you will only hurt yourself further by keeping up an impossible hope."

Thus it was a miracle for all to see when about six weeks later all those nurses, sisters, hospital attendants, and doctors lined the hall of the hospital to wave me good-bye as I was wheeled down the corridor to a waiting ambulance to take me to the train and home. Elder Lee's prophecy had come true. My work was not yet finished, but I had no idea at that time of what my work was to be.

Elder Lee had a rare gift of hearing the voice of the Lord and blessing those who were ill. Years later I was appointed to accompany him as we organized the Iowa Winter Quarters Stake across the Missouri River from Omaha, Nebraska. We had settled on President William D. Hardy as the new stake president, and he had asked for Brother Roy C. Cochran as his first counselor. Brother Cochran was the general superintendent of the Union Pacific Railroad repair shops in Omaha.

When President Lee called him to serve in the new stake presidency, he replied that he was desirous of serving but had just been informed by physicians that his wife was dying of terminal cancer and had only been given three months more to live. Under these circumstances he did not see how he could take care of her and at the same time do the necessary work involved in the organization of a new stake.

Upon hearing this, Elder Lee asked him if he believed in the power of the priesthood. Brother Cochran replied that he did. President Lee said, "The Lord has called you to a prominent position in this new stake. You are needed there. We will bless your wife that you can fill that position."

Brother Cochran then said that if his wife were blessed he had faith that she could recover. We talked with Sister Edna Cochran and told her of her husband's call, and she asked for a blessing. I was asked to anoint her, which I did, and Elder Lee was asked to seal the anointing. As he did so, he rebuked the cancer and promised her that she would live to see her husband complete his assignment. That she did and was also alive and well more than twenty years after the doctors had told her she would be dead within three months.

Miracles happen today as they did in the days of the Savior, but only when God touches the heart and mind of a spiritual giant such as President Harold B. Lee. Such experiences with him only partly explain why we loved him so much.

52

Neal A. Maxwell
Member of the Quorum of the Twelve

The Blessings of
Being Tutored
by a Friend

President Harold B. Lee had a great impact upon me, even
though our association really did not get started until the
mid-1960s. My first experience with him occurred around 1950,
when, along with another University of Utah student, I auda-
ciously went to his office to complain about certain courses of
study in some Church manuals. He listened courteously and
thoughtfully, impertinent as his two visitors were. I do not
remember any counsel he gave but only that he took time to
hear me out.

My next personal experience with him occurred during my
days while serving as a member of the Young Men's General
Board, when the general board members went with the Brethren
to stake conferences.

During one conference, he generously called on me to speak
in both the Saturday evening and in the general session on Sunday. He told me, before the Saturday evening session, to take
ten minutes. I took less, both because all of us wanted to hear

more from him and because general board members were told to take less time and leave more time for the General Authorities. When he got up to speak, he noted that I had not followed instructions. He said it playfully, but pointedly, to teach me something.

His thoughtful listening and his persistent teaching were two patterns that remained throughout the remainder of our relationship until his death on 26 December 1973. His last words to me, in his office just a few days before Christmas, were words of affection and thoughtfulness. At the end of our conversation, he said to me, "Tell that angel of yours, Colleen, how much we appreciate her and to have a merry Christmas!"

In between that first visit to his office when he was a member of the Quorum of the Twelve and his parting words to me as President of the Church were experiences that are indelibly inscribed upon my mind and my heart.

While he was still in the Council of the Twelve and I was a Regional Representative of the Twelve, we were assigned to go together to the Idaho Malad Stake to reorganize the stake presidency, releasing President Stephen Smith and his counselors after long and faithful service.

During the course of the afternoon interviews, President Lee nodded to me as a certain man came into the room, indicating this man was to be the new stake president—even before we had interviewed him! The man was Devere Harris, then bishop of the Portage Ward and now a General Authority of the Church.

Later that evening, President Lee determined to call a patriarch and asked to have Brother Facer and his wife come over to the chapel for an interview. It was quite late, and all the meetings were over when President and Sister Facer arrived. President Lee and I sat in two folding chairs just opposite them in a somewhat darkened, upper hall or foyer. President Lee said, "Brother Facer, the Lord would like to call you as a patriarch."

Brother Facer began to weep, and Sister Facer asked, "Why don't you tell him, Moyle?"

After Brother Facer regained his composure sufficiently, he said, "Brother Lee, the Lord told me two weeks ago I was going to be called as a patriarch!"

Brother Lee then turned to me and said, "See, Neal, why General Authorities must operate under the direction of the Spirit?"

It was a memorable teaching experience. Once again President Lee was doing and teaching at the same time under the direction of the Holy Spirit.

I found President Lee to be personally kind, and yet very tough-minded intellectually. Because he knew the gospel to be true, he was fearlessly confrontive. This also permitted him to deal with institutional and personal feedback from a position of security.

He was at home in the world of ideas. For instance, his brief experience in politics and government permitted him to distill from that short period what other men would have taken years to learn. Being secure spiritually and intellectually, he could be eclectic in gathering in ideas, concepts, and truths that would be helpful to the work of the kingdom. Though he had not had the opportunity for extensive education in the secular sense, he could cope with and even use ideas that his remarkable spiritual education encouraged him to reach out for.

In my relationship with him, I found him to be kind and to be an unusually perceptive listener, for what reasons I am not certain. Thus, when I was around him, I felt completely secure rather than anxious. Others, as reported, may have had a different experience. President Lee had the capacity to listen and ponder, but then to be decisive in giving direction or comment. He was actually fatherlike and giving in his relationship to me, knowing undoubtedly how much tutoring I required.

He was so appreciative of what little I did for him from time to time. Yet, his tough-mindedness would appear in interesting ways. For instance, for one of the early seminars for Regional Representatives of the Twelve, in which he was "on-stage" for so much of the time, I had prepared various texts for possible use by him in different segments of the seminar. He had had no time to prepare for one of the segments; and on his way to the pulpit in the 17th Ward chapel, he asked me to quickly give him a sheet of suggestions. He merely glanced at what I had prepared and could immediately see that it did not fit the occasion.

I watched him put the papers down and then speak well and spontaneously. It was exactly the right action to take, because what I had prepared for him in that instance would not fit. He had quickly made that assessment. He did not scold me; he simply did not use it. I admired him for that.

I am certain that I often imposed upon President Lee's precious time, such as inducing him to go see Westminster College when the college administrators were seeking some Church support, which followed after his visit. Likewise, I requested that he go to the University of Utah to bless the president, Alfred Emery, before his surgery, and President Lee was again responsive. In both these instances, he did not regard it as an imposition but went gladly and gave himself fully to the needs of each circumstance.

I have seen him overcome what might have remained a stereotyped view of another person. As more and different data came in, President Lee generously revised his perceptions accordingly.

I've seen him give reproof to others, but this was then followed by that outpouring of redemptive affection just as the scriptures call for; concrete efforts soon followed to help the individuals who had been reproved and counseled. I have seen him act with reconciliation even as he coped with some very difficult challenges.

I know what it was to be blessed by him, which he did once for me in connection with a special assignment I received. I know what it is like to be trusted by him with confidences, so many of which to this day have not been, and will not be, shared.

I felt loved by him, secure around him, taught by him, and even respected by him.

I appreciate the tutoring friendship of Harold B. Lee, eleventh prophet and President of the Church in this dispensation — a seer and a special witness of Jesus Christ. The cessation of his leadership here was a glorious inauguration there among those with whom, as foretold, he continues his special labors.

I live in anticipation of a reunion and a resumption of his tutoring friendship that has meant so much to me in my life and ministry.

Index

— A —

Aaronic Priesthood, 198
    place of, 103
Aaronic Priesthood MIA-Young
    Women, 123–25
Accidents, 135, 137
Accountability, 122
Administering to the sick, 16–19, 38–39,
    65, 91–93, 136–39, 141–44, 176–77,
    181, 184, 234–36
Administration, 189–91
Adult Correlation Committee, 84,
    120–22
    See also Church Correlation Committee
Adultery, 35
Adversity, 19–20, 223–24
Albuquerque, New Mexico, 29
Alldredge, O. Layton, 83–84
Allen, James B., 78–82
America. See United States of America
Amherst, Massachusetts, 26–27
Anderson, Ina, 132
Anderson, Rees, 15
Anointing of the sick, 17, 234
    See also Administering to the sick
Antelope Valley Stake, 155
Anti-Mormon literature, 147
Apostles, 112, 156, 162, 208
    patriarchs chosen by, 113–15
    witnesses of Christ, 81
Apples, 219–20
Apricots, 86
Area conferences, 207, 227–29
Ashton, Marvin Owen, 83
Ashton, Wendell J., 43, 83–89, 122, 232
Assembly Hall, 127
Austria, 187

— B —

Bach, Johann Sebastian, 2
Ballard, Melvin J., on James E. Talmage,
    3
Bangerter, William Grant, 179–80
Baptisms, 27, 109, 196
Barker, Howard, 67
Basel, Switzerland, 165
Beckwith, Betty, 26–27
Beckwith, Kenneth, 26–27

Beehive Clothing, 186
Beesley, Joseph, 197
Belnap, B. West, 80–81
Benjamin (Nephite prophet-king), on
    becoming children of Christ, 5
Bennett, Theda, 90–93
Bennett, Wallace F., 90
Bennett, Wallace G., 90–93
Benson, Ezra Taft, 7–10, 155
    president of European Mission, 186
Berchtesgaden, Germany, 165
Berlin, Germany, 187
Berrett, Golden L., 145
Births, 76
Bishops, 13–14, 59–61, 95, 170, 176
    instructions to, 43, 52
    stake president opposed by, 68
Bishop's Training Course and Self-Help
    Guide, 43–44
Blacks, and the priesthood, 85, 215–16
Blessings, fathers', 30, 86
Blessings, priesthood, 58, 75–76, 146,
    164–65, 176–77, 184, 229, 240
    See also Administering to the sick;
    Ordinations; Settings apart
Boise, Idaho, 55, 57
"Book of Lee," 146
Book of Mormon, 26, 86, 147, 193
Boston Stake, 168, 170
Bowen, Albert E., 112
Brady, Mitzi, 94
Brady, Rodney H., 94–101
Brazil South Mission, 179–80
Brazilian Mission, 178–79
Brigham Young University, 59, 71, 79,
    105, 142, 222
Brown, Victor L., 55, 64–65
Burt, John R., 12
Burton, Minnie, 166, 234–35
Burton, Suzi Gibbons, 76–77
Burton, Theodore M., 166, 233–36
Burton, Theodore T., 234
Burton, Timothy A., 77
Butler Ward, 52

— C —

California, 221–22
California Mission, 30–31, 115
California Palmdale Stake, 155

Callings. *See* Church callings
Cancer, 64–65, 236
Cannon, Elaine A., 205–12
Cannon, George I., 118
Cannon, George Q., 203
Cannon, Jim, 209
Cannon, Sylvester Q., 209
Carbon College, Price, Utah, 233
Caruso, Enrico, 2
Cazier, Edna, 20
Chapel dedications, 57
Chicago, Illinois, 234
Chicago Stake, 110–11
Chiemsee, Germany, 165
Child, Hortense H. (Smith), 125
Children's Hospital of Los Angeles, 157
Children's Primary choruses, 82, 127
Christensen, M. Elmer, 102–7
Church activity, 44, 48
Church administration, 189–91
Church Administration Building,
    99–100, 140–41, 149, 231
Church auxiliaries, 106
Church Building Department, 67
Church callings, 48, 55, 63, 84, 103,
    113–15, 123–24, 148, 156–57, 232,
    238–39
Church Correlation Committee, 79, 84,
    119–22, 124
Church curriculum, 120
Church history, 163
Church Home Teaching Committee, 103,
    105, 113
Church leaders, training of, 168–70
Church Leadership Committee, 231–32
Church magazines, 43
Church security plan, 185
Church service, 45, 76, 112, 123
    See also Service
Church Welfare Committee, 102–3, 166,
    186
Church welfare program, 8, 15, 78, 83,
    96, 100, 102–3, 110, 164, 166,
    185–86, 215
Civic problems, 103–5
Clark, J. Reuben, Jr., 22, 24, 186, 198
Clemens, Samuel, 2
Clifton, Idaho, 7
Cochran, Edna, 236
Cochran, Roy C., 236
College students, 205–6
Comfort, 137–39
Conference addresses, xi, 35–37, 160–61
Confirmations, 196

Conversion, 5–6, 108–9
Cook, Gene R., 32–37
Cornell, George W., 213–17
Cornell, Jo Ann, 215–17
Cornell, Marion Emma, 213–14
Correlation, priesthood, 53, 78, 106–7,
    120–21, 205, 227, 232
Cottonwood Stake, 103
Council in heaven, 7
Council of the Twelve. *See* Quorum of the
    Twelve
Counsel, 49, 60–61, 65, 68–70, 96–99,
    104–5, 107, 110, 122–23, 176, 180,
    204, 210–12
Counselors, choosing of, 170
Cowdery, Oliver, 24
Creation, 80
Critchlow, William J., Jr., 66, 70
Cromwell, Oliver, 3
Curitiba, Brazil, 179
Curriculum, 120

– D –

Dallas, Texas, 138
Davey, Leland, 104
Davidson, Floyd Thomas, 108–9
Davidson, R. Viola, 108–9
Dearborn Stake, 113
Death, 137, 223–24
Delegation, 168–70, 226
Dempsey, Jack, 2
Denning, Gracia, 198–99, 202
Denning, Paul, 198
Denver, Colorado, 42, 192–94
Denver Stake, 111
Department of Health, Education, and
    Welfare, 94–100
Depression, Great, 8, 185
Deseret News, 2, 209
Detroit Stake, 113
Devils, casting out of, 29
Discernment, power of, 176
Divorce, 60–61
Dolls, 213–14, 217
Dunn, Paul H., 206, 221–30

– E –

Earth, creation of, 80
East Germany, 186
East High School, 123
East Jordan Stake, 52
East Millcreek Stake, 83–84

Easter, 140
Eastern States Mission, 141, 187
Eastern States Mission Home, 145–46, 215
Edison, Thomas A., 2–3
Edmunds, Jasmine, 115
Edmunds, John K., 110–17
Elbert Farms, 28
Elggren, A. Lewis, 42
Elisha, 163
Emery, Alfred, 240
Emigration Stake, 127
Endowment sessions, 116–17, 152–53
England, 91–92
    area conference in, 228
England East Mission, 151
English language, 207
Enoch, 34
Episcopal Church, 214
Equitable Life Assurance Society of New York, 213
Eternal families, 208, 210–11
European Mission, 186
Evans, Marius O., 103
Evans, Richard L., 115
Evil spirits, 176
Example, 34, 134, 153–54, 223
External Communications Department of the Church, 88

– F –

Facer, Moyle, 238
Faith, 9, 49, 139, 173, 225, 236
Families, 120, 123, 174
    eternal, 208, 210–11
Family home evening, 105–6, 197, 202
Family prayer, 88
Fasting, 16, 136, 142, 156, 203
Fathers, 9
Fathers' blessings, 30, 86
Faust, James E., 43, 231–32
Faust, Ruth, 232
Featherstone, Dave, 56–57
Featherstone, Merlene, 55–57
Featherstone, Ron, 56
Featherstone, Vaughn J., 54–58
Federal Heights Ward, 127, 207
Federal welfare program, 96, 100
First Council of Seventy, 28, 34, 226
First Presidency, 32, 36, 38, 43, 53, 65, 78, 84, 149, 157, 162, 178, 226, 229
    letter to Richard M. Nixon, 72–73
First Quorum of the Seventy, 34, 47, 226

First Vision, 86
Florida Mission, 20–21
Ford, Henry, 2–3
Forgiveness, 219–20
Fort Douglas, Utah, 11
Frankfurt, Germany, 187
Fraternities, 206
Friends, 71
Funerals, 1, 80, 87, 142, 222–24
Funk, Mark, 123–25
Funk, Ruth Hardy, 118–26
Fyans, Helen Cook, 51–52
Fyans, J. Thomas, 51–53

– G –

Galileo, 2
Garden of Gethsemane, 173
Gardiner, L. Ray, 127–30
Genealogical work, 201
General Church Welfare Committee, 102–3, 166, 186
General conference, 8, 43–45, 99–101, 159–61
General Home Teaching Committee, 103, 105, 113
General Priesthood Committee, 78
General priesthood meeting, 35
George VI, King of England, 49
Germany, 186–87
    area conference in, 207, 227, 228
Gibbons, Francis M., 75–77
Gibbons, Helen, 75–76
Gibby, Joseph Clifford, 131–34
    Technical Illustration, Procedure and Practice, 133
Gifts of the Spirit, 9
Goates, Helen Lee, 86
Goates, L. Brent, 1–6, 43, 149
    Harold B. Lee, Prophet and Seer, xi, 121, 192
Goates, Les, tribute to Babe Ruth, 2–3
"God Be with You Till We Meet Again" (song), 200
Government welfare program, 96, 100
Granite District Board of Education, 103
Grant, Heber J., 91, 110, 185
Grant, Ulysses S., 73
Graves, F. Charles, 88
Great Depression, 8, 185
Great Lakes Naval Training Center, 111
Greatness, 1–6
Groberg, John H., 59–61
Guillain-Barré disease, 16
Gulf States Mission, 56

— H —

Hahn, Elizabeth, 202–3
Hardy, William D., 236
Harold B. Lee, Prophet and Seer (book),
    xi, 121, 192
Harris, Devere, 62–63, 238
Hawaii, 222–24
Hawaii Honolulu Mission, 149
Haycock, D. Arthur, 71, 73, 87, 123, 204
Healings, 18–19, 38–39, 64–65, 91–92,
    109, 157–58, 181, 234–35
    See also Administering to the sick
Heavenly Father, 139
    love of, 126
Highland High School, 135
Hill Cumorah Pageant, 86
Hillside Stake, 54
History of the Church, 24
Holt, Diana Bird, 135–39
Holy Ghost, 28, 37, 147, 160, 211–12
Holy Land, 82
Home, 120
Home teaching, 44, 53
Homosexuality, 35
Honolulu, Hawaii, 222–24
Hope, 139
Hospice program, 138
Hotel Utah, 122
Hughes Tool Company, 94
Humor, 44–45, 207
Hyatt, Alfred H., "The Link Divine," 87
Hyde, Charles S., 234

— I —

Idaho Falls 26th Ward, 59
Idaho Falls Temple, 63
Idaho Malad Stake, 62, 238
Iguacu Falls, Brazil, 180
Illnesses, 16, 19–21, 111–12, 233, 236
    See also Administering to the sick
"Inactives," 44, 48
Income tax evasion, 35
Independence, Missouri, 196, 201–2
Indiana University, 59
Infections, 233
Inspiration, 23–25, 27, 31, 56–57, 61,
    62–63, 72, 113–15, 120, 137, 180,
    187, 238–39
    See also Revelation
Internal Communications Department,
    53
Internationalization of the Church,
    226–27
Iowa Winter Quarters Stake, 235–36

It's a Wonderful Life (film), 4
Ivins, Antoine R., 51

— J —

Japan, 108–9
Jensen, Leo D., 218–20
Jesus Christ, 140–41, 144, 173, 201, 204,
    236
    Apostles witnesses of, 81–82, 114
    appearance in Salt Lake Temple, 116
    becoming children of, 5
    head of the Church, 199
    intercessory prayer of, 27
    love of, 126, 220
    on friends, 71
    perfect example of leadership, 5
    recognized by devils, 29
    testimony of, 82
    "Jesus: The Perfect Leader" (article), 5
Jordan River, 163
Joseph, "called Barsabas," 114
Joseph Smith, Sr., Family Organization,
    196–204
Joseph Smith, Sr., Family Reunion,
    199–202
Journal of Discourses, 203
Judas Iscariot, 81, 114
Julius Caesar (play), 1
June conference, 118

— K —

Kapp, Ardeth G., 125
Kennedy, Michael A., 203
Keys, 162
Kimball, Camilla, 38
Kimball, Spencer W., 9, 33, 53, 88–89,
    215–16
    "Jesus: The Perfect Leader," 5
    on leadership of Christ, 5
    open-heart surgery of, 38–39
Kirton, Wilford W., 160
Knight, John M., 192, 194
Korean War, 13

— L —

Lafayette, Indiana, 233–34
Laguna Beach home, 72
Lambda Delta Sigma, 206
Landau, Elliott D., 145–47
Language Training Mission, 71–72
Lansing Stake, 113
Latter-day Saint Student Association,
    206, 229

at University of Arizona, 138
Larned, J. N., *A Study of Greatness in Men*, 3–4
Larson, Clinton F., 197
Laws of the land, 35
Leadership, 4–6, 45, 63, 168–70, 189–91
Leadership Committee, 43, 45, 121
Lee, Fern Tanner, 46, 178–81, 194
  death of, 87, 165, 187, 222
  funeral of, 87
Lee, Freda Joan, 20, 86, 95, 100–101, 115, 130, 166, 198, 203, 217
Lee, Harold B.

Personal History

boyhood, 7–8, 180
missionary in Western States Mission, 192–94
Bible books sold by, 46, 182, 194
schoolteacher, 131–34
seminary teacher, 182
principal of Woodrow Wilson School, 194–95
president of Pioneer Stake, 8, 15, 22, 28, 102, 110, 162, 176, 185, 195, 220, 234
member of Salt Lake City Commission, 104
nomination for governor declined by, 163
called as member of Quorum of the Twelve, 8, 15, 35, 163, 185, 195, 208
godfather, 214
managing director of Church welfare program, 15, 78, 102–3, 110, 164, 166, 185–86, 215
chairman of Church Correlation Committee, 78–79, 119–22, 227, 232
contributions to correlation, 53, 106–7, 205
death of wife, 87, 165, 187, 222
death of daughter, 224
miraculous blessing of, 21
stomach surgery of, 21
teacher development program originated with, 171–73
Acting President of the Twelve, 43
President of Quorum of the Twelve, 166
First Counselor in First Presidency, 32
Sustained as President of the Church, 131, 160, 188, 199, 225–28
death of, 9, 73–74, 77, 89, 116, 138–39, 153, 167, 188, 204, 217

funeral of, 204
biography of, *xi*, 20, 121, 192
film biography of, 9

Beliefs and Opinions

declaration to fathers, 9
inspirational thoughts of, 48
on adultery, 35
on appearance of the Savior in Salt Lake Temple, 116
on blacks and the priesthood, 85, 215–16
on "Book of Lee," 146
on challenges involving women, 122
on Christ as head of the Church, 199
on Church sorority and fraternity, 206
on conversion, 34
on counsel, 49, 60–61
on delegation, 168–70
on dependence on the Lord, 8
on example, 34, 223
on faith, 49
on family home evening, 105–6
on following the Brethren, 9, 13–14
on friends, 71
on Holy Land, 82
on homosexuality, 35
on "inactives," 44, 48
on income tax evasion, 35
on learning English, 207
on medical treatment, 65
on missionary work, 48–49
on obedience to laws of the land, 35
on personal revelation, 34–37
on priesthood correlation, 122
on prophets, 33
on reality of Satan, 128
on revelation, 85–86
on strengthening home and family, 122, 123, 174
on teachers, 172
on testimony, 147, 180
on theories, 80
on true record of his service, *xi*
on United States of America, 49–50, 72
on youth, 122, 123

Personal Characteristics and Experiences

adversity experienced by, 19–20
blessings given by, 16, 18–19, 38–39, 65, 75–76, 91–93, 96–98, 136–39,

141–44, 146–47, 165, 176–77, 181, 184, 229, 234–36, 240
book by (*Youth and the Church*), 183, 184
BYU basketball game attended by, 105
callings issued by, 55, 63, 84, 103, 113–15, 123–24, 148, 156, 232, 238–39
chapels dedicated by, 20, 51, 57, 223
Christlike, 160
Christmas cards sent by, 173, 201, 204
compassion of, 221, 224
conference addresses of, 35–37, 160–61
counsel of, 68–70, 96–99, 104–5, 107, 110, 122–23, 176, 180, 204, 210–12
courage of, 7–8, 88–89
debate with ministers, 193
dedication of, 18–22, 111–12
door held open by, 129
efforts to unite family of Joseph Smith, Sr., 196–204
encouragement of, 173
example of, 134, 153–54
faith of, 225
familiarity with scriptures, 152–53, 193
family home evenings with, 197, 202
foreordination of, 7
friend, 131–34, 150, 185–88
friendliness of, 128–30
funeral addresses given by, 80, 223–24
genius for delegating, 226
gift of healing, 181
gift of making people feel important, 117
gifts of the Spirit, 9
Godlike, 150
greatness of, 6
health problems of, 19–21, 111–12
home of, 87
inspiration received by, 12–14, 23–25, 27, 31, 60–61, 113–15, 180, 187, 190, 211–12, 238–39
interviews with news media, 85–86
kindness of, 158
letter to Richard M. Nixon, 72–73
letters from, 124–25, 133–34, 166
light encircling head of, 193–94
love for youth, 23
love of, 52–53, 55, 58, 126, 220, 232
love of others for, 148, 150, 184
luminous radiance surrounding, 120
mantle of apostleship, 208
mantle of a prophet, 199, 228
marriages performed by, 51–52, 77, 107, 207–12

meetings with missionaries in temple, 116, 151–54
memory of, 45, 64
"miracle" file of, 77
ordinations performed by, 56, 60, 84, 229, 231
piano played by, 87, 192
prayers offered by, 88, 114, 142, 179
presidency predicted, 29, 194
prophecies of, 17–19, 41
prophet, 9–10, 162–63, 173
radiance of, 100
radio address by, 140
recognized by a devil, 29
seer, 22, 25, 44, 126
sense of humor of, 44–45, 207
settings apart by, 46, 56, 84, 115, 116, 149, 173, 184
spiritual communication by, 37, 160
spiritual experiences of, 28, 156
spirituality of, 172
strength of character of, 7
teaching ability of, 41, 45, 47, 52, 53, 63, 64, 74, 79–80, 148, 182–83, 190–91, 222, 229–30, 238
testimony of, 82, 88, 180
tour of Brazil, 178–81
tour of California Mission, 31
tour of Florida Mission, 20–21
tour of missions in Germany, Austria, Switzerland, 187
tour of Midwest, 234
tour of New England Mission, 27
tour of Northwestern States Mission, 47
tour of South Pacific, 222–24
tour of Swiss Mission, 165
vision of, 200
Visit to Hillside Stake, 54
visit to North Box Elder Stake, 40–41
"visiting with the Lord," 100
wisdom of, 58, 64, 88, 107, 126, 172, 239
witness of Christ, 140–41
Leukemia, 157
Lillywhite, John P., 40
Lincoln, Abraham, 2–3, 73
"Link Divine, The" (song), 87
London, England, 186
Long Odyssey, The (film), 9
Los Angeles, California, 95, 115
Los Angeles Stake, 81, 99
Los Angeles Temple, 133
Love, 81, 126, 220, 232
Lying, 219–20

— M —

McConkie, Bruce R., 28–29, 156
McConkie, Oscar W., 29–31
McConkie, Oscar W., Jr., 26–31
McKay, David O., 32, 44, 70, 166, 178, 186, 227, 228
Malad, Idaho, 62
Malarial fever, 175
Manila, Philippines, 109
Marriage counseling, 60–61
Marriages, temple, 107, 109, 198–99, 208–12
Martin, Janice, 150
Martin, Robert J., 148–50
Maternal blessings, 75–76, 165
Matis, Henry A., 110
Matthias, 81, 114
Maxwell, Colleen, 238
Maxwell, Neal A., 43, 62, 121–22, 232, 237–40
Medical treatment, 65
Melchizedek Priesthood, 196, 203
Melchizedek Priesthood MIA, 232
Mendenhall, Wendell, 67
Mexico, area conferences in, 156, 228
Michelangelo, 87
Mid-Michigan Stake, 113
Military service, 11–13, 29–30, 108
Military servicemen, 111, 165, 208–9
Miracles, 16–21, 77, 108–9, 235–36
Mission homes, 179–80
Mission presidents, 52, 165
Mission representatives, 34
Missionaries, 17, 19, 20, 26–27, 31, 47, 51, 56, 92–93, 165, 184, 187, 192–94, 208
    meetings in temple, 116, 151–54
Missionary Training Center, 71
Missionary work, 48–49, 53, 226
Mitchell, John, 97
Monson, Frances, 12
Monson, Thomas S., 11–14, 43, 95, 97, 98, 121, 171, 231
Moses (statue), 87
Motives, 3
Mount Jordan Stake, 95
Moyle, Henry D., 17, 186, 221, 231
Munich, Germany Area Conference, 207, 227, 228
Music, 118, 123
Mutual Improvement Association, 218–19
Mutual Improvement Association General Music Committee, 119

— N —

Naaman, 163
Napoleon Bonaparte, 2–3
Nauvoo, Illinois, 196–97, 199
Naval Training Center, 11
Navy, 29–30, 108
Nephi, 225
New England Mission, 26–27
New Jersey Stake, 21
New Testament, 26–27
New York City, 86–88, 145–46, 187, 213
New York Stake, 87, 111
New Zealand Mission, 17, 19
News media, 85, 89
Nile River, 118
Nixon, Richard M., 72–73, 97, 98, 100
Normandeau, Lorena, 202–3
North Box Elder Stake, 40
Northwestern States Mission, 47
Norwich, England, 153

— O —

Obedience, to counsel of the Brethren, 8–9
    to laws of the land, 35
Ogden, Utah, 66
Olympus High School, 70
Olympus Stake, 87
Omaha, Nebraska, 236
Oneida Stake Academy, 7
Opportunity, 3
Ordinations, 56, 60, 84, 196, 203, 229, 231
Oxford, Idaho, 131–33

— P —

Packer, Boyd K., 40–41
Packer, Donna, 40
Pageant of the Nations, 132
Pain, 135–38
Palm Springs, California, 190
Palo Alto, California, 75
Palo Alto Ward, 175
Papa and the Playhouse (musical play), 118
Parables of James E. Talmage, The (book), 3
Parents, 9, 136
Parker, Arthur Kapewaokeae, Sr., 223
Pasteur, Louis, 2
Patriarchal order, 123–25
Patriarchs, 113–15, 238–39

Peace, inner, 142
Penitentiaries, 60
Pennsylvania, 44
Pentecostal Church, 86
Pentecostal experiences, 229
Perschon, Phileon F., 185
Peter, 114
Petersen, Mark E., 38–39, 145, 155, 198
Phelps, W. W., 24
Philippines, 109
Piccolomini, "The Link Divine," 87
Pinnock, Anne Hawkins, 43
Pinnock, Hugh W., 42–45, 232
Pioneer Stake, 102, 162, 185, 195, 234
Pogue, Steven R., 151–54
Portage Ward (Idaho), 238
Porter, L. Aldin, 57
Porto Alegre, Brazil, 180
Prayer, 16, 27, 88, 114, 142, 156, 163, 179, 198, 200, 203, 224
  family, 88
Prayer circles, 157
"Prayers or apricots," 86
Premortal life, 137
Presiding Bishopric, 55, 64, 83
Priesthood, 78–79, 162, 226
  Aaronic, 198
  and blacks, 85, 215–16
  Melchizedek, 196, 203
  patriarchal order of, 123–25
  teacher development sponsored by, 171
Priesthood blessings, 58, 75–76, 146, 164–65, 176–77, 184, 229, 240
  See also Administering to the sick
Priesthood correlation, 53, 78, 106–7, 120–21, 205, 227, 232
Priesthood Correlation Committee, 227
Priesthood leaders, 226
Priesthood Leadership Committee, 43, 45
Primary children's choruses, 82, 127
Priorities, 174
Prophecies, 17–19, 41, 62–63, 72, 106–7, 203, 235
Prophets, 32–33, 162
Public Communications Department, 84–85
Purdue University, 233

— Q —

Quinn, Gerald B., 155–58
Quinn, Libby, 157
Quinn, Robbie, 157–58

Quorum of the Twelve, 20, 38, 65, 156, 162, 190, 226
  patriarchs chosen by, 113–15

— R —

Reorganized Church of Jesus Christ of Latter Day Saints, 193, 197, 200–201, 203
Reese, Glenna L., 159–61
Regional Representatives, 43, 45, 53, 113, 166, 173, 232, 238
  seminars for, 121, 166–67, 189–90, 239
Reimann, Maybeth, 163
Reimann, Paul E., 162–63
Relief Society General Presidency, 186
Responsibility, 61, 75
Revelation, 35–37, 85–86, 120, 125, 153, 180
  See also Inspiration
Richards, Franklin D., 46–50, 142
Richards, Stephen L, 103, 140
Richardson, Elliot L., 94, 97, 100
Ricks College, 49, 72
Rigdon, Sidney, 162
Rio de Janeiro, Brazil, 178
Rochester, New York, 141
Rochester Ward, 142
Romney, Marion G., 22, 23–25, 44, 53, 54, 66, 70–71, 72, 89, 110, 113, 119, 120, 156, 164, 186
Rudd, Glen L., 15–22
Rudd, Glen Lee, 15–20
Rudd, Matthew, 16, 18
Russon, John M., 164–67
Russon, Lyn Redding, 167
Russon, Mary, 164–67
Ruth, George Herman (Babe Ruth), 2–3

— S —

Sacred Grove, 86
Sacrifice, 63
Salt Lake City Airport, 128
Salt Lake Hillside Stake, 54
Salt Lake Temple, 38, 56, 65, 77, 100–101, 115–17, 172, 199, 209
  appearance of the Savior in, 116
  missionary meetings in, 116, 152–53, 229
Salt Lake Theater, 118
San Antonio, Texas, 51
San Diego, California, 11, 190
Santos, Joseph M., 11

Satan, 128, 176, 224
Schreiner, John, 168–70
Scouting, 103
Scripture study, 146, 152–53
Sealing authority, 116
Sealings, 107, 109, 198–99, 208–12
Self-reliance, 7–8
Seminaries, 182–83, 221–22
Service, 4–6, 45, 76, 112, 122, 123, 138
Servicemen, 111, 208–9
  conference in Berchtesgaden, Germany,
    165
Settings apart, 46, 56, 84, 115, 116, 149,
    173, 184
Seventeenth Ward meetinghouse,
    121–22, 232, 239
Shakespeare, William, 1, 2
Sharon Stake, 103, 105
Sigma Gamma Chi, 206
Skidmore, Rex A., 171–74
Smith, C. Dennis, 140–44
Smith, Donna Lee, 203
Smith, Emma, 198–99, 200
Smith, George Albert, 186
Smith, Hyrum, descendants of, 200
Smith, Israel A., 203
Smith, Joseph, Jr., 162
  descendants of, 196–203
  First Vision, 86
  Harold B. Lee likened to, 23–25
  Teachings of the Prophet Joseph Smith, 7
Smith, Joseph, Sr., uniting family of,
    196–204
Smith, Joseph F., on priesthood, 106
Smith, Joseph Fielding, 32–33, 53, 73,
    84, 149, 156, 166, 172, 197, 198–99,
    228
Smith, Lucy Mack, descendants of, 197,
    200
Smith, Lyman E., 200
Smith, Merritt, 87
Smith, Michael, 143
Smith, Samuel Harrison, descendants of,
    200
Smith, Stephen, 238
Smith, W. Wallace, 197, 200–201, 203
Smith, Wallie, 142
Smith, Willard R., 199
Smoking, 103–4
Snow, Lorenzo, 116
Socrates, 2
Solemn assemblies, 35, 131, 188
Solemn assembly room, 116
Sonne, Alma, 176–77, 186

Sonne, Richard B., 175–77
Sorensen, Asael T., 178–81
Sororities, 206
South African Mission, 84
South Davis Stake, 148–49
South High School, 182, 218
South Ogden Stake, 66
South Pacific, 222
Spanish-American Mission, 51
Spirit world, 54, 180, 201, 203, 204
Spiritual communication, 36–37
Spirituality, 74
Springfield, Massachusetts, 27
Stake missionaries, 46
Stake presidents, 34–35, 62–63, 168–70
Stanford University, 75
Stapley, Delbert L., 84
Stewart, Jimmy, 4
Stohl, Betty B., 182–84
Stohl, Clark, 183–84
Stover, Walter, 165, 185–88
Study of Greatness in Man, A (book), 3
Stuttgart, Germany, 187
Success, 1–6
Suffering, 137
Suicide, 175–76
Swallow, LaPreal, 4–5
Swiss Mission, 165–66
Swiss Temple, 133, 165
Swiss-German Mission, 165
Switzerland, 187

– T –

Tabernacle Choir, 87, 159–60
Tacoma, Washington, 44
Talmage, James E., 3
Tanner, N. Eldon, 53, 55, 70–71, 72, 74,
    84
Teacher development program, 171–72
Teaching. *See* Lee, Harold B., Personal
    Characteristics and Experiences,
    teaching ability of
Teachings of the Prophet Joseph Smith
    (book), 7
Tears, evoked by Holy Spirit, 54–55,
    160–61
*Technical Illustration, Procedure and
    Practice* (book), 133
Temple Department, 63
Temple marriages, 107, 109, 198–99,
    208–12
Temple meetings, 116, 152–54, 229
Temple ordinances, 116, 198–99

Temple View Stake, 12
Temples, 63
  murals in, 133
Testimonies, 147, 180, 183
Theories, 80
Thomas, Madison, 16
Tokyo, Japan, 108
Tragedies, 175–76, 223–24
Twain, Mark, 2

— U —

Union Pacific Railroad, 213
United States of America, 49–50, 72
  Department of Health, Education, and
    Welfare, 94–100
United States Naval Reserve, 11–13
United States Navy, 29–30, 108
USS *Hornet* (ship), 108
University of Arizona, 138
University of New Mexico, 29
University of Utah, 11–12, 147, 209,
    237, 240
University students, 205–6
Uruguayan Mission, 52
Utah Historical Society, 163
Utah Stake (Provo), 105–6
Utah State University, 70

— V —

Vandenberg, John H., 67
VanValkenburg, Mac, 76
Veil, 180
Virginia Roanoke Mission, 56
Visions, 200

— W —

Waldorf Astoria Hotel, 88
Wallace, Ann Widtsoe, 147
Wallace, J. Clifford, 189–91
Washington, George, 3
Washington, D.C., 46, 94–100
Washington, D.C., Stake, 111
Watergate scandal, 72, 98
Weber Heights Stake Center, 66–70
Weber State College, 66
Webster, Daniel, 1
Weeping, 54–55, 160–61

Welfare program, Church, 8, 15, 78, 83,
    96, 100, 102–3, 110, 164, 166,
    185–86, 215
  government, 96, 100
West, Wilburn G., 142
Westate News (mission newspaper), 42
Western States Mission, 42–43, 192–94
Westminster College, 240
Westwood Ward, 95
White House staff, 97
Wilcox, Keith W., 66–74
Wilcox, Viva May, 70
Wilkins, Ernest, 75
Wilkins, Maurine Lee, 75, 87
  death of, 224
Willey, Verl, 40
Williams, Ariel L., 110
Williams, Frederick G., 162
Winder Stake, 105
Women, 122
Wood, Leah, 136–37
Woodrow Wilson School, 194
Woodruff, Wilford, 33
Woolsey, Harriet E. Jensen, 192–95
Work, 7–8
World War II, 11, 30, 186, 208

— Y —

Yokosuka, Japan, 109
Young, S. Dilworth, 26
Young Men's General Board, 237
Young Men's Mutual Improvement
    Association, 218–19
  General Board of, 102, 106
Young Women, 123–25
Youngreen, Buddy, 196–204
Youth, 23, 122–23, 183
Youth and the Church (book), 183, 184
Youth conferences, 199, 228–29

— Z —

Zobell, Albert L., Jr., *The Parables of
    James E. Talmage*, 3
Zollikofen, Switzerland, 165
Zundal, Eberhard, 40
Zundal, Laura, 40
Zurich, Switzerland, 165–66